Games and Play
in the Theater
of Spanish American
Women

Games and Play
in the Theater
of Spanish American
Women

Catherine Larson

Lewisburg
Bucknell University Press

Associated University Presses
2010 Eastpark Boulevard
Cranbury, NJ 08512

The paper used in this publication meets the requirements of the American National Standard for Permanence of Paper for Printed Library Materials Z39.48-1984.

Library of Congress Cataloging-in-Publication Data

Larson, Catherine, 1950–
    Games and play in the theater of Spanish American women / Catherine Larson.
        p.   cm.
Includes bibliographical references and index.
    ISBN 0-8387-5569-0 (alk. paper)
1. Spanish American drama—Women authors—History and criticism.   2. Spanish American drama—20th century—History and criticism.   3. Games in literature.   I. Title.
    PQ7082.D7L37   2004
    862'.609357—dc22

                                                        2003021613

To Nadine Holman Madden

. . . Sometimes the whole playground
Ran like one animal harrier
Screaming after you,
Challengers and thwarted in turn
Hounded and hounding, with grins
Like tired hounds.

And after the exhilarated spell
As the fox, the defiant
Scapegoat who dares all comers.

Always finally out of breath
You laugh and let yourself
Be touched, collapse thrilled
And exhausted to crouch panting
Hands on knees as you watch the herd
Speed on after the twisting shifting
Hero sooner or later always depleted
Of strength, unpetulant, capitulated
To the great ongoing
Entropy of the game.

—Robert Pinsky

Contents

7

Acknowledgments

I OWE A GREAT DEAL TO A GREAT NUMBER OF PEOPLE, INCLUDING GEORGE Woodyard, Vicky Unruh, Jacqueline Bixler, Margarita Vargas, Teresa Cajiao Salas, Charles Ganelin, Kathleen Myers, William García, Gustavo Sainz, Hernán Feldman, Steven Wagschal, Josep Sobrer, and Timothy Compton. I am also grateful to Indiana University, whose Arts and Humanities Initiative grant aided me in the completion of this project.

I would like to thank the following for allowing me to publish here emended versions of studies that appeared elsewhere first: Mara García and Robert Anderson, editors of *Baúl de recuerdos*, for my essay on Felipe Ángeles; *Hispania*, for my analysis of *La dama boba* by Lope and Garro; and *Latin American Literary Review*, where my early study of game playing in Spanish American theater appeared in 1991.

Games and Play
in the Theater
of Spanish American
Women

1

Introduction: Games, Play, and Theater

"This wasn't a game. This was theater."
—Glen Roven

LIKE MOST TOPICS THAT APPEAR UNIVERSALLY COMPREHENSIBLE AND instantly recognizable, play and games are elusive concepts. On the one hand, they are both frequently identified with childhood, joyfulness, and leisure time. In the United States, we might imagine the family gathered around the television to watch a basketball game, perhaps with the children nearby playing card or board games, or we might hark back to our own lazy summers and endless hours of "Tag" or "Red Rover." We might also consider the Kennedy weekend football scrimmages as familial bonding experiences and preparation for the political games that the players would later encounter. Most of us know well the board game that invites us to "play the game of Life." One of the bestselling books of the summer of 2001 was *The Games We Played*, a collection of reminiscences from a host of celebrities subtitled "A Celebration of Childhood and Imagination." In Spanish America, similar examples of play form part of the collective experience and memory. The games may have different names, but they exemplify universally recognized activities that define childhood.

Still, game playing also incarnates some darker—and often adult—connotations. "Don't play games with me!" we exhort in anger. We say that an unfaithful spouse is playing around or that a cheater is playing dirty. Some organized games have their unpleasant sides: the child not selected for a team, the losers in a tournament, or those who bet and lose thousands of dollars on the talents of other game players would remind us that games are often neither innocent nor simple. Indeed, their surface can obscure the remarkable complexity of the games played daily by children and adults, men and women, around the world. As a field of academic inquiry, game playing had to prove itself;

13

it was not taken seriously for many years. Nonetheless, it has since resonated in fields as diverse as education, psychology, anthropology, and literary studies. This book is intended to illustrate how an examination of games and play can illuminate our understanding of the theater of Spanish America. More specifically, it foregrounds the drama of many of the women writers from Mexico to Argentina during the last half of the twentieth century: games and play serve a central and unique function in a number of their dramatic texts,[1] enabling us to see in a new light these women playwrights and the contexts in which they are writing.

In Spanish America today, increasing numbers of women are writing for the stage, a situation that illustrates the growing acceptance and participation of women in the arts and in society. In many ways, this change is really quite revolutionary. Like so many other realms in Spanish America, the theater was long considered a man's domain: canonical texts seldom included those written by women, and female dramatists found that their plays were infrequently staged.[2] Even as recently as 1990, Catherine M. Boyle saw the problem as immense. Although she acknowledged that a few women participated as half of famous husband-and-wife teams—writing plays, establishing companies, or becoming the patrons of both dramatists and actors—Boyle emphasized that women's greatest presence in the theater has been as actresses, playing "roles generally created by men, ranging from the intelligent and strong woman—the matriarch—to the spinster, the good-hearted whore or the unfortunate waif—all of which gave an incomplete, faulty and misleading portrayal of women. . . . the real voice and expression of women remain muted."[3] Female characters and women's issues were most commonly seen from the perspective of the male dramatists who created and examined them; the representation of women was filtered through men, creating in the process a somewhat skewed vision of how women think, act, and react to their world.

Now, however, the Spanish American stage is more frequently populated with the works of formerly marginalized women writers who are working collectively and individually to write and produce dramas that express their own vision of the Hispanic experience. These playwrights treat women's concerns, more radical feminist issues, and human problems, expressing through the dominant tradition and in open challenge to it what it is like to be a woman in Spanish America today. As part of this literary and theatrical awakening, a number of women dramatists confront the problems inherent in machismo, breaking away from the stereotypical view of woman as object, as

Other, as madonna or prostitute, that defines the standard representation of women dating from the time of the conquest of the New World.[4]
Some playwrights examine women's position in society by embracing
more mimetic approaches to the theater; others reflect the influence of
such European writers as Artaud, Brecht, Ionesco, or Beckett. Still
others have experimented in a different way, questioning theatrical
tradition by writing plays that deal overtly with issues of gender and
representation, the impact of political repression on Spanish American women today, and the relationships between signs and referents,
biology and society, the masculine and the feminine.[5] These issues are
often tied to the playwrights' use of the game metaphor: in a significant
number of dramas, the exploration of roles in Spanish American society surfaces when dramatists deal with the very essence of play and its
relationship to the performative elements of social interaction.

Jacqueline Eyring Bixler's provocative study of game playing in
Spanish American theater, "Games and Reality on the Latin American
Stage" (1984), posits that in a rather large number of dramatic texts,
women writers have gone beyond using game playing only as a theatrical convention, or as an aspect of the *theatrum mundi* metaphor, and
instead have self-consciously incorporated games into their plays'
structures to highlight from a woman's perspective the idea that life,
as well as the theater, is a game. When the entire drama consists of
games within games, when characters knowingly assume roles inside of
roles and "stage" plays inside the play itself, the dramatist underscores such concepts as the nature of human identity, the relationship
between the theater and reality, and the methods by which authority
and control are manifested and maintained in real life. Issues of power
and authority are, of course, central to discussions of women in Spanish America and consequently may serve as strategic vehicles for these
women writers, who seem to use the game metaphor even more frequently than do male playwrights.[6] Indeed, as Bixler asserts, "Female
dramatists have found in gamesplaying a particularly effective form of
communicating their own personal feelings of repression as women in
a male and power-oriented Hispanic society."[7]

Bixler's work on the topic sparked my own interest in seeing how
ludic elements have influenced the corpus of women-authored plays of
the last fifty years in Spanish America. In "Playwrights of Passage:
Women and Game-playing on the Stage" (1991),[8] I looked at a larger
number of texts (two plays by Susana Torres Molina, one each by
Roma Mahieu and Mariela Romero, two by Griselda Gambaro, and
one by Rosario Castellanos), and drew several conclusions about the

playwrights' use of the game metaphor. I suggested there—as I do here in this more comprehensive study—that game playing, as both a structural and thematic element of the dramas, seems to serve as a strategy for allowing these women writers to talk about hierarchical relationships, power, and control and the ways in which they relate to gender-oriented issues such as sociocultural gender roles and identities. Ultimately, I concluded that in their utilization of game playing, which is tied so clearly to power games and hierarchical notions of winning and losing, the women playwrights who employ games in their dramas seem to simultaneously uphold and subvert patriarchal models. That study was a significant step in the journey toward the present book. Nonetheless, I knew that I wanted to examine even greater numbers of plays to test the thesis that contemporary women dramatists seem to be using the game metaphor to do something else—something important—in the theater. This book is an attempt to elaborate upon those early ideas, to catalogue the types of games played in the dramas of these women writers, to further examine the role of ludic theory in elucidating the playtexts, and to offer new ideas as to the function and prevalence of game playing in Spanish American women-authored texts.

It really is not at all surprising that playing a game should be a part of the theatrical experience. The ludic quality of theatrical representation has been examined by a number of scholars, with Johan Huizinga's *Homo Ludens: A Study of the Play Element in Culture* serving as the seminal exploration of game playing in human existence.[9] In the years since the appearance of *Homo Ludens*, scholars from diverse fields have continued the investigation of game playing and, often, its links to the stage.[10] The theater is an especially rich medium for linking games and art: from the time of the ancients, through Shakespeare and the Spanish baroque dramatists, to the eighteenth and nineteenth century's Moratín (*La comedia nueva o el café*) and Tamayo y Baus (*Un drama nuevo*), and into the present, the world/stage metaphor has underscored the self-reflexive nature of the theater, in which characters stage interior plays and play games with each other as part of the dynamic of the battle of the sexes or as a strategy for gaining power, authority, or control. "Playing a game" has long been associated with the theater, with the dramatic text, with the play.[11] In a real sense, all games played within a theatrical context are inherently metatheatrical, functioning like inset plays within the outer, framed play, and reminding the readers and spectators that they are witnessing a scene that foregrounds the conjunction of illusion and reality—in the game as well as in the dramatic fiction. The games represented symbolically in the theater allow authors to explore the social world and expose some of its most profound problems. Both game playing and the theater show us that what might appear to be "only a game" is frequently "more than a game," illuminating paradigmatic events that involve us in substantive issues of human subjectivity.[12]

It should be noted, however, that games can also echo patriarchal relationships: they promote hierarchies in their opposition of winners and losers, stress the value of following rules, and emphasize the use of power (through physical strength, intellectual machinations, or emotional manipulation) to reestablish order.[13] In the dramas of these women writers, games serve as a theatrically self-conscious way to articulate the construction of cultural roles and to discuss society, history, or politics, illustrating what Victor Turner called performative reflexivity.[14] Amalia Gladhart's description of game playing in the theater is particularly apt:

> Imaginative games duplicate theatrical performance in their linkage of freedom and control: improvisation within a rigid framework, insistent repetition, determinate yet arbitrary roles. Even games invented by the players as they go along take on a life of their own, establishing the boundaries of the game context, solidifying a seemingly casual choice into an incontrovertible rule. The metaphor of ritual game playing has provided many playwrights with a vehicle for theatrical exploration and sociopolitical commentary. Games have been presented as an escape from an unbearable reality, as a self-contained and often violent reality in themselves, and as a representation of the empty or commercialized relations between individuals in an impersonal society.[15]

As the examples of this study indicate, games and play are manifested in a variety of ways, but the dramas themselves often share certain central concerns as they point to a number of problematical issues by means of the game-theater metaphor.

The seventeen plays described in this representative survey of the last fifty years were selected because they illustrate a broad range of types. The playwrights use game playing in dramas that deal principally with men, in those that treat the relationships between men and women, and in plays that depict female relationships. Manifestations of play and games range from overt to metaphorical presentations, from self-consciously articulated games, contests, or competitions to more generalized examples of spontaneous play, from a lighter ludic perspective to one eminently more threatening. The playtexts present realistic children's games and those much more adult or even perverse in nature, and the players are both children and adults, although adults predominate. The games are both physical and verbal. Some dramas utilize real or metaphorical toys, while others emphasize make-believe play involving single or joint pretense. Many of the dramas have a strong foundation in ritual, reminiscent of the ancient links between play, ritual, and the theater.

The plays are often serious in tone; several have a strong sexual subtext, with both hetero- and homosexual implications, and in both cases, violence and cruelty seem to be linked to the manifestation of sexual tension. A second—and related—subtext appearing in the majority of the dramas is sociopolitical in nature; the game often serves as a symbolic representation of the violence and torture that occur on political levels and for domestic interactions that can take place within the family unit. In this sense, the dramatic text can be used, as Gladhart observes in her discussion of performance, as a pretext or cover that transmits a coded message to the audience in times of censorship or heightened political or social tensions.[16] In every case, game and play are presented from a perspective that subverts associations with innocence, joyfulness, and childhood. The dramatists' ironic employment of the game-play dyad[17] allows them to utilize simulated realities to speak to more authentic ones, related specifically to three general categories: sociopolitical issues, the domestic sphere, or the theater itself.

Two significant issues in discussing the appearance of the game as theme, technique, and structure of women-authored dramas are the selection of playtexts and the means of ordering them in a meaningful way. Each of the dramas studied offers a specific type of game at its core. Some are so overtly about games that the word appears significantly in their titles (*Juegos a la hora de la siesta, El juego*); others reflect in less direct or more metaphoric ways game playing or play in general, while still others approach the topic by means of metatheatrical treatments of role or the nature of the theater, presenting themselves as a kind of global game played between the dramatist and the reader or spectator. In every drama examined, however, a game of some sort plays a key role—be it central or not—in the construction of the playtext. Clearly, the plays examined do not exhaust the number of women-authored texts that treat the topic, but I have tried to find examples that illustrate a wide variety and range of approaches and that cover approximately fifty years of dramatic production. Moreover, although many of the dramas come from Mexico and Argentina—both possessing relatively strong and ongoing theater traditions—I have included numerous others from countries as diverse as Puerto Rico, Venezuela, Bolivia, and Paraguay, suggesting in the process that this textual strategy and the issues it problematizes are relatively typical across the Spanish American theater scene; game playing appears to transcend national borders and boundaries.[18] It also, of course, transcends gender. Although I recognize that games and play occur in many of the same ways in male-authored dramas that foreground game playing, this study focuses on women and their use of the strategy, with an eye to exploring the ways that their texts differ from those penned by men.

I have grouped these representative samples in the five chapters that form the heart of this study, but those textual analyses are preceded by an examination of the essence of play. Consequently, chapter 2 ("Ludic Theory: Games and Drama Criticism") discusses many of the elements of ludic theory that have guided my approach to the playtexts.[19] In this part of the study, I survey the topic of games and play, both as popular cultural practice and as the subject of increasingly serious academic inquiry in a number of fields. I end the chapter with an examination of game playing in literature, most specifically, the theater. I analyze individual texts in chapters 3–7: "Games in the Theater: Representation, Roleplaying, and the Search for Identity in Dramas by Elena Garro, Maritza Wilde, and Susana Torres Molina," "Violent Games in Plays by Roma Mahieu, Mariela Romero, and Griselda Gambaro," "Games and Gender Issues: Becoming Other in Dramas by Rosario Castellanos, Susana Torres Molina, and Diana Raznovich," "Games and/in Spanish American Society in Plays by Myrna Casas, Griselda Gambaro, and Josefina Plá," and "Games and the Historical-Political Realities of Spanish America in Dramas by Griselda Gambaro, Jesusa Rodríguez, and Sabina Berman." There is great overlap between and among the texts; several of the plays clearly fit into more than one category, but I have made an attempt to group them coherently and to cross-reference or examine them to a lesser degree in chapters with which they share specific points of contact.

Theatrical self-consciousness surfaces as a motif, albeit in varying degrees, in all the dramas, highlighting the links between playing games and the dramatist's use of the role within the role, the play within the play, and the ceremony within the play, concepts that Richard Hornby discusses with clarity in *Drama, Metadrama, and Perception*.[20] Indeed, the kinds of games seen in these plays by Spanish American women both underscore their own self-referentiality and stress the dual connections between theater as ritual and game playing as ceremony, as well as the related influence of Antonin Artaud and his work on the nexus of the theater, ritual, and cruelty. Because theatrical games are, to some extent, present in each of the playtexts, their study forms the basis of chapter 3, "Games in the Theater: Representation, Roleplaying, and the Search for Identity in Dramas by Elena Garro, Maritza Wilde, and Susana Torres Molina." The principal texts analyzed are Elena Garro's *Felipe Ángeles* (Mexico, 1967/1979, first staged in 1978) and *La dama boba* [The Lady Simpleton] (1963), Maritza Wilde's *Adjetivos* [Adjectives] (Bolivia, 1997, premiering in 1990), and Susana Torres Molina's *. . . y a otra cosa, mariposa* [Moving On] (Argentina, 1988, first staged in 1981). In each of these dramas, different types of real and metaphorical games allow the reader/spectator to contemplate the nature of the theater, the question of identity, and the relationship between illusion and reality.

The relationship between the game and violence is the theme of the fourth chapter, "Violent Games in Plays by Roma Mahieu, Mariela Romero, and Griselda Gambaro." In this chapter, the most overt uses of game playing emerge in Mariela Romero's *El juego* [The Game] (Venezuela, 1977), Roma Mahieu's *Juegos a la hora de la siesta* [Games at Siesta Time] ([Poland] Argentina, 1976), and two plays by Griselda Gambaro: *Los siameses* [The Siamese Twins] (Argentina, 1967), and *El campo* [The Camp] (1967). These dramas spotlight games of the most serious and sordid type in order to explore the degree to which human beings are capable of inflicting pain on others.

Chapter 5, "Games and Gender Issues: Becoming Other in Dramas by Rosario Castellanos, Susana Torres Molina, and Diana Raznovich," treats the relationships between men and women, sexual orientation, and connections between mothers and daughters and among female friends in Rosario Castellanos's *El eterno femenino* [The Eternal Feminine] (Mexico; completed in 1973, first staged in 1976), Torres Molina's *Extraño juguete* [Strange Toy] (1977), and Diana Raznovich's *Casa matriz* [Dial-a-Mom] (Argentina, 1981). In the plays examined, the games present distinctly feminist perspectives on gender as their authors turn conventional relationships upside down.

Certainly all of the plays studied here deal with Spanish American society. Still, in Myrna Casas's *El gran circo eukraniano* [The Great USkrainian Circus] (Puerto Rico, 1986), the associations between the ludic and the circus facilitate the examination of numerous elements of Puerto Rican society. Gambaro's *El despojamiento* [Striptease] (1974) invites the reader to contemplate the interconnectedness of

gender, economics, and the world of the theater. Finally, Josefina Plá's
Historia de un número [Story of a Number] ([Spain] Paraguay, written in 1949, but first published in 1967) points to a type of game playing in which numbers are all that matter.

In the seventh chapter, "Games and the Historical-Political Realities of Spanish America in Dramas by Griselda Gambaro, Jesusa
Rodríguez, and Sabina Berman," the social game acquires a more historical or political tone. In the dramas analyzed, the theater seems to
serve most obviously as a vehicle for encouraging audiences to think
about—if not act upon—the issues that have shaped the countries in
question—in this case, the two most powerful countries in Spanish
America: Argentina and Mexico. Games, rules, winners and losers join
together as the playwrights explore events and times of fundamental
importance in their countries' historical and political evolutions.
Gambaro's *Información para extranjeros* [Information for Foreign-
ers] (1973) speaks to the Argentine body politic. Jesusa Rodríguez's
Sor Juana en Almoloya [Sor Juana in Almoloya] (1995) and Sabina
Berman's *Krisis* (1996) explore different and related moments in Mexican history and politics by means of theatrical games.

The game is both a structural and thematic element of these dramas.
Their authors seem profoundly interested in the dynamics of game
playing, in the kinds of hierarchical relationships that, by definition,
assert themselves in those games, in the concept of winner vs. loser or
game leader vs. game player, and in the consequences of following or
breaking the rules of the game. The games studied here are fundamentally about power and control, but the results of several of those games
indicate that although the dominant player may win, winning the game
may nonetheless turn out to be an ironic defeat, since the winner and
loser are so closely tied together in a mutually co-dependent relationship that the end of the game threatens the psychological survival of
the dominant player. In a number of the other plays, however, the
game appears to be one of many more to come; it will be reborn in
other forms, but with the same cast of characters.

It is important to note that women writers are not alone in using
games and play as the central metaphors of their dramatic works.[21]
José Triana's *La noche de los asesinos* represents a model for utilizing
game playing as both the structure and theme of a play, as the characters appear to use the game as a preparation or rehearsal for a future
horrific act. Carlos Gorostiza's *¿A qué jugamos?* posits a game in
which characters act out what they would do if it were the end of the

world. Other male-authored dramatic texts, such as Jorge Díaz's *El cepillo de dientes*, Alejandro Tantanián's *Juegos de damas crueles*, and Sergio Vodanović's *El delantal blanco*, also employ games as central elements. Yet the significant number of women who have appropriated the metaphor invites us to ask why this particular construct has attracted so much interest.

As the seventeen women-authored dramas described in this study will show, this technique relates to the ways in which Spanish American women are finding their voice and expressing their perceived roles in society. Game playing, role playing, and theatrical self-consciousness join together as strategies for allowing these women writers to define themselves and the world around them through the theater. By foregrounding game playing—itself a performance—within the text, these playwrights offer a complementary critique of the theater.[22] Moreover, as Bixler has observed, "many contemporary Latin American dramatists have discovered in the inherent playfulness of the theatre a means of revealing non-playful aspects of their daily reality. . . . Under the pretense that all is a game, the dramatist subtly attacks the power structures that dictate the rules by which one must play in order to survive."[23] The games of power and control represented on stage often reveal a feminist response on the part of the dramatists, a protest against what Sandra Gilbert describes as women's alienation from the sources of power—alienation that occurs on a personal, political, philosophical, aesthetic, and literary level.[24] In that sense, these women-authored dramas may function as parodies of the national stories of the countries from which they are derived, illustrating how the marginalized subject reacts to the social and sexual contracts that define her identity.

A necessary result of my consideration of game playing in women-authored texts is the raising of other, more difficult questions. Do these dramatists articulate distinctively female literary, dramatic, and theatrical theses? Have they done what Gayle Greene and Coppélia Kahn describe as "the dual task of deconstructing predominantly male paradigms and reconstructing a female perspective and experience"?[25] Is the status quo maintained or challenged? Although these questions will be examined in much greater detail in subsequent chapters, at this point, when we consider the plays collectively, we may justifiably answer them in both the affirmative and negative. It would be inaccurate to signal *significant* differences between these plays and those of Vodanović, Díaz, Tantanián, Gorostiza, and Triana. The plays written by the women's male counterparts also employ the innocence of children's games (as well as games between both same- and different-sex characters and those of distinct social classes) to examine issues of social and political power. The couple in Díaz's *El cepillo de dientes*, for example, interacts in a markedly similar manner to Ana I and Ana II of Romero's *El juego* and to the "brothers" of Gambaro's *Los siameses*; children enact horrific adult games in Triana's *La noche de los asesinos* and in Mahieu's *Juegos a la hora de la siesta*; class differences and theatrical self-consciousness play significant roles in Vodanović's *El delantal blanco* and Torres Molina's *Extraño juguete*. Yet it would be difficult to cite a play written by a man that even attempts to make the kind of feminist statements about the possibilities for female agency that emerge in *El eterno femenino* or *Casa matriz*. Moreover, there is a tendency in the women-authored plays to stress more domestic, female-oriented issues or, as *Adjetivos* and *El despojamiento* make evident, to analyze gender via the theater. Consequently, although it is difficult to insist that all of these dramas about game playing articulate a feminist ideological stance, certain shared characteristics do appear to suggest at least a degree of unanimity of purpose.

The ironies and ambiguities inherent in this discussion of the dramatists' uniqueness as *women* writers may, at least to a degree, be addressed via a return to Huizinga. *Homo Ludens* tells us that "[a]ll play means something," that play "can be very serious," and that "society expresses its interpretation of life and the world through play."[26] In that sense, we may glimpse the workings of the metaphors that lie at the heart of these dramas and that serve as both their subject and object. It might be sustained that their authors have produced so many dramas treating games and play because they have found the metaphor especially relevant to their concerns. This may, in turn, help to explain why game playing seems to occur in such a comparatively large number of women-authored plays and why so many of the characters in these particular dramas are female: women have been forced by their cultures—and they are cultures decidedly still controlled by men at the beginning of the new millennium—to follow socially scripted rules and to play games that stress gender hierarchies and submission to stronger, more powerful "players," and they frequently express their social roles and identities in a theatrically self-conscious manner. Role and identity are, in effect, social scripts; as Helene Keyssar observes, many dramas re-present history in order to

call into question conventional notions and theatrical representations of sexuality and the relationship of power to gender. . . . Many of these plays exploit the very nature of theatre to demonstrate the distinction between gender and sexuality. It is not in biologically defined social identity but in social gender roles that power is allocated and enacted on stage.[27]

By utilizing play (both literal and theatrical) to foreground social gender roles, women dramatists are able to call attention to the social and cultural realities that define their identities and, in the process, react critically to them.

These playwrights most often use the game, itself allied with power and control, to portray the cultural and literary encoding that links gender with manipulation, repression, and hierarchy. Ironically, however, games are curiously paradoxical choices for women to utilize in structuring their plays, at least in part because of the varied connotations that they generate. Although commonly associated with childhood, innocence, and liberation from the harsh realities of the rest of the world, the kinds of games that surface in these recent dramas by Spanish American women overtly deconstruct such images, rendering their presence ironic in the extreme. Indeed, as the playtexts reveal, game playing is equivocal and unstable, operating on a shifting ground, simultaneously subversive and rule-bound, the ultimate representation of freedom and the consummate expression of authority. Furthermore, games have winners and losers; as Huizinga reminds us, "[Play] creates order, *is* order. . . . Play demands order absolute and supreme."[28] It might seem improbable that so many women dramatists consciously employ the game as a textual strategy, since the kinds of power relationships that operate in games have historically privileged men over women—and since the hierarchical construction of winners and losers, linear movement, and binary oppositions such as order/ chaos, self/other, or dominance/subjugation would tend to uphold patriarchal models. Many of these women-authored dramas, however, emerge as ironic on yet another level, because their authors insert themselves even more dramatically into hierarchical positions at the moment they are exposing the repressive social conditions that surround them. The playwrights evoke a kind of double-voiced discourse, inscribing their texts into the male tradition of contest and competition while simultaneously using its very conventions to destabilize the literary and cultural myths that are encoded in the concept of game playing. In that paradoxical sense, theme and structure act in opposition to one another, allowing us to witness the oscillating movement between men and women and between winners and losers in the games of the theater.

2

Ludic Theory: Games and Drama Criticism

"The course of the world is a playing child moving figures on a board."

—Heraclitus (Fragment 52)

THE NATURE OF PLAY APPEARS EASY TO APPREHEND AND DEFINE. WE ALL played as children; we continue to engage in games and play as adults. As Joseph W. Meeker asserts in his foundational work in the field of literary ecology, "Play is as natural as breathing."[1] Yet, like most universal concepts, the subject has been explored and debated by philosophers, pundits, poets, and psychologists as the quintessential example of popular culture and as a metaphor for explaining the meaning of human existence. In this chapter, I will trace key discussions of play in its relationship to high and low culture, examine attempts to define and describe it in a variety of fields, and outline its application to literary texts and to the theater.

Early references to the play phenomenon can be traced back to Heraclitus, although play has existed from the beginning of time. Jack Maguire, the author of several mass market books on play and storytelling, reminds us that in the earliest days of human existence, both the young and the old shared their pastimes and labors, and "like the distinction between childhood and adulthood, the distinction between work and play for all ages was less clear in the past than it is today."[2] Until around the time of the Industrial Revolution, games were often pragmatic in nature, serving to instruct children and keep older people in shape for their responsibilities by functioning as metaphors for social interactions. No matter what they were called in other countries and languages, "Tag" or "Hide-and-Seek," for example, could mimic stalking wild animals or herding livestock; "Marbles" required dexterity and critical thinking skills; "Prisoner's Base" or "Tug-of-War" imitated war; "Musical Chairs," "Ring-Around-the-Rosy," and "London Bridge" originally reenacted historical events.[3] These games allowed their players to gain symbolic control over stressful situations; others functioned as spiritual rites or incantations "originally designed to impose some order on the mysteries of the universe," or reinforce acceptable sociocultural or religious behaviors.[4] Games were immensely popular:

> In the aftermath of the Roman Empire, game playing became such a bonding element in every facet of group life that great halls were built so that large-scale games could be played indoors as well as outdoors. These halls were commonly called ball houses, because so many games involved balls; but they were also the scenes of running, chasing, singing, and dancing games. The generic name *ball house* accounts for the origin of the current terms *ballad* for a narrative-style song, *ball* for a celebratory dance, and *ballet* for a dance performance.[5]

Around the time of the Great Plague of London (which produced "Ring-Around-the-Rosy"), Western culture began to differentiate childhood from adulthood; the old games were still there, but they were now called "children's games," and adults tended either to create more sedentary and intellectually challenging card and board games, or to replace simpler group games with more complex team sports.[6]

Attempts to theorize about the nature of play and games often begin with the work of Johan Huizinga, whose theories inform most modern approaches to the topic, including my own. In his ground-breaking examination of the nature of play, *Homo Ludens: A Study of the Play Element in Culture* (1938, Dutch edition; 1949, first English edition), Huizinga discusses the two functions of play: it can be a contest *for* something, or it can be a representation *of* something.[7] This, of course, also offers a logical connection to the theater. Related to ritual, tied to relaxation, play is intimately linked with the theater—even the word "play" as a text performed onstage reinforces this point of intersection. Like the theater, play is often a metaphor for our lives and realities. It can make manifest the nature of role and identity, helping us to define who we really are, even as we enter into the world of illusion.

Still, play encompasses much more than the activities of children, contest, representation, or the world of the theater. The topic has emerged as an area of study in numerous fields, although it entered that of literary theory and criticism principally in the twentieth century:

> There is a gamut of applications to which "play" lends itself. It is a polyvalent term which finds currency as an ordering force in anthropology, edu-

cation, mathematics, philosophy, psychology, and theology. . . . With few exceptions play theories through the nineteenth century have been marked by a tangential discussion of play as an aesthetic category. Indeed, comments are usually limited to recognizing the general principle that artistic creation is a play function. Not until the twentieth century is much consideration given to developing play as a specifically aesthetic principle and to applying it to actual literary works.[8]

Ruth E. Burke sets out her own definition of play: "A human and humanizing activity which is aesthetic in nature (i.e., pertaining to one of the highest modes of human experience) and in mediate position between the immanent and the transcendent."[9] Because of Burke's historical overview of the topic, I will begin my theoretical discussion with her survey, which includes the contributions of such luminaries as Huizinga and Roger Caillois, move to the work of Victor Turner and other anthropologists who have had a major impact on the field, and conclude my own overview of the nature of ludic criticism with a few key examples of its application to literature, ending with its emergence as a tool for explicating Spanish American plays of the last fifty years.[10]

Burke's study, *The Games of Poetics: Ludic Criticism and Postmodern Fiction*, traces the history of ludic theory from Plato, Aristotle, and Kant to Friedrich Schiller; Schiller's concept of the play impulse to explain the origin of art (in *Letters on the Aesthetic Education of Man*) would later have a significant impact on the field. She focuses, however, on twentieth-century play theories, beginning with the seminal study on the topic, Huizinga's *Homo Ludens*. Huizinga's classic definition of the play-concept is cited by virtually every study that will follow:

> play is a voluntary activity or occupation executed within certain fixed limits of time and place, according to rules freely accepted but absolutely binding, having its aim in itself and accompanied by a feeling of tension, joy and the consciousness that it is "different" from "ordinary life."[11]

Huizinga's study looked at the function of play in culture, examining key binary oppositions that would be debated for years to come, as his *Homo Ludens* was published in multiple editions and languages across the globe. Particularly noteworthy were the oppositions of play/work, play/everyday life, imaginary/real, and play/seriousness. Jacques Ehrmann summarizes the "remarkable scope and insight" of Huizinga's work:

> Huizinga is in fact the first to have undertaken, in a systematic way, to establish certain relationships between various human activities (law, war, poetry, art, etc.) which at first glance might appear to have nothing in common. His great merit is specifically to have discovered in the play-element of these activities a common denominator and an important factor of culture.[12]

Following Huizinga, the second major play theorist of the twentieth century was Roger Caillois, whose *Man, Play and Games* (1958) offered an elaborate system of play categories and refined terminology.[13] Caillois insisted that play is free and voluntary; make-believe and unproductive; rule-governed; circumscribed within fixed and predetermined limits of space and time; and uncertain in its course or results.[14] Much of this description echoes that of Huizinga, and, in truth, both have been criticized for a degree of narrowness of interpretation or unresolved contradictions, just as both are cited by virtually every critic treating the topic since the publication of their studies. Caillois's categorization of play is probably the best known aspect of his writings. He suggests that play be divided among four categories or attitudes, depending upon which of the following is dominant: competition ("the desire to win by one's merit in regulated competition," or *agon*), chance ("the submission of one's will in favor of anxious and passive anticipation of where the wheel will stop," or *alea*), simulation ("the desire to assume a strange personality," or *mimicry*), or the pursuit of vertigo (*ilinx*). Theatrical presentations belong to the third category.[15] These four categories are elements of an overarching continuum, which runs from *ludus* (controlled play) to *paidia* (spontaneous play).[16]

Huizinga and Caillois represent the two dominant voices in twentieth-century examinations of play and games. Their early work on the topic spawned interest in the field and ultimately led to numerous later critical discussions of the nature of play. Edward Norbeck, for example, would contribute his own description of play:

> Characteristic behavior of mankind at all ages of life . . . and is distinguished by the combination of traits of being voluntary, somehow pleasurable, distinct temporally from other behavior, and distinctive in having a make-believe or psychically transcendental quality.[17]

Still other scholars would enter the debate about what exactly constitutes play and games and the differences between them. In *The Games of Poetics*, Burke summarizes other key twentieth-century studies of the role of play, which I briefly mention here for their significant impact on the field. These include Eugen Fink's *Le jeu comme symbole du monde* (1960), which explores play within the larger study of philosophy; Hans-Georg Gadamer's *Truth and Method* (1960); Jacques Ehrmann's edition of a special issue of *Yale French Studies, Game, Play, Literature* (1968), which includes a number of key essays in the areas of philosophy, literary theory, and the practice of the game; a special issue of *Sub-Stance*, "A Polylogue on Play," (1980), edited by Robert Chumbley; Jean Duvignaud's *Le jeu du jeu* (1980); and Peter Hutchinson's *Games Authors Play* (1983), the first study to demonstrate "how a writer can 'signal' a game and draw the reader into deductive and reflective dialogue with the text."[18]

Burke describes the publication of other diverse studies of play since 1980, many of which treat the topic via sports, metafiction, or postmodernism. She concludes that virtually every critic analyzing play since the time of Huizinga "insists on play's freeness or voluntariness of participation, its special position in time and space, and its quality of make-believe (acting as if). All forms of play therefore contain an element of transcendence in that they provide momentary escape from ordinary perception and existence."[19] Burke ends her historical and theoretical overview with her own views on play as a mode of critical analysis, discussing the connections between play and wit, humor, irony, dream, fantasy, reflexivity, and postmodern fiction, and applying her ideas in analyses of six modern and postmodern novels. Like the work of Hutchinson, Burke's study is fundamental for its presentation of the state of the field and for its union of theory and practice. Nonetheless, it took the work of an anthropologist to fully bring ludic criticism to the study of theater.

The studies of the anthropologist Victor Turner have, indeed, enlightened the relationship between the theater and play or games. In *Dramas, Fields, and Metaphors* (1974), Turner discusses social dramas and ritual metaphors, ideas he had originally put forth in *Schism and Continuity in an African Society* (1957). Seeing the social world as constantly "becoming" and social relations as inherently dynamic, Turner notes the dramatic quality of the metaphor ("My metaphor and model here was a human esthetic form, a product of *culture* and not of nature").[20] He posits that social dramas can occur in the family or in the state and "can be isolated for study in societies at all levels of scale and complexity. This is particularly the case in political situations." Like Greek drama, "where one witnesses the helplessness of the human individual before the Fates," social dramas are governed by conflict: "People have to take sides in terms of deeply entrenched moral imperatives and constraints, often against their own personal preferences." "Social dramas, then, are units of aharmonic or disharmonic process, arising in conflict situations. Typically, they have four main phases of public action, accessible to observation"; these are *breach* of regular, norm-governed social relations, a phase of mounting *crisis, redressive action,* and either *reintegration* of the disturbed social group *or their agreement to differ.*[21]

In *From Ritual to Theatre: The Human Seriousness of Play* (1982), Turner elaborates upon his earlier definitions. His union of social dramas and the theater is particularly useful for this study: "By means of such genres as theatre . . . performances are presented which probe a community's weaknesses, call its leaders to account, desacralize its most cherished values and beliefs, portray its characteristic conflicts and suggest remedies for them, and generally take stock of its current situation in the known 'world.' "[22] Relating performance to experience, Turner states, "For me, the anthropology of performance is an essential part of the anthropology of experience. In a sense, every type of cultural performance, including ritual, ceremony, carnival, theatre, and poetry, is explanation and explication of life itself. . . . Here the etymology of 'performance' may give us a helpful clue, for it has nothing to do with 'form,' but derives from Old French *parfournir,* 'to complete' or 'carry out thoroughly.' A performance, then, is the proper finale of an experience."[23] This particular type of experience is especially related to the experimental theater so common in the 1960s and 1970s in the United States and echoed in Spanish America. Turner looks back to Greek comedy and tragedy to analyze the essence of their "play": these theatrical events are " 'social metacommentaries' on contemporaneous Greek society, that is, whatever the nature of their plot, whether drawn from myths or reputed historical accounts, they were intensely 'reflexive.' If they were 'mirrors held up to nature' (or rather to society and culture) they were *active . . .* mirrors, mirrors that probed and analyzed the axioms and assumptions of the social structure. . . ."[24]

Turner distinguishes the differences between the "liminal" and the "liminoid" by "associating the first with obligatory, tribal participation in ritual and the second as characterizing artistic or religious forms voluntarily produced, usually with recognition of individual authorship, and often subversive in intention towards the prevailing structures."[25] The issue of liminality relates directly to the connections between play, theater, and society. As Richard Schechner asserts,

"Turner sought to integrate the notion of liminality—the threshold, the betwixt and between—so decisive to his grasp and experience of ritual as anti-structural, creative, often carnivalesque and playful—with his emerging understanding of the relationship between social drama and aesthetic drama. Performance is central to Turner's thinking because the performative genres are living examples of ritual in/as action."[26]

Turner returns to the etymology of the word "play," noting the early sense of "fight" or "battle" as well as that of "recreation." The liminal "in-between" nature of certain types of theater (for example, the Theater of the Absurd or the Theater of Cruelty, which Turner prefers to call "liminoid") brings him again to the links between ritual and theater. "Theater," he notes, "is a liminoid process, set in the liminoid time of leisure between the role-playing times of 'work.' It is, in a way, 'play' or 'entertainment' (which means, etymologically, 'held-in-between,' that is, it is a liminal or liminoid phenomenon)." Turner observes that the theater, like all cultural forms, can be both conformative and subversive: "I am merely arguing that the rise of modern and postmodern theatre contains within it the seeds of a fundamental critique of *all* social structures hitherto known."[27] Schechner articulates the essence of his colleague's philosophy:

> He taught that there was a continuous, dynamic process linking performative behavior—art, sports, ritual, play—with social and ethical structure: the way people think about and organize their lives and specify individual and group values. . . . I think he was so long interested in performance—theatre, dance, music, ritual, and social drama—because performance is the art that is open, unfinished, decentered, liminal. Performance is a paradigm of process.[28]

In "Body, Brain, and Culture," Turner analyzes play as that which doesn't fit in: "Play is, for me, a liminal or liminoid mode, essentially interstitial, betwixt-and-between all standard taxonomic nodes. . . . Like many Trickster figures in myths . . . play can deceive, betray, beguile, delude, and gull."[29] As Schechner puts it, "in Turner's terms, play is categorically uncategorizable, the 'anti' by means of which all categories are destabilized."[30] This radical, destabilizing stance points to the obvious connections between performance, social commentary, and play—connections that offer a theoretical underpinning for the present study of the play concept as theme and structure in numerous Latin American dramatic texts.

Other anthropologists have also contributed a great deal to the study of the nature and function of play in society, offering significant implications for the examination of game playing in the dramas of Spanish American women.[31] A primary subset of the study of plays and games is that of children's play, an area that offers a great deal of applicable data and theories to the field.[32] Helen B. Schwartzman, in *Transformations: The Anthropology of Children's Play*, reminds us of one of the key points to which play theorists subscribe—even if they also continue to debate the issue:

> Perceptions of play are intimately related to one's culture. In the West, our understanding of play has been most significantly influenced by shared attitudes of what play is *not*. Play is not *work*; play is not *real*; play is not *serious*; play is not *productive*, and so forth.[33]

Studies of children's play have explored such topics as language play—play languages, verbal dueling (ritualized insults), riddles, vocabulary games, narratives—games requiring physical skill, those requiring strategy, and sports (which often combine both). Children's play and games are often viewed as models of adult behaviors, illustrating the preparatory function of play as children mimic adult behavior. For example, "Capture the Flag" offers a "perfect model of the male contest, allowing boys to experience power and prestige; it promotes fraternity despite the aggressiveness of the game."[34]

Brian Vandenberg describes the two prevailing approaches to studying child's play: "play as handmaiden" and a child priority approach. The "play as handmaiden" school sees the relationship between play and other developmental factors. It could, for instance, serve as a handmaiden to more central features of development, such as problem solving or creativity, or, in the case of fantasy play, enhance the development of social and cognitive skills. The child priority approach stresses the idea that since "children boldly state what we adults only dare whisper," we can "ask how children's myths illuminate important adult needs"; such myths can be religious, political, economic, or scientific in nature.[35]

Although we often think of play in terms of children ("it's mere child's play") and relaxation, the topic has serious repercussions for the adult world. Huizinga emphasizes the idea that play is order and creates order: "Into the confusion of life, it creates a temporary perfection."[36] It is rule-governed, with "spoilsports" those who ignore or transgress the rules of the game.[37] Play is seldom free in any absolute sense. More often, it establishes hierarchies, as leaders and followers, winners and losers illustrate its natural flow, its "characterization." It is a means by which authority and control are effected and maintained.

At this point, it is relevant to note that game theorists—the majority of whom are anthropologists, psychologists, or sociologists—have differing opinions regarding whether or not "game" and "play" are synonymous terms. In questioning categorical differentiations, the debate has explored issues such as spontaneity and organization (or lack thereof) of the play or game; the amount of convention, formalization, and institutionalization exhibited; and the presence or absence of rules in play.[38] Huizinga and Caillois, whose early research in the field has sparked a renewed interest in the topic, tended to use the terms interchangeably, suggesting that both play and games have rules, a point that later critics have questioned. Yet, concludes Klaus V. Meier in "Play and Paradigmatic Integration," "most social scientists are no longer ensconced at the stage of appealing to Huizinga and Caillois as almost canonical authorities."[39]

Meier, in his overview of the state of the field in 1986, observes that current theory tends to support either Piaget's typology of play types and model of child development or Bateson's view that play is a signal or "meta-message" (e.g., the signal "this is play"), "a frame demarking a class of behaviors not to be taken seriously."[40] The conflict between joy and seriousness with regard to play is another area of contention among those who study the topic. Although a number of scholars believe that play is motivated by joy, others have countered with examples of play that is "furtive, brutal, and cruel . . . not entered into voluntarily and not producing positive results."[41] These instances hold great implications for the study of the role of play in contemporary Spanish American theater, since so many dramas are characterized by their violence and negative conclusions.

Related to the dichotomy of joy and seriousness in play research is the relationship between play and reality. Schwartzman notes that some anthropologists see children's play as a distortion of reality in which, over time, illusions come to correspond to reality, reflecting a developmental movement of play → games → reality; she suggests, however, that play "creates and contains its own 'reality'," alluding to, rather than distorting, events.[42] Meier again clarifies the issue: "Play is not necessarily based upon an avoidance of directly dealing with reality. Rather, it involves a change of perspective on the part of the participant to effect a temporary transformation or suspension of normal social dictates."[43] This "temporary transformation or suspension" is clearly reminiscent of the "willing suspension of disbelief" that characterizes the theater audience's acceptance of the "reality" it sees depicted on stage, just as it also signals the presentation of "real-seeming artifice" in our traditional understanding of the tension between illusion and reality in the theater. Indeed, Gadamer reminds us in *Truth and Method* of the paradox inherent in the theater and in all art: art is a type of game that is both set apart from real life and vitally related to actual existence.[44]

In addition to the studies of Ruth E. Burke and Peter Hutchinson, a number of scholars have utilized the work of the philosophers and social scientists mentioned above to investigate the role of the ludic in literature; a few salient examples will help delineate the state of research in the field. Huizinga saw those links in his insistence that all literature involves game playing, noting that the "players voluntarily suspend reality to engage in mutually-acceptable communication."[45] Numerous other studies have insisted upon the essential position that art is by definition play.[46] Pointing to the role of "language as a potential medium for play and a means for describing" it, Chick observes that "Literature, in its many forms, thus provides a remarkably fertile area for play research."[47] Nancy A. Benson, in "Play Theory and an Elizabethan Sonnet Sequence," posits that the "use of ludic theory as an analytic tool can . . . throw new light on works previously neglected or misunderstood."[48] Benson focuses less on examples of play *in* the text than on the author's play *with* the text, analyzing such elements as games of pretense, variations on conventional models and strategies, the interrelated roles of time and repetition in play and poetry, and the exploitation of the phonic possibilities of language as techniques that can clarify our understanding of the works in question and the relationship between play and literature.

Gene Koppel employs a game approach to analyze an Anne Tyler novel, concluding that "The psychology and spirit of game-playing permeate *Breathing Lessons*, shaping its characters, events, themes, and basic form. And in its central concern with game-playing the novel explores the nature of art itself."[49] Koppel examines rules, roles, the spirit of play at work with each character, the issue of choice in playing games, the function of game playing (for its own sake, for social or financial prizes or awards), the game as "playing with" people's lives without their consent or knowledge, and the role of the author in luring us into the game and keeping us playing until the end.[50]

In the area of Hispanic literature, Catherine Bellver uses games "as a metaphor for the process of conflict resolution at work in the reading of *ultraísta* poetry." The reader, Bellver observes, who is willing to "'play' the text—to remain open to polysemy and ambiguity and to actively engage in its completion—can find allusive connotations that allow literary communication to take place."[51] Also analyzing play and Hispanic poetry, Gordana Yovanovich has recently utilized ludic theory to examine the presentation of black women in the early poetry of Nicolás Guillén: through play the black woman "finds her dignity and realizes her humanity by playfully engaging the very circumstances that threaten her." Yovanovich follows Turner in thinking that play not only implies the fluidity and energy of a "higher power" but also emerges as "a powerful mode of resistance against authority, including social and political authorities."[52]

We can see similar approaches in studies of game playing in the works of several Spanish American dramatists. A number of critics have explored the ludic qualities of metatheatrical texts from the Americas, and others have noted briefly the use of games in specific plays as part of their discussions of other issues. In 1991, Pilar V. Rotella presented a paper entitled "Games People Play: Oppressors and Oppressed in Three Plays by Latin American Women Writers (Castellanos, Hernández, Gambaro)," which explicitly looks at the game from a sociopolitical perspective. Rotella posited that these three women writers "explore issues of dominance and dependence, victimization and subordination, and the visible, outward rituals which embody complex inner motivations. Each writer, however, chooses to highlight a different section in the vast tapestry of human emotions woven on the basic pattern of power: who gets it, who wields it, who suffers its effects."[53] Nora Eidelberg's 1985 *Teatro experimental hispanoamericano 1960–1980: La realidad social como manipulación* divides Spanish American theater into three categories—ludic, didactic, and popular—in order to illustrate the methods employed to define reality during those two key decades of social and political unrest. Grounding her approach to the first category in Rubén Monasterios's definition of the ludic (from *Un enfoque crítico del teatro venezolano*, 1975), Eidelberg states that ludic theater is deductive and indirect, trying to present both the known and the unknown, the unique and the commonplace in a series of games, "tautological at times, symbolic and/or poetic," that are centered around "a deliberate search for the essence of reality."[54] Eidelberg posits that ludic theater, by nature veiled, is accessible only to an intellectual elite. Her examination of five plays (Juan Carlos Ghiano's *Corazón de tango*, Susana Torres Molina's *Extraño juguete*, Vicente Leñero's *La carpa*, Isaac Chocrón's *La revolución*, and Julio Ortega's *Mesa Pelada, cuatro ensayos*) illustrates how each dramatist portrays reality and how that reality is then elevated to a symbolic or ideological level. The critic focuses on two principal techniques utilized by the five dramatists: the creation of a play within the play (or game within a game) and the incorporation of intertextual elements (texts within the text).[55] She avers that the dramatic action of ludic theater is centered on the game itself, with no didactic or utilitarian goals as requisite elements. A statement particularly relevant to this study is Eidelberg's contention that games are either child-like, erotic, or evil in nature.[56] The plays I analyze fit well into these categories, which serve as useful descriptors and structuring devices. Finally, Amalia Gladhart's *The Leper in Blue: Coercive Performance in Contemporary Latin American Theater* contains a chapter analyzing games in the theater. Focusing specifically on Mariela Romero's *El juego*, Gladhart points to an aspect of game playing that is reflected in many of the dramatic texts examined in this book: "Like performance, game-playing is inherently polysemous, conventional in its reproduction of rule structures, subversive in its refiguration of reality."[57]

The critic most deeply involved with the topic is Jacqueline Eyring Bixler, who has written several essays treating game playing in Spanish American theater, using Huizinga as a prime theoretical resource. One essay also uses reader-response criticism to examine a play by Osvaldo Dragún ("The Game of Reading and the Creation of Meaning in *El amasijo*"), a text characterized by its ludic nature and the necessary participation of the reader: "It is at once a puzzle and a process."[58] In "Los juegos crueles de Egon Wolff: ¿Quién juega?," Bixler analyzes a number of plays by Wolff, in particular *Kindergarten* and *Háblame de Laura*, that highlight ludic and agonistic intensity, often achieved by means of ritualized roles and games. Probably the most significant study by Bixler was mentioned in the first chapter, "Games and Reality on the Latin American Stage" (1984), which treats three of the texts that will be examined in this book: Romero's *El juego*, Torres Molina's *Extraño juguete*, and Mahieu's *Juegos a la hora de la siesta*. Her comments on the game within the theatrical game merit emphasis:

. . . the games being played on the Latin American stage today are not the chaotic, seemingly nonsensical games of absurdist drama, but rather organized, purposeful games that reflect metaphorically an extratextual, socio-political reality. While pretending through play to escape from their banal, miserable existence, the characters unconsciously produce a distorted, mirror image of that very same reality. Under the pretense that all is a game, the dramatist subtly attacks the power structures that dictate the rules by which one must play in order to survive. . . . The fact that all three works were written by women was not a determinant in the selection of these texts, although it does suggest that female dramatists have found in gamesplaying a particularly effective form of communicating their own personal feelings of repression as women in a male and power-oriented Hispanic society.[59]

This last, apt statement reflects my own position vis-à-vis the use of game playing in women-authored dramatic texts, because, as Bixler stresses, game playing acts as both the text and the context in their works.[60] Games function to create the female subject—often, by using play to grant the woman metaphorical authority and control—and in so doing, they interrogate and subvert the cultural, political, and social power structures that have created the rules women have been forced to follow for decades and even centuries.

Bixler sees game playing in the theater occurring on at least two levels: "one, the on-stage playing of roles, and two, the spectator's suspension of disbelief, or pretension that this illusion is reality. The possibilities of further levels of game playing are infinite as the actors play games in which they create or adopt new fictional roles."[61] Bixler is describing metatheatrical role-playing within a role, which is by definition a kind of game—most frequently, both for the other characters onstage and for the audience. This type of metatheater is probably the most prevalent form of game playing found in the dramas examined in this book, as characters move from one role to the next, shifting identities in a great theatrical game reminiscent of the great theater of the world of Calderonian drama.[62] These games of the theater—including their theoretical underpinnings—will be investigated in much greater detail in the next chapter, but a few key elements merit mention here, as well, due to their relationship to ludic theory in general.

The functions of game playing within the drama as theme and/or structure are multiple. First, games underscore the self-reflexive nature of the theater itself, in that many games involve role-playing, inset dramas, etc. Second, they establish irony by definition: when children's games are used in violent, sadistic ways by adults, the audience is quick to notice the distance between expectations and reality. In fact, the shock value of using the games of innocent childhood to enact unspeakable horrors clearly emphasizes those horrors all the more. Consequently, the game metaphor can allow the dramatist to explore socially or politically dangerous topics within an innocent context, setting up critiques by means of this veiled technique. Such topics might include the position of woman in the Spanish American patriarchy or the protest against such events as the Argentine Dirty War or the Mexican Tlatelolco massacre. Bixler sees many of these same characteristics in her analysis: "Within the texts lie deeper resemblances: a nakedness of dialogue and stagecraft, a language deep in ambiguity, symbolism, and political undertones, and a metatheatrical usage of gamesplaying. . . . The games themselves are the vital link between the stage and the real world, for the games performed in the theatre are an obvious metaphor of the games played in today's society."[63]

This chapter has presented the evolution of ludic theory and practice, highlighting some of the most significant connections between anthropology and the theater in the process. In the direct application of the topic of play and games to literary texts, critics have tended to emphasize Huizinga's groundbreaking work in the field. Early work in the area of Spanish American theater has signaled the relationship between the theatrical game and those played in society. The goal of the current study is to expand upon those concepts in order to provide a more global and comprehensive understanding of the impact of the ludic upon a representative group of Spanish American women writers. In so doing, we will explore, as the anthropologist Norbeck proposed for his own field,[64] play as a mirror of the pervasive values and attitudes of the societies these writers (re)present. By looking at the nature and number of the games played, we will examine how, in these dramas, play is utilized as a means of social control; the connections between play and aggression, gender, history, and politics; the manifestation of power in the games played among and between the characters in the texts studied; and the ways in which theatrical games function to illustrate the textual strategies that these women writers share.

3

Games in the Theater: Representation, Roleplaying, and the Search for Identity in Dramas by Elena Garro, Maritza Wilde, and Susana Torres Molina

"All play **means** something."
—Johan Huizinga, *Homo Ludens*

IN A VERY REAL SENSE, EVERY DRAMA STUDIED IN THIS BOOK IS ABOUT theatrical games. The playwrights, ever conscious of the fact that the theater itself is a grand illusion, implement games that highlight the *theatrum mundi* metaphor and emphasize role-playing within the role. In some dramas, the theatrical game is the central thematic or structural element of the playtext. Others highlight metatheater while maintaining a central focus on issues such as social interaction or political repression. Indeed, David William Foster contends that not only does metatheater "formalize in an overdetermined way the inescapable nature of human relations," but it also "is designed to underscore [the] sociocultural role of the spectacle."[1] Each of the dramas discussed in this chapter displays a distinctive slant, providing an overview of the range of possible approaches to the topic. Elena Garro's *Felipe Ángeles* offers an overtly metatheatrical play that consistently underscores the connections between the theater and games, calling attention to its own theatricality as it presents the sham trial and subsequent execution of one of the heroes of the Mexican Revolution. Maritza Wilde's *Adjetivos* [Adjectives] also unites theater, history, and game playing in its self-conscious examination of what human beings are capable of doing to each other. Garro's *La dama boba*[2] [The Lady Simpleton] highlights metatheatrical allusions (what Richard Hornby calls literary and real-life references)[3] in an intellectual and intertextual game that asks the reader or spectator to find echoes of the literary past in her drama. Susana Torres Molina's . . . *y a otra cosa, mariposa* [Moving On] stresses role-playing within the role as it explores gender issues. Indeed, much of what these playtexts illustrate may be seen in the following quotation from the radical psychiatrist R. D. Laing, which appears as the epigraph of the first printed version of Torres Molina's *Extraño juguete* [Strange Toy]:

> están jugando un juego.
> están jugando a que no
> juegan un juego.
> si les demuestro que veo que están jugando,
> quebraré las reglas y me castigarán.
> debo jugarles el juego de no ver
> que veo el juego.[4]

[they're playing a game. / they're playing that they're not / playing a game. / if I show them that I see that they're playing, / I'll break the rules and they'll punish me. / I should play on them the game of not seeing / that I see the game.]

The present study utilizes Lionel Abel's theories as a starting point for examining both the nature of self-conscious theater and contemporary explanations of how readers of the classics transform themselves into rewriters, recasting canonical texts into new forms for new audiences. In the past thirty-five years, most Hispanists have based their discussions of self-referential theater on Abel's *Metatheatre: A New View of Dramatic Form*, although they have frequently utilized only his basic definition of the phenomenon. In Abel's study, "metatheater" describes a new genre, which is neither comedy, tragedy, nor tragicomedy, but something else. Metadramas are "theatre pieces about life seen as already theatricalized," in which

> the persons appearing on stage in these plays are there not simply because they were caught by the playwright in dramatic postures as a camera might catch them, but because they themselves knew they were dramatic long before the playwright took note of them. What dramatized them originally? Myth, legend, past literature, they themselves.[5]

Due, in great measure, to its broad scope, Abel's study left a number of unanswered questions, but it nonetheless prepared the way for the kinds of modifications and practical applications that have made the word "metadrama" one of the most common terms in theater criticism.

In recent years, discussions of metatheater have evolved considerably. Studies by Keir Elam, James L. Calderwood, Robert Egan, Sidney Homan, and June Schlueter attest to both a continuing interest in the topic and a concomitant desire to move beyond Abel's general formulations and toward a more precise means of examining metadramatic texts. Elam's analysis of metatheatrical functions adds a new perspective to previous theoretical and practical considerations:

> They bring attention to bear on the theatrical and dramatic realities in play, on the fictional status of the characters, on the very theatrical transaction. . . . They appear to be cases of "breaking frame," since the actor is required to step out of his role and acknowledge the presence of the public, but in practice they are licensed means of *confirming* the frame by pointing out the pure facticity of the representation.[6]

These cases of "breaking frame" tend to occur most frequently in periods that are particularly self-conscious. Manfred Schmeling observes in *Métathéâtre et intertexte* that metadramatic reflection makes the text a type of dramatized literary history. Examples of theater within theater often emerge in those historical periods in which theatrical norms (such as the well-made play) are challenged by dramatists confronting accepted ideologies.[7]

Hornby's *Drama, Metadrama, and Perception* (1986) gives what is arguably the most comprehensive approach to the concept of self-conscious theater, going beyond much early work in the field by detailing a concise classification of metadramatic techniques, clarifying a number of muddy areas of understanding, and offering a truly useful tool for unlocking such plays as those analyzed in this study. *Drama, Metadrama, and Perception* is more descriptive than prescriptive. It begins traditionally, noting that, at its most basic level, a metadrama is a drama about drama, in which the subject of the play is drama itself. Hornby goes on to examine a curious effect of metatheater on the reader/spectator: we must feel that we are "seeing double"; that is, we must recognize that the dramatist has broken the illusion of the fictive world presented onstage. That recognition can vary with the degree that metadramatic techniques are employed in the play, but the resulting effect will always be a disruption of the imaginary world that has been established up to the moment those metadramatic techniques are used. Those techniques may be categorized into five principal types:

1. The play within the play
2. The ceremony within the play
3. Role-playing within the role
4. Literary and real-life reference
5. Self-reference[8]

Hornby's work in the field provides a number of tools for textual explication that can help to illuminate what the dramatists discussed in this chapter accomplished in their own metaplays.

Finally, it is useful to note a uniquely Spanish American perspective on metatheater. As Daniel Zalacaín has proposed, contemporary Spanish American dramatists often utilize the techniques of circularity and metatheater to illuminate the search for reality of humans trapped in a world of isolation; basically, he suggests, this theater reveals a profound social critique while simultaneously attempting to penetrate the extreme aspects of humanity's mysterious position in the world.[9] As we will see, metatheatrical techniques and social criticism go hand in hand in the dramas of Garro, Wilde, and Torres Molina.

Elena Garro's *Felipe Ángeles* chronicles the trial and execution of the Mexican general who allowed himself to be sacrificed for what he termed the ideals of the Revolution. The play (written in 1954, first published in 1967, staged in 1978, and published in its final form the following year)[10] describes a man of whom Garro had often heard her family speak with admiration: "He is a figure whom I still consider astonishing. He is the typical Revolutionary character who has been forgotten. All revolutions suffer the same process: they devour themselves."[11] *Felipe Ángeles* dramatizes this view of Mexican history, elucidating the clash of power (military, political, gender, personal) between opposing Revolutionary forces as a giant game. Garro weaves multiple references to game playing into her text. The entire trial—a farce in all senses of the word—is, ironically, set in a theater, and metadramatic allusions abound, as the reader/spectator becomes aware of the theatrical games at work. In addition, Garro's characters speak often of card games, children's games, power games. Rules are established, questioned, and broken, and the two opposing sides define themselves in terms of winning and losing. In this play, the dramatist uses the game as a central structuring device and as a metaphor to talk about both the Revolution and the years encapsulated by the twenty-five-year span between the work's original composition and its rebirth on the stage.

Garro structures *Felipe Ángeles* in an overtly metatheatrical manner. The first thing that the reader/spectator notices is the setting: the General's trial is to take place in a theater in Chihuahua—ironically, the Teatro de los Héroes. As Sandra Cypess observes, a theatrical space is converted into an improvised prison cell, suggesting the synecdochical relationship between this theatrical space and the entire country. In other words, Garro has turned the theater into the Mexican world and the world into the theater, creating a metatheatrical situation.[12] Virtually every character alludes to the entire "farce" as a theatrical game. In act 1, for example, three women meet with General Diéguez to protest the court martial of their hero. Diéguez states that he prides himself on being a man who knows all that there is to know about justice, since he is charged with imparting it, but the woman replies, "¿A organizar esta función de teatro le llama usted justicia, general?" [You call organizing this performance "justice," General?] (14). A number of the male characters use similar language as they discuss their orders from Venustiano Carranza to find Ángeles guilty and execute him:

DIÉGUEZ: Siento tener que hablarles en esos términos, pero he recibido instrucciones concretas de México.
   [*I'm sorry to have to speak to you in those terms, but I have received concrete instructions from Mexico City.*]
ESCOBAR: [*Señalando el teatro.*] Ahora me explico por qué vamos a juzgarlo en un teatro.
   [(*Indicating the theater*) *Now I understand why we're going to judge him in a theater.*]
DIÉGUEZ: [*Serio.*] ¿Qué quiere usted decir, general?
   [(*Serious.*) *What do you mean, General?*]
ESCOBAR: ¡Nada! Que a mí me cuesta trabajo aprenderme los papeles de memoria. (17)
   [*Nothing! It's just that I have trouble memorizing my part.*]

. . .

ESCOBAR: ¡Ojalá, General Diéguez, que no tenga yo que asistir a su función teatral! (18)
   [*I hope, General Diéguez, that I won't be forced to attend your show!*]

. . .

DIÉGUEZ: [*En voz muy alta.*] ¡Falta mucho para ese estreno, General Escobar! (18)
   [(*In a very loud voice.*) *There's a lot yet to be done before opening night, General Escobar!*]

. . .

DIÉGUEZ: He dado órdenes de anunciar el fusilamiento en el cerro de Santa Rosa, para desalojar un poco la ciudad de revoltosos. Esta misma noche empezará el éxodo. ¿Usted cree que van a perder el espectáculo? (54)

[*I have given orders to announce that the execution will take place on Santa Rosa Hill, so as to clear out the rebels from the city. This very night the exodus will begin. Do you think they're going to miss the spectacle?*]

. . .

ESCOBAR: Me quedo hasta el final de esta función de teatro. (56)
[*I'm staying till the end of this performance.*]

In response to General Diéguez, numerous characters stress the connections between the trial and the illusion of the theater: each of them is an actor in a play already scripted by Carranza. The final act has been written, and the actions and dialogue that precede it are preordained, since the actors are not allowed room to improvise. Garro's characters seem aware of their own inherent theatricality, self-consciously cognizant of their roles as actors in the dramas of others. As Diéguez tells Sandoval, "Tú lo único que tienes que hacer es declarar que Ángeles y sus hombres hicieron fuego sobre ustedes" [All you have to do is say that Ángeles and his men opened fire on you] (13).

Garro insinuates links to both farce and classical tragedy into her lengthy list of allusions to the theater. If Diéguez and Carranza are masterminding a cruel farce, making fun of concepts such as justice and honor, Ángeles behaves like a tragic hero, repeatedly describing his role in provoking his own death, noting his personal failings and tragic flaws of character, and refusing to escape when given the chance, thus sacrificing himself as a martyr.[13] In addition, as Delia Galván points out, the women characters appear to serve as the chorus of classical tragedy, powerless observers of the masculine power structure.[14]

The trial, which occupies the second act of the drama, functions as a play within the play, specifically, what Hornby terms the ceremony within a play. The inset play, by definition, creates esthetic distance between the playtext or its staging and the members of the audience, who, recognizing the trial as a play within the play, "see double," recalling the inherent illusory nature of the theater and, by extension, that of all human existence.[15] Part of the theatrical self-consciousness of the trial is its relationship to rite or ritual. Echoing Martin Esslin and Octavio Paz, Galván suggests that the ritualistic nature of the trial reflects the social needs of humanity since the times of primitive societies, producing a cathartic effect for the public in the light of history—in this case, Mexican history:

El equivalente de la danza guerrera de los dioses eran para los aztecas las guerras floridas que culminaban con el sacrificio de los prisioneros de guerra. Ángeles era enemigo de Carranza y por lo tanto una especie de dios perdedor de una de estas guerras. . . . A lo largo de la historia de México, sobre todo en épocas de crisis, se sigue observando cómo todavía existe una conexión subterránea entre los ritos y los actos políticos de dominación como se observaba en los aztecas, es decir: ". . . el modelo inconsciente del poder siguió siendo el mismo: La pirámide y el sacrificio" [cita a Paz]. De ser así, para Felipe Ángeles el escenario del Teatro de los Heroes de Chihuahua es su pirámide de sacrificio.[16]

[The equivalent of the war dance of the gods was, for the Aztecs, the flower wars, which culminated in the sacrifice of prisoners of war. Ángeles was Carranza's enemy and therefore like the gods on the losing side of these wars. . . . Throughout Mexican history, especially in times of crisis, you can find a subterranean connection between rites and political acts of domination, as was observed in the Aztecs; i.e., "the subconscious model of power was still the same: the pyramid and sacrifice" (quoting Paz). Consequently, for Felipe Ángeles, the stage of the Theater of the Heroes in Chihuahua is his sacrificial pyramid.]

The theatrical game is also tied to the relationship between truth and falsehood, illusion and reality. As one of the General's attorneys comments early on, "No hay que desesperar. Haremos que de esta farsa surja la verdad y el Gobierno tendrá que retroceder" [There's no need to fear. We'll make the truth rise from this farce and the Government will have to back down] (21). As the trial progresses, Ángeles nobly argues that those who have perjured themselves to convict him can never erase the truth of history:

Es una lástima que tengamos que recurrir a la mentira para justificar nuestros apetitos y nuestros actos. Y, ¿justificarse delante de quién? Los hechos existen por ellos mismos y están más allá de nuestro poder. Nuestro pasado es irrecuperable e invariable y ninguna mentira es capaz de borrarlo o de transformarlo. (34)

[It's a shame that we have to recur to a lie to justify our appetites and our actions. And justify to whom? What's done exists for its own sake and it's beyond the scope of our power. Our past is neither recuperable nor invariable, and no lie can erase or transform it.]

Language is key in this game of "Truth and Dare": "¡Compañeros, Ángeles tuerce las declaraciones de los testigos!" ["Comrades, Ángeles is twisting the witnesses' testimony!"]; "No, compañeros, no es Ángeles el que tuerce las declaraciones, son los testigos los que se enredan porque sencillamente están mintiendo" ["No, comrades, it's not Ángeles who is twisting the witnesses' testimony, it's the witnesses who are implicated in this mess because they're simply lying"] (45). And once again, Garro reminds her audience of the ludic nature of the situation as the characters lie and "play dirty": "Felipe Ángeles se queja de que queremos matarlo con mentiras. ¡Hay que jugarle limpio, compañeros!" [Felipe Ángeles complains that we want to kill him with lies. We have to play fair, comrades!] (45); "Insisto en que hay que jugarle limpio" [I insist that we have to play fair] (46). Theater, game playing, language, and history fuse in Garro's interpretation of this Mexican revolutionary hero.

Although several studies of the play have mentioned its metatheatricality in passing (usually, simply noting the theatrical setting and the play-within-a-play technique), none has examined yet another self-conscious aspect of the text: its relationship to a seminal drama of the Revolution, Rodolfo Usigli's *El gesticulador*. One is struck by the similarities between Garro's text and Usigli's 1937 play. In each historical drama, a general of the Revolution returns to the north and is martyred for his beliefs, saving his people from further killing; in each, truth and justice are central themes, and in each, the author stresses the key role of language—the power of the word—in history, in power struggles between people and between conflicting ideologies. Most significantly, each drama is a clear example of metatheater, emphasizing the play within the play, roleplaying within the role, and self-conscious references to the theater within the text,[17] and each uses this structuring technique to examine the continuing impact of the Mexican Revolution on the country years after the events depicted in the drama. In *Felipe Ángeles*, Garro seems acutely aware of Usigli's earlier play about a martyred "fictional" general as she writes about an actual figure from the days of the Revolution. This would add yet another level of metatheatrical game playing to her own text since, as Hornby avers, a major characteristic of self-conscious theater is the utilization of literary and real-life references. *Felipe Ángeles* offers each of these two types of allusions, further reinforcing the reader's or spectator's recognition of Garro's manipulation of reality and illusion.

In the life-and-death game played out in the Teatro de los Héroes, Garro constantly reminds her audience of the ludic nature of the action. Indeed, the word *jugar* surfaces ironically as the dramatist underscores the sense of staking one's life on something:

ESCOBAR: Si hubiéramos pensado en la disciplina militar, jamás hubiéramos tomado las armas.

[*If we had thought enough about military discipline, we would never have taken up arms.*]

GAVIRA: Era diferente. En ese tiempo nos alzamos contra la usurpación y a-demás nos jugábamos la cabeza.

[*It used to be different. Back then we rose up against usurpation and staked our lives on it.*]

ESCOBAR: Felipe Angeles también se la jugó entonces.

[*Felipe Ángeles also staked his life, then.*]

DIÉGUEZ: Y se la juega ahora, pero contra la Revolución. (17)

[*And he's staking it now, but against the Revolution.*]

Or, as General Bautista tells Ángeles at the beginning of the third act, when he suggests that the prisoner escape, "He decidido después de pensarlo todo el día, jugarme la cabeza con usted" [I've decided, after thinking about it all day, to stake my life on you] (57).

The characters also make frequent overt references to actual games and game playing. When General Diéguez comments upon Carranza's illegal prosecution of Ángeles, he notes that it would have been far better to have killed him in the country and say that he had died in an ambush: "Nada más está enseñando demasiado el juego" [He's showing his hand too much], to which Gavira replies, "Cuando la carta es buena hay que enseñarla. ¡Tenemos un as en la mano!" [When the card is good, you have to play it. We're holding an ace!] (19). In a similar vein, Ángeles's attorney tells his client not to be so pessimistic: "No olvide que Carranza se juega todas sus cartas sucias a la palabra legalidad" [Don't forget that Carranza is staking all his dirty cards on the word "legality"] (24). In yet another example, General Ángeles, discussing the role of innocence and culpability, destiny and free will in the matter, concludes that there is a self-determined common destiny guiding all of the players; he is interrupted by Colonel Bautista, who asserts that some will win and others will lose, to which Ángeles replies, "No, coronel, aquí no hay ganadores. Aquí todos hemos perdido por parejo" [No, Colonel, there are no winners here. Here, we've all lost at the same time] (23).

Garro's characters suggest the theme of playing games in more indirect ways, as well. In addition to the multiple overt references to games, some characters comport themselves on stage like children:

AGENTE DEL MINISTERIO PÚBLICO: El licenciado López Hermosa ha dicho que no soy honrado, por citar la confesión del acusado respecto al enemigo. Me permito suplicar al señor Presidente del Consejo, se sirva decir al señor

López Hermosa, que se sirva retirar estas palabras, porque no está en lo
justo al hacer tal apreciación sobre mi persona.
[*Attorney López Hermosa has said I'm not honorable, because I cited the
confession of the accused with respect to the enemy. Allow me to ask that
the President of the Council tell Mr. López Hermosa to take back his
words, because it's not fair to attack me personally.*]

LÓPEZ HERMOSA: Disculpe el señor Agente del Ministerio Público, ya que no
eran mis intenciones lastimarlo, y en obsequio a su deseo retiro las palabras que le hirieron.
[*I beg your pardon, Mr. Agent of the Public Ministry, as it wasn't my intention to injure you, and in deference to your request, I take back the
words that hurt you.*] (29)

This exchange, although cast in the formal language and reflecting the
protocol of the legal profession, is nonetheless reminiscent of childhood accusations and attempts to "take back" injurious words. Moreover, it subtly reminds the audience that the male players in these
games of power and male honor often act more like children than
adults. Cypess looks at this issue from a different but related perspective when she emphasizes the affirming role of the female characters
in the play. Indeed, one of the women reminds General Diéguez that
politics change and admit multiple interpretations (49), a view that
contradicts the single-minded, right-or-wrong position of the male
characters. Diéguez, however, reverts to traditional games between the
sexes as he attempts to disarm Ángeles's female supporters: "Le ase-
guro, señora, que no siempre es grato ser inflexible, y menos frente a
la belleza. Este es el juego de siempre, señora, las dos caras de la me-
dalla" [I assure you, madam, that being inflexible is not always pleas-
ant, and even less so when faced with such beauty. This is the same old
game, madam, the two sides of the coin] (49). Such macho verbal
games of courtship and power contrast with the actions of those same
male characters. Diéguez, for example, hides during the court martial,
and most of the other military officers leave town before Ángeles's execution.

In yet other connections between male legal and military comportment and game playing, Angeles's lawyers repeatedly ask the tribunal
to follow the official rules of the "game"—for example, to grant them
the time allowed by military law to provide disputed documentation.
This request is, ironically, denied in yet another power game because
the attorney is told he should already have had that documentation in
his possession to present at the court martial. The tribunal is clearly
a power game of the highest rank(s). Those in charge consistently dem-

onstrate their authority: "Señor general, evite las insinuaciones o nos veremos precisados a quitarle la palabra" [General, avoid such insinuations, or we'll be forced to deny you the right to speak] (41). The threat to silence Ángeles, here a foreshadowing of the physical act that will end the play, is emblematic of their game of power and the dramatist's attempts to illustrate the relationship between speech, lie, and silence—truth, fiction, and the suppression of true democratic dialogue—in the game of Mexican history. In another major point of disagreement in Angeles's trial, the lawyers and military judges debate the legality of trying Ángeles (who is no longer in the military) under military law. On the surface, this issue illuminates yet again the military's flagrant disregard of fact and law as they rush the court martial through to its inevitable conclusion. In addition, however, the dramatist insinuates into the text language that reminds the reader or spectator of the artificial nature of the entire event; characters frequently use words such as *aparato de legalidad* (legal show) or *función* (performance) to describe the trial (43). Garro repeatedly underscores the relationship between childhood games and the legal and military games of the adults in this drama.

The game is intimately linked to history, again stressing the idea of winning and losing. Gavira defends the military's actions, ignoring possible consequences: "Nosotros ganamos la partida. Los vencidos nunca tienen razón. La historia está con nosotros" [We're winning the game. The vanquished are never right. History is with us] (19). As Cypess asserts, Ángeles plays a synecdochical role as the victim of the distortions of the Revolution and [its] dissipated promises: "Garro questions not only the political bases of the promise offered by the Revolution, but also the very concepts of 'history' and 'reality.' She raises the problematic issue of the multiplicity of fictions, the impossibility of knowing the truth" (my translation).[18] Mexican politics is, as General Diéguez observes, a dirty game: "La política no es academia de ciencias. Aquí todos nos jugamos la vida. ¡Hay que escoger a cuál vida le vamos!" [Politics is no academy of sciences. Here, we're playing for our lives. We have to choose what kind of life we're going for!] Still, another general replies, "Ángeles jugó y perdió. ¿No es eso? Pero algo me dice que no perdió del todo. ¡Compañero Diéguez, nunca sabemos a cuál vida le vamos . . . !" [Ángeles played and lost. Isn't that it? But something tells me that he didn't completely lose. Comrade Diéguez, we never know what kind of life we're going for . . . !] (46). Garro thus leads us to her re-vision of the Mexican Revolution: "Eso no es la Revolución, es el viejo juego del poder, el quítate tú para ponerme yo"

[This isn't the Revolution, it's the same old power game, the "down with you and up with me"] (47). Indeed, General Diéguez, one of the principal perpetrators of the court martial, sees the irony: "Años y años peleando para seguir fusilando. La política no tiene fin, el poder no tiene fin" [Years and years of fighting only to fight some more. Politics has no end, power has no end] (48). "El juego de la política" [the game of politics] is alluded to throughout the play, as Garro explores new ways of interpreting her country's past. Ángeles sees his self-sacrifice as a possible means of effecting change:

> Ahora, después de este fracaso, entre todos, quizás podríamos inventar la historia que nos falta. La historia, como las matemáticas, es un acto de la imaginación. Y la imaginación es el poder del hombre para proyectar la verdad y salir de este mundo de sombras y de actos incompletos. (52)

> [Now, after this failure, among all of us, maybe we could invent the history we're lacking. History, like mathematics, is an act of imagination. And imagination is man's power to show truth and leave this world of shadows and unfinished actions.]

In fact, it could be posited that Ángeles's sacrifice (viewed by several characters as suicidal) is in itself a kind of noble game intended to influence the course of his country's history. He returned to Mexico after two years of exile (and once again, note the use of the word *juego*):

> para conciliar a los mexicanos y terminar con esta guerra fraticida entre los generales que traicionaron a la Convención y los revolucionarios que fueron fieles a la Convención y a los principios por los cuales luchamos todos antes de que entraran en juego las ambiciones personales. (32)

> [to reconcile the Mexican people and put an end to this fratricidal war between the generals who betrayed the Convention and the revolutionaries who were faithful to the Convention and to the principles for which we all fought, before personal ambitions entered the game.]

We return again to the game and the idea of winners and losers as Ángeles's execution approaches:

ESCOBAR: Comprendo que hay gente que juega para perder.
   [*I understand that there are those who play to lose.*]
ÁNGELES: No se pierde nada. Yo no jugué para perder, ni para ganar. Yo luché por unas [*sic*] principios. (65)
   [*Nothing is lost. I didn't play to lose, or to win. I fought for principles.*]

In the final moments of his life, the protagonist evokes his childhood, and the image of the game fuses with that of his country: "¡Niño Felipe Ángeles, te busca tu papá! No quiere que sigas jugando en las peleas de gallos . . ." [Felipe Ángeles, child, your daddy is looking for you! He doesn't want you to keep on playing in cockfights . . .] (67).

In *Felipe Ángeles*, Garro employs an extraordinarily large number of references to games and game playing in order to call attention to what she appears to perceive as the flaws of the Revolution and to her new vision of Mexican history and politics. The dozens of references to children's games, to the theater as a game, and to fiction in general structure her play, which emerges as a three-act game (prologue, trial, execution) with set roles and rules, winners and losers. The game motif reveals Garro's themes and illuminates her characters. The games within her drama illustrate the play within the games of power operant in Mexico dating from the time of the Revolution. Garro seems to suggest that by understanding this aspect of her country's past, one can bring about some real change in the present—in the Revolution that continues into the 1950s, when the play was conceived; into the 1960s, when the play was first published; and into the 1970s, when it was finally staged and published in an edition that would reach more readers. Of course, a key event in Mexican history, viewed by some as the reflection of the Revolution's legacy, occurs right in the middle of that time span. Intended or not, *Felipe Ángeles* speaks to the Mexico of Tlatelolco as it looks back on the country's past and toward its future.

Felipe Ángeles, set in a theater, making theater out of a trial and execution, emphasizes games and play as tools for discussing history's truth and fictions. Maritza Wilde, a Bolivian director and dramatist,[19] uses remarkably similar techniques in *Adjetivos* ([Adjectives], which premiered in 1990 and was published in 1997), a one-act drama that also underscores the illusion and reality of history by means of theatrical metaphors, games, and play. Willy O. Muñoz submits that the text unites the two themes that characterize Wilde's dramaturgy, women and dictatorship (the latter accompanied by violence and oppression), to present the message that each of us is capable of committing atrocious acts at any given moment.[20]

Wilde's play is set in a theater on a night during Carnaval, with the characters, Él and Ella, rehearsing the last scene of a drama in which they play the roles of Nicolás and Elena Ceausescu during their trial, sentencing, and execution. The depersonalized voices of the prosecutors are heard offstage, along with the background noise of a beating heart. After their prompter leaves, the two actors are left alone in the theater, soon discovering that they have been accidentally locked inside. Faced with solving the problem of how to spend the night, the actors (especially Ella) explore the interpretation of their roles ("Creo que hay algo falso, algo que no encaja" [I think there's something false, something that doesn't fit];[21] "¿por qué me es tan difícil lograr este personaje?" [why is it so hard for me to get into this character?] (517); "No puedo entrar en la piel de este personaje. Intelectualmente, aquí, (*se señala la cabeza*) me repugna, pero visceralmente, emocionalmente, me es extraño, indiferente" [I can't get in this character's skin. Intellectually, here, {*she points to her head*} she repulses me, but viscerally, emotionally, she's strange, indifferent] (523), contemplating the nature of the real people they will portray onstage and anguishing over the capacity of human beings to commit unspeakable acts: "Sé que quien dice: 'somos seres humanos,' es realmente humano y sin embargo hizo cosas inhumanas" [I know that someone who says "we're human beings" really is human and yet she did inhuman things] (517).[22] Their ontological and metatheatrical questioning alternates with Él's repeated attempts to seduce Ella—and when words do not help him achieve what he wants, he does not hesitate to use force. It would appear that the dictator's and actor's displays of power make a strong statement about issues of power and authority in gender relationships. Ella, however, is far from the drama's innocent victim: seizing the opportunity to play a sadistic game with Él, she ties him to a chair and, claiming control of the game, performs an erotic dance and begins to caress him while he is rendered immobilized and powerless. Yet the tables are turned not once, but twice: Él escapes his bonds and prepares to rape Ella, but at that very moment, the actors are interrupted by the theater's drunken *portero* (caretaker). The two actors then return to their roles as the Ceausescus, and the accusing offstage voice of the prosecutor ends the play and brings it full circle.

Wilde explicitly uses the concept of the game to analyze the relationship between Él and Ella. After his clumsy attempts to get Ella to have sex meet with repeated failures, Él appears to give in, announcing that she has won the game: "Está bien. Tú ganas. Te prometo que no te volveré a molestar. ¡Te lo juro! ¡Esta vez en serio!" [Okay. You win. I promise I won't bother you again. I swear it! This time, I mean it!] (522). Still, Él continues his assault on his costar ("¿Jugamos a algo?" [Shall we play?] 522), trying to get her drunk, dancing with her, and refusing to let her go when she asks him to stop embracing her; the stage direction says that their struggle becomes violent (525). Ella responds by creating new rules for the game of seduction that they have been playing:

> Está bien, acepto. Pero será a mi manera. . . . Tendrás que someterte a mis condiciones. . . . Yo empezaré haciendo un número para ti, pero tendrás que quedarte quietecito en este lugar (*lo sienta en la silla del personaje Ceausescu*) y para que no hagas trampa, te amarraré así (*Ella se ha procurado una cuerda sin que él se dé cuenta*), y después de mi número, ya veremos. (524–25)

> [Okay, I accept. But we'll do it my way. . . . You'll have to submit to my conditions. . . . I'll begin doing something outrageous to you, but you'll have to stay quietly right here (*she seats him in the chair used by the Ceausescu character*) and so that you don't try anything, I'll tie you up like this (*She has come up with a rope without him realizing it*), and after my little number, then we'll see.]

What follows is a game in which Ella has total control. Él begs her to let him go, but she threatens him with a knife: "Tenemos toda la noche por delante. ¿No decías que podíamos pasarla bien?" [We have the whole night ahead of us. Didn't you say that we could have a good time?] (526). The game Ella "directs" is presented as a rehearsal designed to allow Él to show that he is capable of displaying emotion:

ELLA: . . . Vamos a jugar a ensayar, ¿de acuerdo?
    [*We're going to play "Rehearsal," okay?*]
ÉL: ¡Mujerzuela!
    [*Whore!*]
ELLA: ¿Viste? No podía faltar el insulto. Tú que abusas de los adjetivos calificativos. ¿Dónde quedó tu respeto, tu compañerismo y tu deseo por mí?
    [*You see? There had to be an insult. You, who abuse qualifying adjectives. Where's your respect, your team spirit, and your desire for me?*]
ÉL: (*Tratando de levantarse*). ¡Vamos ya! No soy tu juguete, ¡suéltame!
    [*Trying to stand up. Come on, already! I'm not your toy, let me go!*]

      . . .

ÉL: ¿Qué es lo que estás haciendo conmigo?
    [*What are you doing with me?*]
ELLA: Jugar.
    [*Playing.*]
ÉL: ¿Jugar? ¿Llamas a esto jugar?
    [*Playing? You call this playing?*]
ELLA: Por supuesto. Te molesta porque no tienes sentido de humor.
    [*Of course. It bothers you because you don't have a sense of humor.*]

ÉL: ¡Esto es una provocación . . . !
   [*This is a provocation . . . !*]
ELLA: ¡Bravo! ¡Ya estás hablando como el personaje!
   [*Bravo! Now you're talking like the character!*]
ÉL: ¡Qué personaje ni qué mierda! (526, 527)
   [*Screw the character and screw this shit!*]

Él's game involves role-playing within his role, and he duplicates that of Nicolás Ceausescu in order to lure Ella to get close enough that he can overpower her: "Ya que soy un reo, ¿me podrías dar un trago?" [Now that I'm a prisoner, could you give me a drink?] (528). The actor who plays a prisoner really *is* a prisoner; here, he ironically uses the role to free himself. Ella's "rehearsal" has backfired on her:

ÉL: ¡Se acabó tu juego, compañera! Vamos a ver qué haces ahora, ¡presumida, pretenciosa, provocadora! Te crees muy inteligente, ¿no? A ver si lo eres para librarte de mí! Sólo sabes hablar, ¡gran sabionda!
   [*Your game is over, my friend! We'll see what you'll do now, you con- ceited, pretentious provoker! You think you're intelligent, huh? Let's see if you're smart enough to get away from me! All you know how to do is talk, you big know-it-all!*]
ELLA: Por favor, ¡suéltame! ¡Yo estaba jugando!
   [*Please, let me go! I was playing!*]
ÉL: ¡Yo también estoy jugando! Esto te va a servir para poner en práctica tus métodos de actuación de los que tanto te jactas. (528)
   [*I'm playing, too! This will help you put the acting skills you keep brag- ging about into practice.*]

Wilde has interwoven the play within the play and role-playing within the role in blatantly self-conscious games of power, violence, and tor- ture, which are intended to remind us of the games human beings play with each other. Describing her decision to use the Ceausescus as key elements in her play, the dramatist comments that they offer the pre- text for an analogy between an institutionalized dictatorship and ev- eryday aggressions. Wilde finds no difference between political dictators of the left or right and ordinary men who resort to force to satisfy their sexual needs.[23] Wilde further emphasizes that both the male and female are equal opportunity aggressors. What we had thought was an exploration of female victims and male victimizers has been diverted from its gendered nexus, just as our expectations re- garding the civilized and civilizing role of the theater have been turned upside down by actors who show themselves able to act barbarously even as they discuss method acting.

The reconfiguration of expectations is, of course, part of the play's setting during Carnaval, replete with its connotations of the world turned upside down as characters don disguises and assume new identities. As Muñoz accurately observes, outside the theater building yet another type of theatrical event is taking place, one that emphasizes the ritualistic nature of the theater, but in this spectacle, the entire population participates, illustrating the reification of the great theater of the world.[24] The sexual abandon occurring outside contrasts with the enclosure of the locked theater and its trapped actors—as well as the inset play's idea of the Ceausescus as condemned prisoners.[25] Moreover, the contrast of ritualized theater and Carnaval speaks to the idea of audience. Wilde seems to play with us as she reveals multiple layers of spectators, constantly destabilizing expectations by emphasizing the wearing of masks and disguises and showing the results of both social transgression and passivity in the theatrical and real-life worlds in which rules are subverted.[26]

Wilde's theatrically self-conscious drama, based on game playing, moves seamlessly between Spanish America and Europe, exploring the essence of dictatorships in both the political and personal spheres. In its explicit game playing, *Adjetivos* also plays with male-female relationships: its games are fundamentally about power and sex, and Él's use of force is matched by Ella's seductive and erotic dance.[27] Wilde emphasizes these issues by having her characters blatantly discuss the rules of the games they play and the consequences of breaking those rules. Wilde's Él and Ella blur the boundaries separating reality from the illusion created by both the theater and the game. Character/actor, man/woman, oppressor/oppressed: all play the game of *Adjetivos*, as Wilde asks her audience to participate in the unmasking of the face of evil. Her point, though, is that the face we unmask could well be our own.

In *La dama boba* ([The Lady Simpleton], first published in 1963, but also contained in the second [1983] edition of *Un hogar sólido* [A Solid Home]), Elena Garro treats the oscillating movement between appearance and reality by writing a play about audience members who enter the world of theatrical illusion and make it real.[28] What makes this drama particularly interesting, however, is that Garro's metaplay doubles and redoubles Lope de Vega's earlier metaplay; the new version builds layer upon layer in a repetition of the past that still manages to speak to the imperatives of the present. In a real sense, both Lope's and Garro's versions of *La dama boba* function as games on a macro level, because the dramatists invite the reader or spectator to participate in finding the interior games and plays inside the text and to decipher their relationship to the whole. In each case, the ultimate games are played with theatrical conventions, and the players are Lope, Garro, and their audiences. The metadramatic elements of the Mexican drama offer a means of exploring the links between theater history, tradition, and modern adaptations, as well as the related issues of writing and reception. The issue becomes even more complex when we examine what happens when a writer (self)consciously imitates his or her literary ancestors. In her game of reworking Lope's classic, Garro is clearly cognizant of her theatrical precursor. The reader of Lope thus emerges as the rewriter of Lope; her recontextualizing and modernizing of the classical text place her in an ongoing diachronic trajectory within literary history, as she both echoes and breaks with the tradition of which Lope was a part. Garro's drama is, above all, a play about the theater, and it uses many of the same varieties of metadrama that abound in Lope's text, although the examples differ in both nature and number in Garro's adaptation. Consequently, the metadramatic points of contact between the two plays serve as a means of deciphering how Garro, the reader cum writer, understood, appropriated, modified, or rejected the self-conscious elements found in her precursor's text. All of this is, of course, a type of game, as characters don costumes and play at and with new roles. Garro's text is filled with characters who play games with each other— even though some of them seem not to know that they are participants in those games—as Garro, in a real sense, plays an even bigger game with her audience. A ludic spirit permeates the new incarnation of *La dama boba*, just as it did in the original.

Lope's *La dama boba*, a clear representative of its age, foregrounds the conflict between appearance and reality: the protagonist, Finea (the *dama boba* or lady simpleton), is transformed by love from her original role as a simpleton to her later role as an intelligent (if manipulative) woman. In order to achieve her goal of marrying the man she desires, Finea self-consciously engages in role-playing. When she finds it necessary to revert to her former state of foolishness so that no one will suspect her conniving, she puts on a convincing show; indeed, Finea spends much of the last act of the play moving back and forth between being witty and circumspect and being a simpleton. In *Metatheatre*, Abel contends that all of the characters in a play are either dramatists, would-be-dramatists, or actors; Hornby expands upon that idea, emphasizing that since "all human roles are relative and learned," role-playing within the role necessarily examines questions of both character development and human identity.[29] Finea's roleplaying is clearly voluntary, and it is presented so overtly, so self-consciously, that the entire notion of imposture becomes a major theme of the play. This type of role-playing produces ontological questioning in the reader or spectator. Herbert Weisinger's description of the effects of the *theatrum mundi* metaphor is particularly relevant to this case:

> The strain between what we know ought to be there and what we actually see breaks down our hold on our instinctive acceptance of our three-dimensional, perspectived, space-time, cause and effect universe. The results of our ordinary processes of perception and logic are deliberately and systematically reversed, misdirected, and even repudiated, and we are thus startled into a fresh perception of experience but often at the cost of our confidence in that as well. The metaphor and like devices must by their nature carry with them the overtones of suspicion and anxiety: one can never be sure any more, either in the displaced or the new vision, for, having been tricked once, we feel sure we will be tricked twice. Once the actor has stepped out of his role, can we be sure that he really has returned to it. . . ?[30]

Weisinger's description of metadrama's effects is central to any analysis of both role-playing and game playing in *La dama boba*, as well as to the study of other self-referential strategies in the play. As we will see, role-playing within the role is merely one of a number of techniques that produce just such overtones of suspicion and anxiety.

Garro's version of *La dama boba* plays with Lope's text as it borrows heavily from it. Her characters stage Lope's play a number of times, and she utilizes many of the same self-referential techniques that her predecessor employed. As Garro's play opens, a troupe of professional actors from Mexico City is performing Lope's comedy for the Indians of the rural village of Coapa. Consequently, from the very first scenes Garro indicates her debt to Lope and displays the techniques that she will use to defamiliarize the original version of the play. The play-within-the-play device, the identical title that her version shares with Lope's comedy, and the references made to performances, actors, and the theater in general indicate an extremely self-conscious opening strategy. This strategy will be further developed in subsequent interior performances of Lope's play and in repeated allusions to the theater, to role-playing, and to the conflict between illusion and reality.

That conflict is underlined when one of the members of the audience, Avelino Juárez, the mayor of the neighboring village of Tepan, mistakes theatrical illusion for real life. Garro's version has joined Lope's comedy in the scenes featuring Finea's school lesson, in which a tutor tries to teach the *dama boba* how to spell, with disastrous but comical results. Don Avelino is so convinced by the acting of the character playing the schoolteacher that he kidnaps him so that the illiterate villagers of Tepan can be taught to read.[31] In a move reminiscent of the ludic Maese Pedro episode of *Don Quijote* (II, chapters 25–27), Don Avelino's apparent inability to distinguish actors from their roles serves to draw attention to the nature of the theatrical experience and to the oscillating movement between fiction and reality that forms the basis of Garro's adaptation of *La dama boba*.

Briefly, it should be noted that Garro's decision to include the scenes showing Finea's school lesson was, undoubtedly, not made lightly. First, these scenes parody the kind of exchange that occurs in a real classroom, although they are also reminiscent of the childhood game of "playing school." Moreover, the school lesson has a clear comic function, stressing Finea's *bobería* by making her words and actions ridiculously inane. In this comic scene, the *boba*, Finea, is unable even to understand the letters of the alphabet; she responds to her teacher's spelling "B, A, N, BAN" with:

LUPE. ¿A dónde van?
   [*Where are they going?*]
MAESTRO. ¡Gentil cuidado!
   [*Be careful, heathen!*]
LUPE. ¡Qué no van! ¿No me decías?
   [*What do you mean, they're not going! Didn't you say so?*]
MAESTRO. Letras son, míralas bien.
   Di aquí: B, E, N, BEN.
   [*They're letters; look at them carefully. Say it: "B, E, N, BEN."*]
LUPE. ¿A dónde?[32]
   [*Where?*]

The scene repeats this kind of wordplay at length, with Finea's teacher growing increasingly frustrated, while his student continues to bungle the alphabet and spelling and to misapprehend the links between language and reality. Finea perceives reality only on a literal level; her verbal confusion draws attention to the signifying process by showing how such confounded signifiers undercut the production of meaning. This linguistically self-reflexive scene only further emphasizes the self-consciousness of both Lope's and Garro's plays, since audience recognition of the use of metadiscourse here allows for the acceptance of other self-conscious strategies employed later in the drama. Moreover, it focuses attention on the ludic quality of the theater and of Garro's games with her audience.

The actor/teacher, Francisco Aguilar, ends up spending several months in the village, and in that time, he does teach the Indians how to spell. In that sense, he fulfills the wishes of the mayor of Tepan; the teacher who is not a teacher ironically performs the role he was kidnapped to perform. Yet Francisco also learns a great deal. He begins to fall in love with Lupe, Don Avelino's daughter, who teaches Francisco that he has been perceiving the world in a limited way. Lupe introduces Francisco to alternative realities and to more sophisticated means of describing them. She becomes his teacher, and she therefore duplicates Finea's experience in Lope's version of *La dama boba*: in both cases, the foolish pupil becomes her teacher's teacher, showing that she is much more intelligent than appearances would otherwise suggest.

Francisco is torn between his desire to escape from Tepan and his growing fascination with Lupe and with the mysterious world of the Indians of the village. The situation becomes further confused when the town turns out to honor its "teacher" by dressing in seventeenth-century period costumes. At that exact moment, Francisco's fellow actors finally come to rescue him and are astounded at the living anachronism they see:

FINEA. ¡La Dama Boba!
  [*The Lady Simpleton!*]
JUAN. ¡Es increíble!
  [*It's incredible!*]
FINEA. Encontramos a Lope de Vega, en lugar de encontrar a Francisco
  Aguilar. . . . (237)
  [*We found Lope de Vega instead of Francisco Aguilar. . . .*]

Garro has created a complex mix of illusion and reality: twentieth-century characters in seventeenth-century costumes greet the very same actors who first wore those costumes when they staged a piece of classical theater. Ironically, the actors are now the ones who are unable to separate fact from fiction. They believe that Tepan is a village in which the people *always* wear seventeenth-century clothing, in which the Colonial period never ended.

Present and past, actors and audiences blend together and then separate again: the professional actors decide to stage Lope's play one last time before taking Francisco away forever. Francisco, who has previously failed miserably at convincing the mayor that he is an actor in a play and not a real teacher, explains in a blatantly self-referential manner what happens in the theater:

> Don Avelino, se me ocurre que debemos darles "La dama boba" para que sepan lo que es el teatro. Verá usted que "La dama boba" es una lección, pero que no es una lección. Sólo existe unos minutos, y no pasa en este tiempo, ni en ningún tiempo. Y los actores vivimos siendo lo que no somos en un tiempo imaginario y somos tantos y tan variados, y vivimos en tantos tiempos diferentes, que al final ya no sabemos ni quiénes somos ni lo que fuimos. (241)

> [Don Avelino, it occurs to me that we should give them *The Lady Simpleton* so they'll know what theater is all about. You'll see that *The Lady Simpleton* is a lesson, but it's not a lesson. It exists for only a few minutes, and it doesn't take place in the present time or in any time. And we actors live being what we are not in an imaginary time and we are so many and so varied, and we live in such different times, that at the end we don't know who we are or who we were.]

This explanation of theatricality offers a perfect parallel to the numerous other theatrically-evident techniques that mark Garro's adaptation of *La dama boba*. Art explicates art, but it does so in such an ironic manner that the "reality" of the theatrical representation, itself a fiction, becomes little more than another excursion into the world of illusion and imagination.[33]

In her version of *La dama boba*, Garro's marginalized Indian characters turn fiction into reality through the sheer force of their own collective will. The theater is, of course, the perfect medium for this kind of creativity. Role-playing, the duplication of levels of drama, the blurring of illusion and reality—all of these elements are used by actors/characters who comment upon the theater from within the play. Moreover, the movement of the characters between their "normal" roles and those of actors and/or audience members serves to remind us of the relative nature of human identity, both in the theater and in real life. Finally, the three performances within the performance illustrate the theme of *theatrum mundi* and, in the process, link the Spanish Baroque age with twentieth-century Mexico by showing that attempts to live literature always—and necessarily—explore the relationship between appearance and reality. Therefore, when Lope's version of *La dama boba* is staged for yet a third time, we cannot help but appreciate both Garro's obvious understanding of Lope and her understanding of the nature of metatheater.

Garro's metatheatrical version of *La dama boba* contains actual segments of Lope's text. These scenes are overt plays within the play, in which the characters wear seventeenth-century costumes, announce their roles as actors to an interior audience, and put on a dramatic performance. Unlike the interior play that Finea writes, stars in, and directs, these scenes from Lope's version are obvious citations of another literary text. When these literary references—or intertexts[34]— appear in Garro's text verbatim, they break the illusion of the main play's imaginary world and cause the audience to "see double." The reminder that one literary work exists implies an acknowledgment that another literary work exists around it, and that reminder leads to an increase in the esthetic distance existing between audiences and texts, as the mimetic level of the fiction is broken once again. Hornby offers a similar reading; he would define intertexts as rather extensive metadramatic citations: conscious, direct references to another literary work, in which, as with adaptation, we see both plays "as separate entities, rather than as blending into a single experience."[35]

As we have seen, Garro inserts scenes from Lope's *La dama boba* into her text on three occasions, playing with the original in her recreation of the Golden Age comedy. A closer examination of the three scenes, however, reveals the dramatist's mastery in using these intertexts separately and collectively to call attention to the oscillating movement between illusion and reality. First, as noted above, Garro's version of *La dama boba* is framed by separate performances of Lope's play, each of which is given to an audience of Indians by the professional acting company from the capital: her text literally begins in medias res—specifically, in the middle of act 1 of Lope's play—and it ends shortly after the company has finished performing the same play. Garro even has the actress who plays the role of Finea offer a modernized version of the *Comedia*'s typical appeal to the *ilustre senado* (illustrious senate) for approval and applause at the end, which acts as an intertextual echo of seventeenth-century theater and as a paratextual indication that the play has ended: "Ahora nos despedimos de ustedes y les agradecemos mucho la atención que nos prestaron. ¡Ojalá que haya sido de su agrado el teatro y su 'Dama Boba'!" [Now we'll say farewell, and we thank you for your attention. We hope the theater and its *Lady Simpleton* have been to your liking!] (244).

When the professional actors perform Lope's play, they follow his text faithfully, with one rather notable exception: the scene that Garro uses as the final scene of her play is actually a very early scene from act 1 of Lope's version, rather than the original final scene of act 3. Instead of ending with the triumph of Finea's manipulative "Toledo" scene[36] and the promise of multiple weddings that occurs at the end of Lope's third act, Garro selected a fragment that features Finea's sister, Nise, her suitors, and their literary academy:

DUARDO. (*A Francisco*) Aquí como estrella clara, a su hermosura nos guía.
  [*Her beauty, like a shining star, guides us here.*]
FENISO. (*Juan*) Y aún es del sol su luz pura.
  [*And her pure light is from the sun.*]
DUARDO. ¡Oh reina de la hermosura!
  [*Oh, queen of beauty!*]
FENISO. ¡Oh Nise!
  [*Oh, Nise!*]
LAURENCIO. ¡Oh señora mía!
  [*Oh, my lady!*]
(*Francisco hace una reverencia. Silencio. Telón de "La dama boba".*) (243)
  [*Francisco bows. Silence. Curtain on The Lady Simpleton.*]

We are faced with an intriguing question: why would Garro utilize a blatantly misplaced fragment to indicate the end of her interior play? Ironically, the "incorrect" fragment could have been used to lend support to the play's verisimilitude, because the celestial imagery and hyperbole of the selection seem so typical of the *Comedia* in general. On the other hand, Garro could well have initiated a literary game of her own, in which only she and a very small number of readers would ever suspect that she was playing with Lope's text on yet another level. Still, no matter which reading we support, as soon as we recognize that Garro has altered the ordering of Lope's text—especially when she implies that she is following it faithfully—we are forced to step back, to "see double."

The third intertext, the citation of Lope's version of *La dama boba* performed in Tepan, is the one that Garro places in the middle of her play, and it differs significantly from the other two performances that frame her adaptation. In this fragment, the Indians of Tepan recreate the school lesson scene with which Garro began her drama. Yet, in this new version, only the professional actor, Francisco, follows Lope's text faithfully. This is not surprising, since the other "characters" are not actors, and they have not memorized their lines. Moreover, the function of the scene is completely different: the villagers of Tepan recreate the school lesson in order to learn how to read, and not to perform a play. Garro's version therefore modernizes and gives a social context to Lope's text, because it is part of a twentieth-century, Mexican experience:

FRANCISCO. Esta es la K: los españoles
   no la solemos poner
   en nuestra lengua jamás.
   Usanla mucho alemanes
   y flamencos.
   [*This is "K": we Spanish / are not accustomed to using it / in our language ever. / The Germans and Flemish do.*]
LUPE. Los mexicanos, sí.
   [*The Mexicans do, too.*]
AVELINO. ¡Muy cierto, maestro! Cuando menos acá por
   Tepan la usamos muy seguido. (214)
   [*True enough, teacher! At least around Tepan we use it a lot.*]

This example contrasts Francisco's faithful rendition of Lope's dialogue with the Mexicans' interruptions of the flow of the scene and with their insistence upon seeking relevance in the words that they utter.

The idea emerges even more explicitly a few lines later, when Francisco asks Lupe about the letters of the alphabet:

FRANCISCO. ¿Y estotra?
   [*And t'other one?*]
LUPE. ¡Esta otra! ¿Qué es eso de estotra?
   [*The other one! What's t'other one?*]
ANTONIO. Lupe tiene razón.
   [*Lupe is right.*]
FRANCISCO. ¡Linda bestia!
   [*Pretty beast!*]
LUPE. No me diga bestia, yo soy una joven. . . .
   [*Don't call me a beast, I'm a young girl. . . .*]
FRANCISCO. Es cierto. . . .
   [*That's true. . . .*]
LUPE. Enterita. (215)
   [*Absolutely.*]

Lupe questions the archaic language of Francisco's discourse and challenges him from a clearly feminist stance, while, again, other characters (and, finally, Francisco himself) interrupt the flow of the action, breaking the dramatic fiction that had been established.

Garro's transformation of Lope serves as a perfect introduction to the scene that will follow, in which the Indians analyze Francisco's "performance" as part of a larger discussion of the ways that language represents reality in the village of Tepan. Like Lope's Finea, Lupe (as drama critic) is definitely not a *dama boba*, as the following examples of her performance review illustrate:

> Yo digo que para nada sirve el maestro. Ni siquiera le entiendo cuando habla.
>
> [I say that the teacher isn't good for anything. I don't even understand him when he talks.]
>
> . . .
>
> Habla muy raro, y luego se enoja con una. Además no cree nada de lo que dice.
> [He speaks very strangely, and then he gets mad at you. Besides, he doesn't believe a single word he says.]
>
> . . .
>
> ¡No conoce las palabras! Las dice como un perro mira a los patos, como si nunca las hubiera dicho.
> [He doesn't know words! He says them like a dog looks at its paws, as if he had never said them.]
>
> . . .
>
> Aquí en Tepan, cuando decimos las palabras, las nombramos y usted nada más las dice. (216)
> [Here in Tepan, when we say words, we name them and you only say them.]

Lupe's critique is not just an example of performance criticism. While her words do signal yet another level of theatrical self-consciousness, they also point to the fact that in Tepan, language is somehow different. Francisco will learn that in this village, traditional definitions of reality do not exist: language acquires new referential power, characters can see into the future, and women assume unconventional roles—indeed, an aura of magic realism seems to surround Tepan. Consequently, Garro's adaptation of Lope's text functions as a metaphor for the metamorphosis that Francisco will undergo in the months that he lives in Tepan and for the transformation of reality that defines the village and her play as a whole. Lope's play, then, ironically serves as the pre-text—in all senses of the word—for Garro's imaginative, self-conscious version.

The concept of roleplaying within the role is also central to Garro's use of Lope's drama. Unlike the play within the play, in which Garro directly cites Lope, here she uses many of Lope's themes and textual strategies—but within the context of her own play about Mexican society. Gabriela Mora has already pointed out that Don Avelino's characterization as the naive Indian who cannot distinguish appearance from reality may merely be a pose, an example of voluntary role-playing.[37] I would add that this voluntary role-playing duplicates Finea's roleplaying within her role in the original text. In like manner, Francisco Aguilar, the schoolteacher, wavers between his assumed role as an actor playing a teacher and that of a kidnap victim who is unable to escape from his captors. In both Lope's original version and Garro's avatar of that play, role-playing within the role assumes primary importance, and that role-playing is almost always voluntary, frequently surfacing when a character moves self-consciously back and forth between roles.

Another strategy that Garro uses while playing with the confrontation between appearance and reality in her metadrama is the creation of situations in which anticipated actions are replaced with ones exactly the opposite of audience expectations. This occurs on two levels. The first level is within the play, itself, where the audience consists of other characters. In one scene, the Indians assembled in Coapa for the performance of Lope's play become completely confused after the actor, Francisco, is abducted. The Indian audience members cannot tell that the play has stopped; Garro's stage direction reads, *"El público contempla la confusión de los actores, como si fuera una escena más de la obra"* [*The audience contemplates the actors' confusion as if it were one more scene of the play*] (180). In another scene, the actresses from the acting company assume that they will be attacked or abducted by the Indians, but they are surprised to find that the shadow "threatening" them is merely an Indian woman who brings them food and sympathy.

This upsetting of expectations expands to include those of the real audience (the readers/spectators), who see the members of the theater company suddenly stop searching for their lost friend and join the Indians in a party. The unexpected action conflates the distance between their two worlds and points to the unifying reality of the Mexican experience: the two groups unite to drink tequila, eat tacos, and sing such ballads as "No vale nada la vida" [Life is Worth Nothing] and "El muchacho alegre" [The Happy Boy]. On one level, we can see that Garro has added to the intertextuality of her play; references to other texts heighten the effect of her inclusion of Lope's drama within her own. In addition, she has succeeded in creating numerous isolated moments that suggest that nothing is as it appears to be: just when we feel that we understand what is going on, Garro undercuts our expectations and distances us from any kind of mimetic reading of her play. The technique is clearly linked to her decision to move between the past and the present, between fiction and reality, and between other texts and her own story.[38]

The use of doubling, of representation, serves to underline Garro's recreation of Lope's text, a twentieth-century version that even bears an identical title. Garro plays with the concept throughout her drama, further reinforcing the doubling that occurs on the level of characterization, in which characters self-consciously assume new roles and act in interior dramas. This is made even more evident with Francisco, who repeatedly attempts to convince Avelino Juárez and Lupe that he is not a teacher, but an actor:

¡Don Avelino, usted está equivocado, yo no soy maestro, soy actor! (200)

[Don Avelino, you're mistaken; I'm not a teacher, I'm an actor!]

. . .

¡Créame, don Avelino, no soy maestro, soy actor! Justamente me vio usted en una represen. . . . (200)
[Believe me, Don Avelino, I'm not a teacher, I'm an actor! You just saw me in a perfor. . . .]

. . .

¡Ya no aguanto más, Lupe! Ya no puedo más, vestido todo el día de mamarracho, y enseñando a leer a imbéciles. Ya me harté de decirles que no soy ma-es-tro. ¡Que soy ac-tor! (222)
[I can't take any more, Lupe! I can't take it, dressed up all day long like a ninny, and teaching imbeciles to read. I'm fed up with telling them that I'm not a tea-cher. I'm an ac-tor!]

. . .

Yo soy actor, me gustan las metamorfosis, por eso me gustas tú, porque en la noche te transformas en mil cosas. (235)[39]
[I'm an actor, I like metamorphoses; that's why I like you, because at night you transform into a thousand things.]

Francisco's insistence on separating these two aspects of his character helps to emphasize the metadramatic nature of the play by making explicit the conflict between appearance and reality in the theater: the character and the actor paradoxically come together while they also divide simultaneously.

Yet, while Garro uses the technique of doubling to reinforce identification with Lope's text, she also defamiliarizes her play at the same time, creating a dramatic text that speaks to—and of—the Mexican experience. Garro's version of *La dama boba* deals with the chasm that exists between the rural, illiterate Mexicans and the educated actors from the capital who represent the federal government's attempt to bring culture to the villages.

Garro injects an element of social criticism into her text: the villagers' pleas for basic services such as education have fallen on the deaf ears of a government that offers, instead, a theatrical representation of a classical Spanish play. What lends her critique a note of irony is that the villagers not only do not recognize the distance between this gesture and their very real needs, but, on the contrary, they find a way to make the presentation of Lope's play the answer to their prayers. The villagers of Tepan are able to convert art into reality. By kidnapping an actor, a maker of illusion, they accomplish their goal of learning to read. In that sense, Garro has shown the relationship between illusion and reality just as surely as Lope did three centuries before, when his Finea won her lover's hand in marriage by using the illusion of turning her attic into "Toledo."

The use of the play-within-the-play device, role-playing within the role, the inset play, and intertexts (literary references or citations) are metadramatic techniques shared by both Garro's and Lope's versions of *La dama boba*. Role-playing within the role appears as a means of advancing the dramatic action and as a way of delineating the complexities of character found in these two dramas. Hornby's observation that the theater is a "human identity laboratory, in which social roles can be examined vicariously" offers a final point of comparison between these two metadramas. Whether the dramatist is discussing the role of women and the value of education in a seventeenth-century Spanish comedy or the same ideas in a twentieth-century Mexican setting, the similarity of themes, textual strategies, and metadramatic techniques leads the audience to that special kind of estrangement produced by "seeing double."

Those tired of the recent wave of self-conscious art might well ask, is there anything really new about Garro's play—has self-referentiality run its course, leaving only faint imitations of the classics in its wake? These valid questions are, I believe, answered by the strength of Garro's presentation. Her play is clearly as much a product of its age as Lope's is of his: the type of questioning that each play induces mirrors the examination of process—as well as product—that typifies each era. Garro's drama, although obviously derived from Lope, emerges as a unique play in its own right. Her text speaks about Mexico, cultural conflict, the role of women, and art; its tight construction enables it to stand alone for audiences unfamiliar with Lope's play, in addition to those who know it well.

Garro's play shares a great deal with Lope's comedy, but it also has moved beyond its source, surfacing as a product of its own age. Her doubling of many of Lope's metadramatic strategies underscores her debt to her predecessor. Yet Garro's reading also does much more, since her direct citations of his play inside her text reformat the original, calling attention to the essential artifice of the theater. Garro's horizons of experience and expectations lead her to filter Lope in a unique way. As a result, her use of Lope's self-conscious devices and techniques both upholds and challenges our own readings of the original text. As we become aware of the two dramatists' similar and distinct representations of multiple layers, endlessly-repeating intertexts, and characters within characters, we ask again with Weisinger:

> Once the actor has stepped out of his role, can we be sure that he really has returned to it; does the dream really end; if objects cast no shadow, are they really real; and if last year is either a dream of the past or a projection of the future, is there really no present?[40]

Through her deconstruction of theatrical conventions, imitation of Lope's self-conscious strategies, utilization of theatrical game playing, and incorporation of a ludic spirit throughout the drama, Elena Garro's reading actualizes Lope's text by incorporating it within a new horizon of expectations. Garro has made the past come alive again in a text that foregrounds illusion, illustrating in the process that a twentieth-century Mexican woman and a seventeenth-century Spanish man can tell us a lot about the nature of the theater.

Susana Torres Molina has been involved in the world of the theater in Argentina since 1975; her work includes acting, writing, directing, and set design, and her dramas have been staged not only in Buenos Aires, but in New York, Madrid, London, and Washington, D.C.[41] When Torres Molina published her best-known play, *Extraño juguete*, in 1978, Eduardo Pavlovsky noted in his introduction to the drama that Torres Molina's theater is one of subtexts.[42] His words were proven accurate in an equally complex dramatic work, . . . *y a otra cosa mariposa*, which premiered in 1981 and was first published in

1988.[43] The drama tells the life stories of four male friends, tracing their relationships with one another and with the opposite sex in a series of five discrete scenes, vignettes that capture key moments in their passage from childhood to old age.[44] At each stage in their lives, the four friends exhibit a wide range of behaviors with regard to the relationships between men and women. Torres Molina's ultimate coming-of-age play examines male bonding, pornography, homosexuality, machismo, bachelor parties, marriage, love affairs, and family conflicts in the interactions of these childhood friends.

Yet, the unique element of Torres Molina's drama relates less to its themes than to its staging: the dramatist insists that each of the four male roles be played by women, and she further frames the play by having the female actors dress (and, at the end, undress) as males while on stage. This technique, which Torres Molina calls the only condition for the representation onstage, self-consciously opens the text to examinations of its metatheatricality and its concomitant links to the nature of human identity. Moreover, it forces the reader/spectator to grapple with the issue of gender. By foregrounding the points of contact between and among theme, characterization, and structure, Torres Molina analyzes not only what men think about women, but what women think the male perspective really is. She therefore moves from the more narrow approach of discussing sexuality from a single, gendered point of view to one that celebrates an overlapping, multivoiced discourse that is at once mutually influential and conflictive. Her drama, echoing texts from the Spanish Golden Age (in the motif of the *mujer vestida de hombre* [woman dressed as a man]) to *M. Butterfly* or *Victor, Victoria*, is as relevant as today's headlines in its interrogation of the culturally determined sexual biases that exist in society at large.[45]

The drama opens with the four actresses undressing onstage and then putting on boys' clothing for the first scene, "La prima" [The Cousin]. In this scene, set in a public square, the four friends, El Flaco, El Inglés, Pajarito, and Cerdín, all twelve–thirteen years old, meet to talk about topics of adolescent interest—especially girls. Their conversation is lively, colloquial, and verisimilar: when Cerdín points to a woman supposedly walking by ("Ché, Inglés, mirá . . . llegó tu novia" [Hey, English, look . . . your girlfriend just arrived]), the other boys laugh as El Inglés responds, "Te confundiste, gordo. Mirá bien, no ves que es tu hermana" [You're confused, tubby. Take a better look; you don't see that it's really your sister].[46] The boys tease and punch each other, drool over a *Playboy* magazine, threaten old men with a

slingshot, and talk about their limited sexual experience. Pajarito tells
the story of seeing his female cousin naked in the bathtub and of his
father's obvious pride when he got caught soaping her down. They
have to explain to Cerdín what a shotgun wedding means, and they
muse on the differences between men and women. When Pajarito suggests that more women than men are crazy, El Inglés replies that he
read in a book that females much more foolish than men and therefore
become mad more easily. Pajarito responds, "Parece que ya vienen
con una glándula de menos, o algo así" [It seems like they come with
one less gland, or something like that] (19).

Throughout the scene, two motifs surface: a preoccupation with sex
and a subtle metatheatricality, which extends beyond the obvious level
of having women play the roles of these four boys and emerges in
other, brief examples of game playing and role-playing within the role.
Torres Molina emphasizes this type of game playing in her stage directions when two of the boys prance around mimicking negative, stereotyped homosexual behavior: "Comienza un juego de seducción entre
los dos 'maricas.' Los otros dos siguen el juego riéndose muy excitados.
Cada vez que pasa Cerdín al lado de ellos, le pellizcan el traste" [A
game of seduction between the two gay males begins. The other two
follow the game, laughing excitedly. Each time that Cerdín passes by
them, they pinch his backside] (15). From the beginning of . . . y a
otra cosa mariposa, Torres Molina establishes both the strong bond of
friendship among the boys and the underlying themes of her play:
male perceptions of females and the ways that men act when they are
with other males.

In each subsequent scene of . . . y a otra cosa mariposa, the four
friends age in years, but their preoccupation with sex remains an im-
mutable aspect of their characterization. The boys are now seventeen
and eighteen years old. As the next scene, "Metejón" [Obsessed],
opens, El Inglés sits alone at a table, trying to convince himself to sum-
mon enough courage to talk to a woman supposedly sitting nearby.
The monologue reveals El Inglés's adolescent angst; he berates himself
for failing to greet her when she came in and for the noise of his ner-
vous stomach, he worries about writing her a love note, and he decides
that he ought to start carrying around a book by Borges so that she
will think he is an intellectual. When his friends join him, however, El
Inglés boasts about his relationship with the woman, initiating a series
of exchanges in which the others brag about their own successes with
the opposite sex, including the obligatory sexual encounter with their
maids. The boys try to goad each other into talking with the woman,

but El Flaco demurs: "No . . . mejor no. Lo dejamos para otro día. Hoy no estoy inspirado" [No . . . better not. We'll leave it for another day. Today I'm just not inspired] (29). The woman then apparently walks by, and each of the boys tries to outdo his friends with *piropos* (flirtatious compliments) and blatant come-ons. They are completely unsuccessful, and as the woman walks out the door, the sexual tension diminishes, leaving each boy muttering excuses about why he needs to go home. At the end of the scene, El Inglés is again left alone in the room, reflecting on a scenic level the structural symmetry that the dramatist establishes for the text as a whole. In "Metejón," Torres Molina shows us how little the boys have changed in the last five years. They are still preoccupied with sex, and they continue to view women only as objects of desire.[47]

The third scene of . . . *y a otra cosa mariposa*, "Despedida de soltero" [Bachelor Party] finds the thirty-year-old friends celebrating El Flaco's approaching wedding. The bachelor party illustrates new levels of the men's sexism. The men tell El Flaco that he is joining the legion of cuckolded husbands; he retorts that although his bride wants to work outside the home, he will not allow it. El Inglés adds that he set his bored wife up in her own boutique so that she could entertain herself and leave him alone, and he tells the group about his ongoing extramarital affair. The group's high spirits disintegrate at the end of the scene, however, when Pajarito tells his friends that he is gay, and two of them pin him down, hurling humiliating questions at him until he is on the brink of tears. Their explicit questions are part of a sexual game inside the play; the stage direction tells us of the two tormentors, "Están cada vez más excitados con el juego" [Each time, they become more turned on by the game] (38). When they finally let Pajarito go, the rest of the group play a second game with themselves—one of self-delusion—because they conclude that their friend must be playing a joke on them. The scene ends with the four friends toasting the fact that no woman has ever come between them and their "manly" friendship.

Twelve more years have passed when the fourth scene, "El bulín" [The Bachelor Pad] opens. The men have met for an evening of sex in an apartment owned by El Flaco; the scene depicts their conversation while waiting for the women to arrive. The four friends' behavior remains focused on the carnal. They plan an evening of extramarital sex (at least for two of them) in an apartment purchased solely for that purpose, they set up a projector to show pornographic films to their dates, and Pajarito emerges from the bedroom as a transvestite. The

men give the unmarried Cerdín an inflatable woman, encourage him
to use it while they watch, and then pull the doll's plug while it is on
top of him. Their sexual game emphasizes the transformation of a
child's toy for erotic purposes. Ironically, while this is going on, El
Inglés brags to his friends about his teenage daughter, but he vows that
he would disown her if she were to have sex before marriage. El Flaco
observes that he will make his wife keep bearing children until she has
a son. El Inglés asks Pajarito to allow himself to be seen in public with
a woman so that his homosexuality won't cause his friends and family
any problems. Cerdín thanks his friend for the abortionist he recom-
mended. Virtually every aspect of their conversation reveals their sexism: "Las minas de ahora la juegan de liberadas y cuando se les
complica la cosa, se desesperan por un macho que las proteja . . . así
es fácil vivir, ¿no?" [Chicks today play at being liberated and when
things get complicated, they're desperate for a male to protect them
. . . it's easy to live like that, isn't it?] (43). And that is precisely the
point of this play. Torres Molina examines every conceivable sexual
configuration and stereotypical sexist attitude in . . . *y a otra cosa
mariposa*. Her drama focuses much more on discourse than on action,
constantly calling attention to male perceptions and behaviors in the
dialogue of the four men.

In the last scene of the play, "Toda una vida" [A Whole Life Long],
the men are between sixty-five and seventy years of age. The drama
has come full circle: like the first scene, it is set in a public square, but
this time the four friends are the victims of children's slingshots. Instead of talking about sex, the men focus on their declining health,
their children's accomplishments, and their diets. Time has altered
their perceptions of marriage. El Flaco tells of his dead wife and previous affairs:

¡Siempre la respeté! Bueno, una que otra vez . . . ¡uno no es de fierro,
tampoco! Pero siempre fueron cositas sin importancia . . . programitas . . .
la familia siempre la mantuve al margen. No como ahora, que los matrimo-
nios se cuentan todo. Cualquier cosa. ¿Así dónde vamos a ir a parar? ¡No
hay dignidad! ¡Todo es puro sexo . . . pura carne! (53)

[I always respected her! Well, okay, once in a while . . . nobody's made of
iron, either! But they were always just little unimportant things, casual
affairs . . . I always kept the family away from them. Not like now, where
couples tell each other everything. Anything. So where will it stop? There's
no dignity! It's all pure sex . . . pure flesh!

Torres Molina underscores the irony of these words in the theatrical game playing of the dénouement. One by one, the old men leave the stage and return wearing the young boys' clothing of the first scene. They emulate their earlier behavior by tormenting the old men and by passing around a deck of playing cards featuring pictures of naked women. Suddenly, they stop and turn to address the audience in a monotone, asking, "¿Pero estas minas, existen de verdad?"; "¿Mirá si te pasás la vida buscando una mina así y nunca la encontrás?"; "Y si no te dan bola?"; "¿Pero dónde están?"; "¡Si las minas están para eso!" [But these chicks, do they really exist?; Look, what if you spend your life looking for a girl like that and you never find her?; And if they don't pay attention to you?; But where are they?; That's what chicks are for!] (56). While they repeat these words, the four female actors begin taking off their makeup and masculine clothing. The drama thus ends with a reminder that all of the machismo we have seen exhibited on stage is part of a self-conscious, theatrical game.

The theatrical device of having women dress like men may be traced back to the early days of the theater. Certainly, it was prominent in the Golden Age *Comedia*, when female characters wore men's clothing so that they could move easily and independently within their patriarchal society, often to recapture their lost honor. Several critics have also noted that for a Golden Age male audience, the sight of an actress in men's more revealing clothing would also have been considered titillating. This was particularly the case when the *mujer vestida de hombre* became the object of desire of another female character, who, unable to penetrate her disguise, would fall in love with the stranger.

In . . . *y a otra cosa mariposa*, the dramatist establishes a tension between the complete absence of female *characters* and the fact that the male roles are played by female *actors*.[48] The women are always present-but-invisible elements of the drama. In their introduction to this play, Eidelberg and Jaramillo suggest that the novelty of the play lies in the fact that the male characters are portrayed by four women who do not reveal that they are women from the moment at the beginning, when they dress as men, until the ending, when they take off their male clothes and dress again as women.[49] I find Eidelberg and Jaramillo's assessment problematic, however, because the reader/spectator could never forget either the gender of those actors or what he or she had witnessed in the initial moments of the play. By opening her text with the female actors' change of clothing, Torres Molina emphasizes the idea of theatrical identity and the distance between subject and object, actor and role, mask and masquerade. We are encouraged to acknowledge those differences, and, in a sense, we are invited to act as voyeurs in a literalization of the "male gaze" metaphor, to witness the disrobing that is part of an act of creation, a becoming-something-new, a fusion of male and female, Self and Other. With this technique, the audience is constantly reminded that the stereotyped male behavior and perspectives witnessed onstage are filtered through both the actors and the dramatist, suggesting that the play presents women's perceptions of male attitudes as much as the attitudes themselves. This may help to explain why the drama offers up such a wide range of sexist behaviors, why the focus of the characters' discourse seldom strays from the topic of sex, and why the men fail to mature and evolve as they age. In other words, Torres Molina appears to be making a strong feminist statement, and she uses extreme examples to make her case, culminating in the play's final moments, when the actresses self-consciously break out of their roles and the dramatic fiction to talk directly to the audience. . . . y a otra cosa mariposa consequently reveals a multitude of subtexts to its reader or spectator, exemplifying the feminist semiotics that Sue-Ellen Case describes when she states that both the study of woman as sign and the study of woman as object are deconstructive strategies that aid in exposing the patriarchal encodings in the dominant system of representation.[50]

Torres Molina uses the game metaphor throughout her play, and she constantly links it to metatheater. On the most obvious level, she encloses the five scenes within the frame of the actresses changing clothes on stage. She thus plays with the dual force of the word exposure, having her actresses strip away their female clothing to become the Other, while at the same time, she exposes the sexism she sees in Argentina. Moreover, her characters often multiply the motif of role-playing within the role by self-consciously assuming other roles within a scene. This underscores the nexus of role and identity; Hornby describes such connections in self-conscious theater when he observes that "Theatre is a kind of identity laboratory, in which social roles can be examined vicariously . . . reminding us that all human roles are relative, that identities are learned rather than innate."[51] Torres Molina uses the word juego frequently in the dialogues and stage directions of . . . y a otra cosa mariposa, and toys—from slingshots to inflatable dolls—fill her text. Throughout, the dramatist emphasizes the idea that sex is a game and that like most games, there are winners and losers, those who maintain power and control, and those who do not. This drama epitomizes Helene Keyssar's description of "plays that exploit the very nature of the theatre to demonstrate the distinction between gender and sexuality. It is not in biologically defined sexual identity but in social gender roles that power is allocated and enacted on stage."[52]

Torres Molina's playtext does, indeed, question gender: its oscillating movement from female to male to female highlights the dramatist's interest in portraying game playing, theatrical role-playing, sexual ambiguity, and the issue of gender. . . . y a otra cosa mariposa is an intriguing theatrical text and a fascinating feminist text, but, above all, it is an experimental text, offering layer upon layer of interpretive possibilities, precisely because it deals with the ways that men and women both perceive their world and communicate their perceptions of it.

As I suggested at the beginning of this chapter, every drama in this book contains some measure of metatheatricality in its employment of game playing. Elena Garro's *Felipe Ángeles* is filled with allusions to the theater: the central event of the play, a trial, is presented as a theatrical event from any number of perspectives, and throughout the text, that trial is associated with games. Wilde's *Adjetivos* employs many of the same techniques in her more literal staging of a trial and her interrogation of history. Again, the dramatist layers her text with references to both theatrical and sexual games. Garro's *La dama boba* likewise plays with issues related to theatrical spectacles, just as Torres Molina's . . . y a otra cosa mariposa links its metatheatricality to a discussion of Argentine sexuality. As the examples presented in greater detail in this chapter illustrate, there exists in all of these women-authored plays an interest in uniting games and play with the conventions of the theater. Their games of "make-believe"—echoed repeatedly in these four plays—suggest that all the world really is a stage and that we are all players in a larger and eminently profound game. The effects of this on the reader or spectator are, certainly, many, but ultimately we begin to apprehend the interaction of the two on a deeper level. To borrow from Keyssar, these dramas "exploit the very nature of the theater" to remind us of the inherent links between the theater and human identity and social/gender roles.

4

Violent Games in Plays by Roma Mahieu, Mariela Romero, and Griselda Gambaro

"In our Play we reveal what kind of People we are"
—Ovid, *The Art of Love*

THE DRAMAS DISCUSSED IN THIS CHAPTER—ROMA MAHIEU'S *JUEGOS A LA hora de la siesta* [Games at Siesta Time], Mariela Romero's *El juego* [The Game], and two plays by Griselda Gambaro (*Los siameses* and *El campo* [The Siamese Twins and The Camp])—possess the same salient characteristic: games grounded in violence. The depiction of violence in the theater has a long tradition in Spanish America. Nora Eidelberg, writing in 1979 about the influence of Artaud's Theater of Cruelty on four male-authored plays, called those dramas examples of present-day Latin American theater of denunciation.[1] In addition to noting the strong connection between the playtexts and Artaud's linking of violence and ritual, Eidelberg asserted that in each drama, time—either completely static or circular—played a major role. Finally, she concluded that by forcing the audience to confront the hostile and suffocating environment that surrounds humanity, the dramatists were trying to make the spectator recognize him/herself in the work as a necessary precondition for creating a new identity within this reality.[2] Violence has also emerged as a central issue in discussions of post-Proceso theater in Argentina, as the work of Jean Graham-Jones so forcefully illustrates. Perhaps the most influential work on the topic, *Violent Acts: A Study of Contemporary Latin American Theatre* by Severino João Albuquerque, is an exhaustive analysis of verbal and nonverbal violence and personal and sociopolitical repression and resistance in dozens of plays from Brazil and Spanish America. Albuquerque comments on the functions of this textual violence:

> In the theatre, as in other art forms, depictions of violence serve to reflect constructively upon the human condition and provide a powerful commen-

76

tary on society's imperfections. The spectator's involvement in the artistic experience entails the recognition of his or her innate violence—even if only latent or sublimated . . . [that] makes possible the completion of the ritualized conveyance of violence. . . . [3]

This suggests two key points of contact with the game playing examined in this book. First, like Eidelberg—and, of course, Artaud—Albuquerque reminds us of the ritualization of violence in the theater: "A theatrical performance shares many of the characteristics of rituals: it has been learned, repeated, and endowed with significance in an atmosphere designed to stress its impact; the actors onstage perform, like priests, magical reiterations of an action deprived of reality to a collective body immersed in darkness."[4] In each of the plays of this chapter (as well as many of the others discussed in this book), games serve as the means of conveyance of such ritualized violence, just as they, too, are characterized by repetition and the performance of actions similar to, but also inherently different from, the reality of everyday existence. Foregrounding the tenuous line separating make-believe violence and serious aggression, these dramas emphasize the high intensity of risk taking and the stakes involved in winning and losing in texts infused with cultural meaning. The games analyzed in this chapter, speaking to both human and societal concerns, invite the involvement of the spectator in the artistic experience: as we relate to the violent games depicted, we are simultaneously encouraged to contemplate and react to the larger issues at hand.

Roma Mahieu's *Juegos a la hora de la siesta* [Games at Siesta Time] is a 1976 drama involving children playing adult games of warfare and sexual domination. In a manner reminiscent of Torres Molina's . . . *y a otra cosa mariposa* [Moving On], *Juegos a la hora de la siesta* also employs role-playing within the role by utilizing adults to play the children's parts. The entire drama underscores the concept of play, both the innocent games of real childhood (e.g., "War" and "Statues") and the chilling games of the adult world. The children's games have rules, leaders and followers, winners and losers, and the ultimate outcome of a game gone out of control is the death of one of the players.[5]

Mahieu[6] is far from subtle in using children's games to expose violence: *Juegos a la hora de la siesta* is such an obvious metaphor for Argentine society that it was banned by the authorities. Nineteen seventy-six was a key year in Argentine history: Perón had returned in 1972 and was elected in 1973, but from 1974 until the military overthrow of 1976 and the beginning of the Dirty War (1976–1983), Argentina saw what Martha Martínez calls the destruction of the country's great hope: "The Argentina of the 70s faces the destruction of its great myths. And the theater has echoed this process."[7] Mahieu's first staged play was *Juegos a la hora de la siesta*, and it was enormously successful, winning the Talía, Argentores, and Molière prizes for 1976 and converting the dramatist into an instant hit. However, as Martínez observes, the reality that Mahieu presented so well in her dramatic works was the face of an Argentina of which many Buenos Aires writers had feigned ignorance. The play premiered in July, 1976 and ran successfully for eighteen months, when it was prohibited from further performance by a decree from the President of the Republic; at the same time, the edition of the play that had been prepared by Talía was also censored by the authorities.[8]

In a revealing 1976 inteview, the author described her approach to the text, stating that she wrote the play as the result of having carefully observed the manifestations of violence in children: "They, who don't have the kinds of cultural limitations that we adults have, and who therefore express themselves much more freely, showed me how fear is in reality the origin of their violence."[9] Mahieu further noted that children don't tend to shy away from conflict in their games of role-playing, leading us to conclude that children's game playing functions as an ideal strategy for conveying adult themes: it offers freedom of expression, an opportunity to explore the relationship between fear and violence, and a built-in invitation to portray conflict. As Charles B. Driskell reminds us, however, *Juegos a la hora de la siesta* is not a play about children; rather, it "serves as a dramatic metaphor for the physical, moral, and emotional violence of the adult world."[10] I would add that the dramatist's decision to have adults play children who are acting like adults, a kind of *Victor/Victoria* of game playing, brings with it not only the obvious level of self-conscious role-playing within the role—with all of the attendant associations with questions of identity—but also a specific and terrifying tone. In *Juegos a la hora de la siesta*, those adults transform childhood innocence into unspeakable violence, and the tragedy at the play's end emerges as even more chilling because it comes from "children."[11]

The drama takes place in the corner of a plaza or park, with a bench and sandbox serving as key elements of the set. The characters include seven children and a childlike young adult who appears to be developmentally delayed. Two of the children figure prominently in the action: the despotic leader, Andrés, and Susana, the outcast of the group,

whose mother's poverty (and, most likely, prostitution) have condemned the daughter to marginalization. The children play dozens of
games, most of which involve role-playing within the role. They pretend to be soldiers, animals, doctors and nurses, magicians, participants in a wedding, funeral directors, souls in flight, and policemen.[12]
The words *jugar* (to play) and *juego* (game) appear countless times, as
Mahieu constantly reminds the audience of her conscious use of the
ludic. Yet these childhood games are not light and innocent. Many contain an ominous subtext, as in the game of "Statues," when Andrés
declares that in this reunion of the most famous, unique, and perfect
statues in the world, a statue with the slightest blemish will be destroyed. In one of the final games, Andrés, assuming the role of judge,
sentences his "prisoner" to squeeze a wounded bird to death.[13] Participation is mandatory: "El juego es el juego. El que no tiene bolas, que
no juegue." [The game is the game. Whoever doesn't have the balls
for it shouldn't play].[14] Individually and collectively, the games lead
inexorably toward murder.

Rupture occurs from the first moment of *Juegos a la hora de la
siesta*. The birds' singing is interrupted by the sounds of war games as
the children, ages five to eight, play "Soldiers" by imitating the actions
of combat planes and the sounds of guns, explosions, and bombs: "Me
estoy desangrando. . . . Estoy empapando esta tierra y de cada gota de
mi sangre surgirá un soldado nuevo para venganza del 'Valiente Desconocido.' Y mis ojos mirarán en sus ojos, y sentirán terror al mirarse
en ellos. Oh cobardes. . . ." [I'm bleeding to death. . . . I'm soaking into
this ground and from each drop of my blood a new soldier will spring
forth to avenge the "Unknown Brave Man." And my eyes will look in their
eyes, and they will feel fear when they look at them. Oh cowards. . . .]
(3). War toys—a plastic machine gun and a helmet—assume significant
roles in the game playing. Andrés repeatedly orders his soldiers
around, asking if they swear on their country's blood and its blue and
white flag to be faithful soldiers (4). When one of the children asks to
borrow the helmet, Andrés refuses: "¿Acaso no sabés que eso se gana
en el campo de batalla?" [Perhaps you don't know that this is earned
on the battlefield?] (5). In one telling scene, Andrés has his deputies
pat down a dissident for a supposedly hidden gun:

> No encontramos nada . . . en algún lado lo habrán escondido . . . estos
> hippies son todos iguales. Sucios y mentirosos. A ver vos, ¿dónde está es
> condido? (*Lo empuja a Sergio con la punta de la metralleta*.) (20)

[We didn't find anything . . . he must have hidden it somewhere . . . these hippies are all the same. Dirty and lying. Let's see—where is it hidden? (He pushes Sergio with the end of the machine gun.)]

The political connection is made even more explicit when the children sing "Somos los muchachos Peronistas" [We are the Peronist Children], which leads Andrés to add, "Mi papá es Peronista. Yo también soy Peronista." [My dad's a Peronist. I'm also a Peronist] (10). The children ambush each other and pretend to finish the other players off with feigned bayonet thrusts. All of these references to war, integrated into the children's games and play, call attention to violence and to the Argentine military. In addition to the political link, they have the cumulative effect of preparing the children for the murder of Susana at the end of the play, when the group attacks the child and smothers her in the sandbox.

Andrés often goes too far, hurting his teammates physically to the extent that they begin to cry or threaten to bring their parents in to punish him. He also attacks through language, calling the other children names, often telling the boys that they are *maricones* (queer) or saying to his sister, "Gorda. Gordinflona. Sapo hinchado. ¿Por qué no reventás?" [Fatty. Chubby. Swollen toad. Why don't you burst?] (7). His preferred linguistic mode is the issuance of commands, and he quickly puts a stop to any questioning of his authority: "El capitán soy yo. . . . Yo mando. . . . ¿Querés probar?" [I'm the captain. . . . I command. . . . Do you want to put it to the test?] (20). No one really appears to have any power to control the bully; he often remarks that he can do whatever he wants. Susana is, in many ways, Andrés's opposite. He leads, establishing the rules of their games, but she cannot even get the children to let her participate in their game playing. He commits numerous—and escalating—acts of cruelty, while she tries to feed an injured bird. He incites another boy to torture a wounded sparrow simply for the joy of making someone else kill; she kills it quickly to end its suffering when it is clear that the boy did not finish the job. Still, Susana does not passively accept the physical and verbal abuse heaped on her: she frequently reacts violently in her own defense. The difference is that her violent moves are defensive, while Andrés's are almost always offensive.

The language of *Juegos a la hora de la siesta* is realistic and typical of children of the ages five to eight. They get into endless rhetorical arguments ("Es mentira." "Es verdad." "No es verdad." [It's a lie. It's true. It's not true.]), threaten and swear at each other constantly

("Mirá gorda bachicha, si abrís la boca, mejor no te acostés de noche porque te saco los ojos con un alfiler" [Look, you fat Eyetalian, if you open your mouth, you'd better not go to bed at night, because I'll stab your eyes with a needle]), use a large number of commissives ("Juro" [I swear]), burst into spontaneous song ("Somos los muchachos Peronistas"), parrot jingles heard on television, and move seamlessly—and often illogically—from topic to topic ("Mi tío Juan se murió y no vino a casa nunca más. . . . Mi tío tiene una lancha en el Tigre. Es toda azul y tiene motor. Cuando se venga el calor me va a llevar en la lancha y me va a enseñar a nadar" [My uncle John died and he didn't come to our house any more. . . . My uncle has a speedboat on the Tigre. It's all blue and has a motor. When it gets warmer he's going to take me out on the boat and teach me how to swim]). At times, the children are able to replicate word for word linguistic formulas they have heard often, as when Andrés, in a game in which he plays the role of a priest, "marries" two of the children.[15] At other times, however, the children do not always know what the adults in their lives mean when they speak. For example, Claudia's mother does not want her to play with Susana because Susana's mother is "una mujer de la calle" [a woman of the streets], but the child's understanding and explanation of the term are less than accurate; Alonso's father locks his bedroom door when he is alone with the maid because, he claims, he wants to avoid drafts—and the son has no idea that there could be a different reading of the situation. Again, the children's apprehension of the adult world and its discourse is entirely age appropriate, although the great irony is that the children's roles are played by adults.[16]

Driskell outlines several key themes of *Juegos a la hora de la siesta*: from a sociocultural perspective, the work can be seen as "an allegory of how the middle-class adult world molds and influences, in part, via television," and, in a tragicomic vein, it "asks the spectator to reflect on his [or her] own reality."[17] Both the consumer and existential elements of the play are, indeed, central to its interpretation, the first (seen in several of their games) through the children's references to what they have learned on television, and the second by means of the (meta)theatrical quality of the children's games and Mahieu's interior game of having the children's roles played by adults.

Driskell suggests yet another area of thematic focus for *Juegos a la hora de la siesta*: "It can be seen as an antifascist work, as a disquisition on power—dependence and submission to it—, which is one of the recurrent themes in contemporary Argentine theater."[18] This political dimension is central to the text, as the dictator, Andrés, leads his soldiers to commit acts of violence against the innocent Susana, literally as well as metaphorically "disappearing" his victim under the sand of the sandbox as the play draws to a close. The "soldiers" who had participated in the attack react to their actions by running away, indicating how complicity in torture and atrocity can be achieved when strong military leaders take advantage of fear and the mob mentality to do their beckoning. And fear is clearly a part of the motivation for this action: afraid of the one who is different and at the margins of their "society," appalled by Susana's "murder" of the injured bird she puts out of its misery, fearful of her supposed rejection of God (seen when Susana grinds her crucifix under her feet), the children join together to eliminate the mutually perceived threat. They are caught up in the emotion of the moment, but they have also been led to that moment by the escalation of oppression and violence in their games; one of their games is even called "Violence." Like the Argentine military, all they need is an excuse, and the killing begins. Timing was, indeed, everything, as the events taking place in the country began to echo ever more forcefully those occurring each night in the darkened theater. Tellingly, Mahieu ends her drama on an even more jarring note: in addition to the fleeing children and the final, empty stage, the stage directions indicate that the audience should be "attacked" by sound and light: "The sound of the birds singing increases in volume until it begins to be annoying. The intensity of the light increases. It will stay like that until the theater has emptied" (33). Awakened to the realities beginning to occur in their country, the members of the audience are forced to "see the light" in a drama that asks them to leave the theater resisting authoritarian rule.

Yet another drama that literalizes the idea that life is a game is *El juego*, written in 1976 and published in 1977 by the Venezuelan playwright, Mariela Romero.[19] *El juego* paints the ugly, sordid world of Ana I and Ana II, who do nothing but play manipulative, cruel, and passive-aggressive games with each other, alternating their dominant and submissive roles as the drama progresses, with Ana II as the principal victimizer in the first act and Ana I assuming that role in the second. The games themselves, following one after the other, are a curious mixture of illusion and reality. A salient example is the way in which the characters use the ultimate symbol of powerlessness, a wheelchair. Ana II teases Ana I by withholding the wheelchair from her, forcing her to crawl toward it, but only moments later, Ana I, now installed in the chair, leaps up and walks across the room, an act that completely destroys the "reality" created up to that point, reinforcing the idea that everything in *El juego* is make-believe.[20] Since the characters are constantly pretending (and since they alternate posing as the dominant member of the dyad), the reader/spectator is often left in the dark as to what will happen next. In that sense, Romero also seems to be destabilizing her own text by playing a game with her audience: she repeatedly withholds information, presents conflicting actions, or shifts the power base to keep the audience off guard.

The games found in *El juego* are numerous and varied. A real children's game is played at the very end of the drama, when Ana I, having hidden a stolen wallet, insists on having Ana II move about the room as she calls out "warmer" or "hot." In many games, the two women assume new roles (queen, beggar, revolutionary hero), but in a number of cases, the main game is a contest, a literal and metaphoric pushing match to see who is in control. The characters often break role to discuss the game or the performance of it ("¡Bravo! Siempre has sido muy buena actriz" [Bravo! You've always been a very good actress],[21] and they use markers to indicate that they are about to reenter the fiction: "¿Comenzamos de nuevo?" [Shall we begin again?] [20]; "¡Prepárate te digo!" [Get ready, I'm telling you!] [21]; "¿Tenemos que comenzar dedes [*sic*] el principio?" [Do we have to start from the beginning?], to which the other player replies, "Sí, mi querida niña. Siempre se comienza desde el principio. La palabra lo dice. Comenzar, empezar, iniciar, to begin" [Yes, my dear child. One always starts at the beginning. The word says it. Commence, start, initiate, begin], 21). The drama opens in a sordid, dirty room, with Ana II straddling Ana I, twisting her arm, while Ana I begs for mercy. Ana II spells out clearly the rules of and the motivations for her game:

> Aquí mando yo. Y no acepto desobediencias . . . ni sublevaciones . . . ni oposición de ninguna especie. . . . Creo que no será necesario repetirte cuáles son las condiciones del trato. Puede que a tu modo de ver te parezcan algo injustas, pero entiende que tengo que mantener mi supremacía sobre ti. De otro modo . . . me destruirías. (17)

> [I'm in charge here. And I don't accept disobedience . . . rebellion . . . or opposition of any type. . . . I think it's not necessary to reiterate the conditions of the agreement. It's possible that from your perspective they might seem somewhat unfair, but understand that I have to maintain my supremacy over you. Any other way . . . you'd destroy me.]

The games that follow, of which I will offer a few key examples, are filled with violent words and actions. As noted previously, Ana II makes Ana I crawl across the floor to her wheelchair, all the while exuding joy at the entertaining spectacle, in which she describes Ana I as a pus-filled earthworm. The wheelchair, symbolic of the characters' social paralysis and enclosure, is ironically a central element of the women's ritualized play, as Amalia Gladhart explores in *The Leper in Blue*: "*El juego*'s rituals extend beyond the representation of the violence between two individuals to the dramatization of paralysis itself."[22]

This game is followed by a recounting of Ana I's dream, in which the two ride bicycles around a strange city; the bicycles, toys, fit well into the ludic elements of the game sequence, as do many other elements of this example of self-concious game playing. Ana I, finding herself separated from Ana II, meets a handsome prince who treats her like a beautiful princess and begins to make love to her. Ana II is extremely upset by the dream, in part because she is not participating ("Es imposible. Eso no puede ser" [It's impossible. That can't be], 24), but Romero also hints that even in the women's dreams, so much happiness is simply not possible. Equally plausible is the idea that Ana II is angry because Ana I has changed the rules, altering the narration of a story that has probably been told countless times before.[23] Ana II keeps calling Ana I a liar, but Ana I repeatedly denies it, until, in a quick reversal, she confesses, "O.K. O.K. No lo soñé" [O.K. O.K. I didn't dream it], telling Ana II that the whole story was invented to torment her. Ana II returns us to the game frame: "Con que es eso, ¿no? Pretendías cambiar las reglas del juego, ¿no es así?" [So that's it, huh? You were trying to change the rules of the game, isn't that right?] (27). In order to reassert her dominance, Ana II transforms Ana I's beautiful, romantic story by turning the prince into a drunken, syphilitic rapist. Ana I reacts by jumping up from the wheelchair: "No juego más. Esta vez has ido demasiado lejos" [I'm not playing any more. This time you've gone too far] (29). The self-conscious discussion of the rules of their game escalates: Ana II accuses Ana I of cheating and Ana I removes herself from the game, leading Ana II to suggest that she'll have to look for a new game player. This part of the game culminates with yet another theatrically self-reflexive exchange:

ANA I: ¡Déjate de teatro! ¡No quiero jugar más!
   [*Enough theater! I don't want to play anymore!*]
ANA II: ¡No estoy jugando . . . esto no es ningún juego! (30)
   [*I'm not playing . . . this is no game!*]

Nonetheless, the game is not over yet, because Ana II, pretending to be the queen of a palace, forces her subject, Ana I, to remove her clothes so that the "queen" can attempt her own version of the seduction that Ana I had originally imagined—only this time, Ana I's sweet dream is transformed into Ana II's heavy-handed nightmare. Once again, the two players step back to discuss the game:

ANA II: No te lo tomes tan a pecho. Fue un juego . . . como siempre hacemos.
[*Don't take it so much to heart. It was a game . . . like we always do.*]
ANA I: Un juego para demostrarte a ti misma que eres más fuerte que yo. Pero por más que lo intentes nunca me podrás dominar del todo. (36)
[*A game designed to show you that you're stronger than I am. But no matter how much you try, you'll never be able to dominate me completely.*]

Finally, the game players talk about yet another "deal," deciding that they can break the old one and make one that is newer and better:

ANA I: Es un juego. Uno de esos juegos que tanto te gustan. . . . Imagínate por un momento que yo soy tú y tú eres yo. . . . Yo trataré de imitarte . . . de comportarme como tú . . . y tú tendrás que actuar como yo. Es muy sencillo.
[*It's a game. One of those games you like so much. . . . Imagine for a moment that I'm you and you're me. . . . I'll try to imitate you . . . to behave like you . . . and you'll have to act like me. It's very simple.*]
ANA II: No le veo la gracia.
[*I don't see charm.*]
ANA I: No te quieres arriesgar, ¿verdad?
[*You don't want to take a risk, right?*]
ANA II: ¿No habías dicho que era un juego? En los juegos no se arriesga nada.
[*Hadn't you said it was a game? In games, you don't risk anything.*]
ANA I: ¡Entonces, acepta!
[*Then accept!*]
ANA II: ¡Sí, acepto! (37–38)
[*Yes, I accept!*]

Clearly, Romero uses these scenes to examine the issues involved in the games the two women play. Incorporating direct references to the theater itself, the dramatist points to the connections between games and the theater that define *El juego*. The games emphasize role-playing within the role, just as they highlight the process—the act of artistic creation—of producing the interior plays.

The games of *El juego* function on many levels, from the individual to the universal. On a personal level, they reveal a great deal about basic human relationships. As I discuss below, they may suggest a committed response to politics and an indictment of many aspects of Spanish American society. Gender is highlighted in Romero's drama as the woman writer has her female characters "play" with patriarchal constructs, creating games that are always about power and control. Moreover, as Gladhart proposes, Romero could also be playing with traditional associations of femininity and passivity by presenting paralysis as a pose, although in the case of *El juego*, both Anas "discard immobility or passivity when challenged."[24] Susan D. Castillo suggested just three years after the play was published that although Romero would probably reject the idea that a feminist intention lay behind her work, her female characters receive special treatment; she stated that few times in Latin American theater have characters that so closely resemble women today been conceived.[25] Of course, the two women's roles are multiple and fluid: some characters in their games become dictators, while others are beggars.

The sadomasochism inherent in *El juego* indicates that the victim and the victimizer are codependent characters. They share their name, differentiated only by number/order of appearance, in a move that simultaneously depersonalizes the two females[26]—adolescents, adults, children, or simply beings, as Isaac Chocrón posits—and presents them as Self and Other, as friends, as real or metaphorical "sisters," as parts of the same mutually destructive whole.[27] Yet as violent as the two women are to one another, they nonetheless join together in their fear of the unseen man, "El Viejo" [The Old Man], who wields ultimate power over them. Romero has set the two mutually dependent women up in opposition to the male oppressor who threatens and controls their every act; as the play draws to a close, the women hear his approaching footsteps and the door to the room opens, leaving the audience with the uncomfortable feeling that an even more grotesque game is about to begin. Albuquerque suggests, "Much like the ringing of the telephone at the end of [Pavlovsky's] *El señor Galíndez*, El Viejo's steps and the mere opening of the door provide a more powerful signation of a figure of repression than would the presence of an actor onstage."[28] Romero's decision not to present El Viejo onstage has powerful implications:

... It is often the horrors that *aren't* shown that are the most disturbing. ... The fascination of the unspeakable or indescribable or unprintable is that [one] always assumes that, whatever it is, it must be worse than the worst that [one] can imagine.[29]

In the unwritten third act, which will only be produced in our night-mares and imaginations, Romero has included us as active partici-pants in the game of *El juego*: we cannot help but react in horror at what will come.

It appears that Ana I and Ana II work for El Viejo as pickpockets or street thieves or, possibly, as prostitutes, and are likely to incur his wrath because they have spent their day playing violent games with each other rather than bringing home money for him. Still, argues Al-buquerque, once we appreciate the terror that El Viejo inspires, we can begin to see the attack and counterattack of the two women as a strategy to resist outside oppression: "Their 'juego' can thus be seen for what it really is: a prolonged attempt at disguising their fragility and helplessness."[30] The behavior of Ana I and Ana II would therefore represent what psychoanalysts would term transference, as they re-place the subject who actually produces the violence in their lives with a safer alternative. Bixler sees a similar function for the games of *El juego*: they are the women's "only means of comprehending and cop-ing with their daily world."[31]

The relationship between the women and El Viejo also has as a sub-text a commentary on the political. Certainly, multiple examples of re-pressive military governments could be found in the 1970s throughout the Americas. As Bixler observed in 1984, "[The dramatists'] games of domination and subjugation, governed by the 'regla general,' parallel very clearly the extratextual, political game being played in many parts of Latin America today."[32] The games taking place in the center of the play deal specifically with the uprisings of the masses, the sanc-tioning of repression by the Church, and the silencing of those who speak out. In a powerful and lengthy game, Ana I sentences Ana II to death for her "crime" of attempting to assassinate the "dictator," while Ana II proclaims, "Soy la voz de la conciencia del pueblo . . . ese pueblo oprimido y asfixiado por la injusticia y la tiranía de tu régi-men" [I am the voice of the conscience of the people . . . those op-pressed and asphyxiated by the injustice and tyranny of your regime] (42, 41). The game, obviously also a metaphor for Ana II's personal domination of Ana I throughout act 1, involves a lengthy discussion of the political or revolutionary angle, but it also combines politics with the sadomasochism that has marked their relationship: Ana II begs Ana I (the monarch/dictator) to shoot her, shouting that she wants to die for her country (43).

In addition, the violence exhibited onstage can be linked to political torture. Reminiscent of the testimony of real-life torture victims, Ana

II counters the accusation that she is cruel with "La crueldad no tiene nada que ver con esto, mi querida niña. Es sólo persuasión. ¿No te sientes ahora como más liberada?" [Cruelty has nothing to do with this, my dear child. It's only persuasion. Don't you feel more liberated now?] (16). Later, when Ana II is jailed and sentenced to death for treason, she is labeled a Communist, a guerrilla, and Ana I is coerced into collaborating with the "authorities" as they interrogate her:

ANA I: Ella me empujó a esto. Me dijo que me enseñaría a pedir limosna. Ella tiene la culpa de todo. Me dijo que era por mi bien.
[*She forced me to do it. She told me she'd teach me to be a beggar. It's all her fault. She told me it was for my own good.*]
ANA II: ¿Por tu bien . . . o por el de las guerrillas? ¡Confiesa! (*La empuja*).
[*For your own good . . . or for the good of the guerrillas? Confess! (She shoves her).*]
ANA I: ¡Yo no sé nada!
[*I don't know anything!*]
ANA II: Mejor me dices de una vez quiénes son los otros. . . . No me obligues a aplicar la fuerza (*Otro empujón*) (56).
[*You'd better tell me once and for all who the others are. . . . Don't make me use force. (Another shove)*]

The clichéd scenarios enacted in *El juego* emphasize violence and torture, although Romero also integrates a few moments of tenderhearted affection into her text. Still, the oscillating movement between acts of cruelty and those of compassion and tenderness might also be seen as examples of torture of the cruelest type, confusing and destabilizing the victim by leaving her never knowing what will come next, granting her hope only to snatch it out of her reach. Romero's play offers up multiple possibilities, speaking both on the level of interpersonal relationships and on that of the national or universal. Nonetheless, the union of the personal and the political is particularly typical of committed theater in Latin America, where, profoundly influenced by Artaud and Brecht, drama has often been used to comment on political repression and stir audiences to action.[33]

El juego makes a powerful statement about contemporary Spanish American society and its theater. Castillo summarizes:

El juego is a good example of the maturity that psychosociological tendencies in Latin American theater have reached. . . . The closed area is a sordid microcosm from which all social institutions are judged. The characters, manipulated and limited by socio-economic forces, survive in the violent rituals of games and recreations. Their small struggle—no matter how futile and unequal it might be—is the only possibility of rupture from the oppressive circle.[34]

The games and rituals of *El juego*, Castillo suggests, mirror the relationships found in the world outside the theater. *El juego* consequently serves as an effective metaphor for both interpersonal conflicts and for those occurring between the individual and society at large. And just as the games that the two Anas play tend to allude to their own external "reality," the numerous self-conscious and highly theatrical games of *El juego* serve as seminal examples of game playing in the theater, reminding us again that life is a game.

In this last section of the chapter, I focus not on one play but, briefly, on two of the earlier works of the Argentine Griselda Gambaro, arguably the best known and most influential Spanish American woman dramatist of the last fifty years. These plays are typical of Gambaro's oeuvre of the 1960s and 1970s; as Becky Boling asserts, they "portray the irrationality of this period in Argentine history during which the country experienced spasmodic changes in leadership. Throughout this period of production, Gambaro concentrates on describing the dynamics of oppression, the strategies of power, and the irrationality of domination as she witnessed them in practice in Argentina."[35] Although elsewhere in this study I explore other texts she has written, two dramas seemed particularly relevant to the theme of violence and to its union with game playing: *Los siameses* and *El campo*. Marguerite Feitlowitz lends support to this contention:

> Gambaro's chief concern has always been violence—its roots, manifestations, and spheres of influence, as well as the ways in which it may be perceived, masked, and denied. Her plays explore the relations between domestic and political violence, repression and complicity, and also the abiding conflations in public life of history and fiction, illusion and substance.[36]

In addition to their basis in violence, *Los siameses* and *El campo*, like so many other dramatic texts Gambaro has written, are characterized by the pervasive use of metaphoric games as their structural underpinnings and thematic centers. In both plays, the dramatist consistently interrogates the interactions of winners and losers, the knowledge (or lack thereof) of the rules of the games played, and the utilization of games as a way of exerting power and control.

Los siameses, written in 1965 and first produced in 1967,[37] portrays not two women but two men, one weak (Ignacio) and the other strong (Lorenzo), who have sustained a kind of Cain-and-Abel, sadomasochistic relationship for years. Sandra Cypess suggests that their relationship "implies two vital complementary aspects of man—one cunning and aggressive, the other trusting and receptive."[38] In this sense, *Los siameses* is remarkably similar to Romero's *El juego*. The principal player is Lorenzo, who engages in countless games of power but who fails to share the rules of the game with Ignacio. *Los siameses* describes the dominant man's humiliating psychological torment of his weaker "sibling,"[39] as well as his obvious instigation of the brutalizing beatings and incarcerations that others give him and that ultimately lead to his death. Curiously, Lorenzo's "game" is to get others to carry out the actual punishment, much as Andrés often did in Mahieu's *Juegos a la hora de la siesta*; he appears to get satisfaction out of setting his brother up, playing dirty rather than dirtying his own hands. Ignacio, metaphorically blind to the harm his brother is heaping upon him, repeatedly allows himself to fall into the traps his sibling sets with manufactured evidence and lies to the authorities. The supposed motivation for Lorenzo's games is a belief that he will be stronger without Ignacio. Yet, at the conclusion of this drama, the stronger man realizes that his brother's death has left him alone, without his necessary victim. Gambaro's drama abounds in violent games; the irony is that by the play's end, the consummate game player has out-tricked himself, since with the death of his twin, he cannot continue doing the only thing he knows how to do: play games.[40]

In "Griselda Gambaro and the Female Dramatist: The Audacious Trespasser," Catherine M. Boyle examines the common argument that in Gambaro's plays, the victimizer becomes the victim and victims are generally accomplices to their victimization. Boyle states that this view is "a simplification of the underlying trends in Gambaro's work, where, to borrow her image, nobody is wholly surgeon or patient."[41] To support that view, the critic mentions *Los siameses* and the idea of the game:

> *Los siameses* deals with degrees of dependence and complicity, with the ability to handle the rules of a game managed through a chain of delegation of duty and responsibility. As Lorenzo creates the evidence that will damn his brother Ignacio, the latter, who has no access to the rules of the game,

pleads with him to stop acting the fool, incapable of grasping the complicity between Lorenzo and the policemen, believing that truth will prevail and that when it does Lorenzo will suffer.[42]

This point clearly pertains to *El campo* (1967),[43] which also centers on a character who participates in his own destruction because he is ignorant of the rules of the game. *El campo*, like so many other texts by Gambaro, employs sadistic game playing, although in this drama, the scale is larger, involving more "players" in a less intimate space. The protagonist, an accountant named Martín, is brought to an ill-disguised concentration camp, supposedly to straighten out some discrepancies with its books. He quickly discovers, however, that he is the latest pawn in a sick game devised by the camp's commandant, who forces him to witness and participate in a number of degrading acts and has him beaten mercilessly. After Martín escapes, the cold reality of his fate becomes clear, for the play ends just at the point when the accountant is recaptured, surely to face even worse torture in the future. Everything has been a setup. The protagonist realizes that even his escape from the camp was part of a prearranged, larger, and infinitely more sinister game.

El campo has another victim, Emma, who appears to have been a prisoner in the camp for quite some time. Emma's head is shaved, she wears rags for clothing, constantly scratches herself, and has a wound on her hand,[44] which she and Franco occasionally pretend does not exist. In fact, Emma constantly asserts things that are contradicted by visual evidence. She presents herself to Martín as a concert pianist, and the tone of her verbal interactions is mannered and highbrow, as the stage directions suggest: "Sus gestos no concuerdan para nada con su aspecto. Son los gestos, actitudes, de una mujer que luciera un vestido de fiesta. La voz es mundana hasta el amaneramiento" [Her gestures don't reconcile with her appearance at all. They are the gestures, attitudes, of a woman who is wearing a party dress. Her voice is society-minded, even mannered].[45] Behaving as if she is really not a prisoner in this grotesque camp, Emma emerges as a key character. On one level, she acts like many real-life prisoners, effectively reducing the horror of her daily experiences by repressing them, pretending they are not happening. In addition, Gambaro indicates that Emma's behavior is forced upon her by Franco; he is the director of the inset play in which she "stars," and he provides her with the script for her performance. This suggests yet another layer of her torture, as the female victim must pretend to both her victimizer and the outside world that everything is wonderful, a possibility with real implications from the perspective of gender. On yet another level, however, Emma may simply be Franco's vehicle for luring Martín into believing that he is free to leave the camp. She could be the bait in a larger game between the two men, one whose point is for the dominant player to give the weaker player the sense that the nightmare is over, only to turn that notion upside down in the course of playing the game. Verbal and physical violence and torture are elements of each of these three possibilities.

Gambaro makes the suffering even more horrific by contrasting it with the sounds of children at play. In the camp, Martín hears children playing outside, but those innocent and joyful sounds are presented against the backdrop of military commands and a kind of generalized moaning. Moreover, although Franco exudes bonhomie when he describes the frolicsome youngsters, one of his earliest acts is to order into the intercom that the children be silenced. His command produces instant results, leading the audience to infer either that the sounds of children's play were prerecorded for Martín's benefit, or that the children have been so brutalized that a single word from Franco can produce quick compliance on their part. When Martín manages his brief escape and returns home, the sound of children playing outside is equally disconcerting—first, because his own younger brothers seem to have vanished, leaving their half-completed schoolwork on the table (Martín proposes, "Se escaparon a jugar" [They must have escaped to play] 87), and second, because a few minutes later, a cry of pain is intercalated into the sound of their play. The sight and sounds of children's play then mysteriously stop, all of which presages and intensifies the final, terrible encounter with Franco's goons. The juxtaposition of innocent children's play with adult games of violence and torture heightens the overall chilling effect of the play, making Franco's game even more frightening by comparison.

El campo underscores the metaphor of torture as a ritualistic game that illustrates the interrelationship of dominance and subjugation. And, like the other Gambaro play of this chapter, it also suggests other levels of interpretation, readings that emphasize the political repression and torture of the innocents that have marked much of Argentina's recent history.[46] Diana Taylor, identifying Gambaro's plays of the 1960s as representative of a "theater of crisis," posits that those dramas are central elements of "a new discourse on fascism and atrocity."[47] In *El campo*, as in so many other dramas she has written, Gambaro seems to be reacting to the earliest indications of violence and repression that were taking place, anticipating the events that will soon overtake and overwhelm her country, and encouraging her audiences to pick up on the signs of the horror to come. Beyond any doubt, these works present a political message.

Gambaro's employment of violent games serves multiple functions in addition to exposing the political realities she sees around her. This textual strategy also allows her to signal the division of the psyche by means of her good and evil twins and examine the issues of domination and repression that operate on other levels of human relationships, including the relationship between men and women in Spanish American society.[48] Sociocultural and gendered readings therefore complement political approaches to these dramas. As Jean Franco proposes, Gambaro's plays "are not written as feminist works; but they are important because they allow us to understand that the social construction of the feminine position within the overall sexual politics of sadomasochism is symptomatic of the State's manipulation of the erotic in order to secure obedient subjects. . . . Further, women incline to perform this script written by the State because their creativity is often a desire for performance.[49] Certainly, this would appear to be the case of *El campo*'s Emma, who gives performances for the representative of the State throughout the play, and who ironically has a piano "concert" with a broken piano, in what Gladhart asserts is really a nonperformance, a coerced, yet impossible recital.[50]

In an interview published in 1987, Gambaro analyzed the social and political critique pervading her works, arguing that "society is modifiable, changeable." She adds that although her plays from the early period involve torture, death, and humiliation, each one "has a positive side, because it appeals to people's lucidity. It's a call to attention. My vision is not necessarily fatalistic."[51] This comment may be surprising, given the horrific actions depicted and the depressing tone of so many of Gambaro's plays, including others (like *Las paredes* or *Decir sí*) with similar themes and techniques. It describes, however, a writer who has not given up, who is willing to take a stand by means of a theater that consistently calls its audience to attention.

The literal and metaphoric games played in the works of Gambaro, Mahieu, and Romero give the plays much in common: the texts exhibit repeated examples of repression, violence, and torture, and they all depict characters who participate in games of whose rules they know nothing, just as they also present other, stronger figures who specialize in manipulating with words and actions. All of the plays have political, gendered, and sociocultural subtexts. Ultimately, all five of these dramas ask the audience to respond to the violent games they have witnessed onstage. As Taylor put it:

> In order to *see dangerously*, to look back at the gargoyles without turning into lifeless stones, Gambaro insists that we must see beyond the theatrical frames and decode the fictions about violence, about torturers, about ourselves as audience, about the role of theatre. . . . She develops a dangerous theatre, one that provokes audiences to resent and reject theatrical manipulation, one that shocks and disrupts, that breaks the frames of theatrical traditions in order to make the invisible visible once again.[52]

Like Gambaro's *El campo* and *Los siameses*, Mahieu's *Juegos a la hora de la siesta* and Romero's *El juego* serve as seminal examples of dangerous theater. Their disturbing ritualized violence challenges both complacency and complicity, forcing us to "see dangerously," to confront repression, and to critique our own participation in perpetuating violence in all of its forms and on all of its levels.

5

Games and Gender Issues: Becoming Other in Dramas by Rosario Castellanos, Susana Torres Molina, and Diana Raznovich

"Sexual role-playing has implications for gender play: the way people perform sexuality influences how they wear their gender."
—Jill Dolan

GENDER HAS LONG BEEN INTIMATELY LINKED TO THE IDEA OF PERFORM-
ance. Indeed, as Laurence Senelick contends, "Gender *is* performance. . . . Whatever biological imperatives may order sexual
differentiation, whatever linguistic patterns may undergird it, it is outward behavior that calibrates the long scale of masculinity and femininity in social relations."[1] In the dramas examined in this
chapter—Rosario Castellanos's *El eterno femenino* [The Eternal Fem-
inine], Susana Torres Molina's *Extraño juguete* [Strange Toy], and
Diana Raznovich's *Casa matriz* [Dial-a-Mom]—gender issues and
performance unite by means of the playwrights' utilization of key
ludic strategies. Many of those strategies are metatheatrical or involve
the direct intercalation of games or play. Others have to do with a general playful tone or ludic spirit, often via the incorporation of humor,
clichés, or caricatures into the text. In all cases, however, the dramas
of this chapter explore woman and her relationships with other women
and with men, illustrating what Nieves Martínez de Olcoz describes as
the depiction of woman's body as a space to allegorize cultural negotia-
tions.[2] Castellanos's magical hair dryer allows a young bride to discover what it means to be a Mexican woman. Torres Molina explores
the games of rich Argentine women and their live male toy, while Raznovich presents yet another perspective by having her protagonist
play with a markedly different type of "doll." In their contests and
representations, these three dramas underscore the ways in which

games and play can make visible the connections between gender and the domestic, sociopolitical, and theatrical spheres.

The Mexican dramatist Rosario Castellanos created an overtly feminist drama[3] with *El eterno femenino*, which was first published in 1975 and staged in 1976; both events took place after the author's untimely death while serving as ambassador to Israel. *El eterno femenino* poses the idea that the eternal battle of the sexes is a kind of game, although it is not always an easy one for women to participate in. Kirsten Nigro describes "the depiction of women so oppressed by the demoralizing roles they play and by the dehumanizing masks they wear that they are now frozen in the poses of the *eternal feminine*."[4] The play suffers from a lack of connection between its three acts and from its constant set and character changes, although, to be fair, Castellanos's introduction states that the play was not written in imitation of realist theater practice, asserting that this is a drama not of characters but of situations.[5]

Highlighting the ludic through farce and caricature, the playwright creates a work rich in game playing. Several critics have commented upon Castellanos's sense of play in—and with—the text. Lucía Fox Lockert calls the *El eterno femenino* a set of nested dolls presenting varied levels of perception.[6] Amalia Gladhart focuses on the protagonist, Lupita, as a spectator in a theater in that "the play she watches is her own (potential) life."[7] Role-playing within the role and the play within the play are central to the drama, as the young bride dreams a series of vignettes in which she stars and meets women from Mexican history who rewrite their life stories. In fact, the entire drama is ultimately about the roles that Mexican women have been forced to play throughout the centuries. When characters in act 3 metatheatrically critique both the very play in which they appear and the dramatist who created that play, one of the women offers a solution to the problems raised in the text, "No bastar imitar los modelos que se nos proponen y que son las respuestas a otras circunstancias que las nuestras. No basta siquiera descubrir lo que somos. Hay que inventarnos" [It's not enough to imitate the models they propose and that are the answers to circumstances other than our own. It's not enough even to discover what we are. We have to invent ourselves] (194). Their claim, "hay que inventarnos," emerges as a kind of battle cry for other North, South, and Central American feminists. This sense of inventing new roles, inherently ludic and theatrical, is simultaneously about gender, about the changes that were taking place in Spanish American

society at that time, which voices like that of Castellanos were beginning to call for. And although her drama may seem a bit dated in the
new millenium, it was ground-breaking in her day. In addition, in its
focus on the media, popular culture, and the anthropological performance of everyday life, *El eterno femenino* could be said to prefigure
current theoretical work in performance and cultural studies.[8]

The play opens in a beauty parlor, where Lupita is getting her hair
styled prior to her wedding.[9] Her hair dryer, however, has been installed with a device that causes her to dream about her future. In
these dreams, Lupita sees herself age from a vital individual into the
stereotypical *mujer sufrida* (long-suffering woman), who shuns her
husband's sexual advances and who finds her world filled with whining
children and a sagging body. Nonetheless, *El eterno femenino* is a
farce, so in her dreams the woman also murders her adulterous husband and ultimately finds fulfillment when she wins appliances in a
Mother's Day contest, although, as I discuss below, she will literally be
buried under the very appliances that symbolize the woman's domestic role.

Four issues related to the ludic figure prominently in this first act.
Role-playing is, as mentioned earlier, central to act 1, as Lupita stars
in a series of inset plays—her dreams of the future—that illuminate
her life via the clichés and stereotypes that define the typical Mexican
woman.[10] In yet another layering of role-playing, however, we find in
the final scene, "Apoteosis" [Apotheosis], that Lupita self-consciously
adopts yet another role within the role: although the vignette opens
with a white-haired Lupita quietly sitting in her rocking chair, the
chiming of the clock on the wall signals her to leap to her feet, take off
her white-haired wig, emerge from behind a screen sporting a traditional Mexican peasant costume complete with sombrero, and dance
the Mexican Hat Dance while singing "Estoy bailando sobre tu tumba,
Juanito" [I'm dancing on your grave, Juanito] (63). This high-energy
dancing and singing continues until someone knocks at the door,
which causes Lupita to don her former disguise and return to her role
as old woman.

The use of disguise is also central to yet another theatrically self-
conscious element of the play. One of Hornby's categories of metatheater, the ceremony within the play, also emphasizes the ludic,[11] and
act 1 contains several examples of such ceremonies. One vignette, the
honeymoon, foregrounds ritualized ceremony involving the bride's
virginity, although in Castellano's ironic version, Lupita asserts that
the carefully arranged red spot on her wedding gown is not catsup, but

plasma, purchased from the blood bank especially for the occasion of her "deflowering." In yet another example, the *alternativa* (or "ritual ceremony of confirmation for a *matador*")[12] is the metaphor for the vignette titled "La Anunciación" [The Annunciation], in which Lupita announces the pregnancy apparently accomplished on her honeymoon. Castellanos plays with macho stereotyping and Catholic tradition as Lupita, wearing tight-fitting toreador pants, performs *verónicas* (cape passes) with a dust cloth and acts out an unseen announcer's description of the "victory" in the bullring, although the young woman soon adds that she is not the bullfighter but rather the noble bull, offering yet another inversion of audience expectations. These ceremonies within the play, like so many of the other metadramatic elements of *El eterno femenino*, are rendered ironic by Castellanos as they express criticism of gendered stereotyping while simultaneously calling attention to the playful nature of the theater itself.

In a third major example of the ludic nature of act 1, the setting, costumes, and stage properties highlight feminine stereotypes. Not only is the space of the beauty parlor (and the domestic space seen in Lupita's dreams) enclosed, but it represents symbolically the place where woman is converted into an object of male desire. As part of the objectification of woman taking place in the salon, key objects assume a ludic function, particularly the masks and costumes that the women wear. Sharon Sieber posits that such theatrical accoutrements, which are used to put the woman on display by first emphasizing ugliness, set up "the binary process of transformation into opposite, woman becoming Other for the Other."[13] Interestingly, however, once the honeymoon is over, the idea of "becoming Other for the Other" is turned on its head: Lupita's mother teaches her daughter that now that she is married, she should let her physical appearance suffer, so in "La cruda realidad" [The Crude Reality], Lupita's mask and costume consist of face cream, hair curlers, and a robe that has seen better days. Once again, Castellanos playfully critiques gender roles via the literalization of the metaphors she uses.

Finally, act 1 underscores games, contests, and the concept of winning and losing. In "Apoteosis," the people knocking on Lupita's door include a horde of photographers, mariachis, game-show entertainers, and a Master of Ceremonies, who informs her that she has won a contest, a raffle, sponsored by the A.B.C. (A: adquiera. B: buenas. C: cosas) [Acquire Good Things] chain.[14] Yet in this dream, winning the game can cost Lupita her life, as the tangible expressions of female-

oriented consumerism—blenders, washing machines, stoves—are
piled on top of her, literally as well as metaphorically threatening to
asphyxiate her.[15] The game within the theatrical game, like the other
ludic elements of act 1, brings to the foreground the larger game,
which is the butt of Castellanos's satire: the roles that Mexican society
forces its women to assume.

In the second act of *El eterno femenino*, the bride dreams again,
but her dreams feature other characters as protagonists. As the beauty
parlor lights dim, we find Lupita at a fair, with its games, hawkers, and
freak shows, a description alluding directly to the ludic, carnivalesque
nature of the setting. Inside a circus tent side show, Lupita first speaks
with a rebellious Eve, "la Mujer que se volvió Serpiente por desobe-
diente" [the woman who turned into a serpent because she disobeyed],
who suggests to a boring Adam (he is consumed with naming everything he sees) that God may really be a Goddess. Lupita then goes to a
wax museum in which famous women from Mexican mythology and
history—La Malinche, Sor Juana Inés de la Cruz, Doña Josefa Ortiz
de Domínguez, the Empress Carlota, Rosario de la Peña, and Ade-
lita—come to life and tell their stories, what Sandra Messinger Cypess
terms "images from the cultural script of Mexican history."[16] Sor
Juana observes that the women's self-representation will be difficult
to relate, because they had been forced to submit against their wills to
a stereotyped, official version of history, but in each case, the women
give a decidedly unofficial reading of their life stories. Again, the comic
inversion of roles attests to the ludic nature of Castellanos's satire.

The revisionist history presented in act 2 is then replaced in the
final act by yet another set of female characters, which Lupita represents by means of projected images and a different type of "disguise."
In this third act of *El eterno femenino*, by donning a series of wigs—
and, once again, the transforming power of these elements of costume
is essential in metatheatrical terms—the young bride metamorphoses
into a host of contemporary Mexican women, including "the old maid,
the streetwalker, the other woman of the *casa chica*, the postiche intellectual, the trendy, liberated woman."[17] Each new wig leads to the assumption of a new role, but the roles are both literally and figuratively
nightmares for Lupita. Later, when the protagonist finds herself in a
group of well-bred society ladies, Castellanos engages in a self-conscious game that pokes fun at herself: she has the women criticize the
very play in which they appear, decrying the feminist Castellanos's
negative representation of Mexican womanhood. Again, the play
within the play adds yet another metatheatrical level, which both re-

minds us of the playful nature of the theater and stresses the themes that have appeared throughout the drama. Even more, the self-parody functions as yet another game within the text. Maureen Ahern suggests that by criticizing herself, Castellanos may have found "an effective way of defusing hostility by anticipating the attacks she knew this play would arouse in Mexican social circles. . . . Here, then, where biography and drama meet, Castellanos once again proves to be the mistress of the ironic reversal."[18] Castellanos appears to be in complete command of the game playing, cleverly executing the ultimate strategy for assuring her success—or, at least, minimizing criticism of her theatrical game.

El eterno femenino plays with its own theatrical referentiality, but it also suggests that being a woman in Mexico by definition means playing a whole succession of roles and being a player in an often-losing game. Castellanos's drama depicts the historical representation of Mexican women as illustrating the bottom rungs of the social, cultural, and literary hierarchies, and it also maintains that the game is still being played in countless incarnations and will continue to be played in this manner until women learn how to invent themselves. In that context, Castellanos further asserts that only by reinventing the rules of this game will modern women be able to break the cycle of stereotyping and submission that has defined them from the earliest encounters between men and women, beginning with Adam and Eve and extending into the present. The literal and symbolic games in *El eterno femenino* allow the dramatist's vision of Mexican women to emerge: game show masters of ceremonies, raffles, and wax museum dolls that come to life enable Castellanos to supply what D. J. R. Bruckner called "a feminist corrective to women's history."[19] By playing games in and with her drama, Castellanos lets her clichéd characters, language, and situations dramatize the predominant gender issues of her time and create theater that could raise the collective consciousness while it made both men and women laugh.

The Argentine Susana Torres Molina's 1977 *Extraño juguete*[20] presents a portrait of two sisters in their mid-to-late thirties, Angélica and Perla, in their encounter with Sr. Maggi, a bizarre traveling lingerie salesman who has knocked at their door. After they let him in, the three characters embark on a series of verbal and physical games, as they play with—and against—each other. The salesman intrigues the sisters with the story of his life and with the unusual contents of his suitcase, which include ladies' lingerie and a stuffed parrot that Maggi takes with him on the job.[21] The sisters begin to play with Maggi as if he really were the strange toy alluded to in the title. They self-consciously misconstrue his comments, find double meanings and alternative readings for virtually every word he utters, and leave him increasingly confused and frustrated. Still, although the salesman is originally put on the defensive, he finally appears to have had enough of the sisters' emotional abuse, and he begins to retaliate. Maggi asserts himself as the dominant player in the game, cracking a whip at the women and forcing them to climb up on chairs as if they were circus animals. The game has become increasingly violent, with Maggi gradually assuming greater control, until he leaves the sisters, literally with their pants down, awaiting a spanking, while he goes to the bathroom. Upon Maggi's return, however, the entire tone of the piece changes. The audience then learns that the salesman was an actor/dramatist whom the two upper-class women have hired to stage the interior play just performed.[22] The major part of the drama has actually been a game inside the play, or a play inside the game. Revealing its metatheatricality at the end of the play, *Extraño juguete* extends the level of game playing to include the reader/spectator, as well. The outer play, however, is not yet over. The drama ends with Maggi negotiating for his expenses and making an appointment for the following Friday's performance, a new enactment of another script—this time, one about a New York drug addict. This game will continue in infinite permutations and in the future stagings of other dramas.

In *Extraño juguete*, Torres Molina makes a number of serious points about Argentine society and the prostitution of art. The rich women, who amuse themselves by producing and acting in their own real-seeming theatrical productions, make their sexual fantasies come alive in an often-degrading game of dominance and subjugation. Their real victim, the actor-dramatist who gives them what they pay for week after week, has only momentary, illusory control in a society in which money confers power. In that sense, the dramatist overturns the traditional male-dominant hierarchy, calling attention to the relationship between power and gender.[23] Torres Molina highlights the connections between sexual roles and identity through the constant shifting of male and female dominance, but she also plays with the idea that sex is a game and that, like *Monopoly*, the ones controlling the cash are the winners.

Extraño juguete explores the complex relationships existing among its three characters by means of game playing, grounding the play in a metadramatic structure. Noting the ties between Torres Molina's drama and Huizinga's *Homo Ludens*, Bixler has observed that "Under the pretense that all is a game, the dramatist subtly attacks the power structures that dictate the rules by which one must play in order to survive."[24] In this chapter, I propose to expand upon the levels of linguistic game playing in *Extraño juguete* by focusing upon the link between the use of self-conscious language within the play and the complementary notion of *homo loquens*: man (and woman, of course), the speaking animal. What happens in the dramatic discourse of *Extraño juguete*—the nature and number of the language games[25] employed—speaks to the larger issue of game playing in the text and to its relationship to gender.

The games revealed on stage are both verbal and physical, and each example highlights the others, leading the audience to the ultimate game of the self-reflexive ending. Just as we will see in Diana Raznovich's *Casa matriz*, Torres Molina's characters become caught up in their roles, self-consciously playing with enactment and the shaping of their dramatic personae. Every word of dialogue uttered acquires new meaning when it is realized as part of a performance within a performance. As such, the dramatic discourse attains an increased degree of importance as performance language, in that the text of the major part of the play loses a measure of its mimetic quality precisely because of our retrospective reassessment of the interior script. In retrospect, the audience's awareness that the interior play was merely a preconstructed dramatic performance leads to a degree of distancing from the events enacted and the dialogue spoken.

Apart from the inherently self-conscious nature of the dialogue in this metadrama, Torres Molina employs other types of self-reflexive language to highlight linguistic game playing. One technique is the use of repetition to draw the audience's attention to discourse itself. A key example is the phrase, "¿Qué quiere que le diga?" [What do you want me to say?], repeated countless times by Maggi as a conversational filler, or, as Bixler observes, as Maggi's way of ingratiating or humiliating himself.[26] This frequently repeated phrase and others like it are self-reflexive in and of themselves because they foreground the act of communication. In addition, the repetition of key lines of dialogue parallels other repetitive acts in the play, such as the constant opening and closing of Maggi's suitcase. Repetition, then, emerges both in terms of physical action and acts of discourse, drawing the attention of the reader/spectator to the physical and linguistic acts indicated.

Another key type of language game in *Extraño juguete* involves playing with words and with the ambiguity and indeterminacy inherent in all discourse. The play abounds with non sequiturs, but each is carefully and, again, self-consciously placed to underscore how communication fails when speakers deliberately obfuscate the sense of the words they utter. Speakers talk at cross-purposes, with the result that no communication takes place. Torres Molina uses this variety of linguistic misfiring frequently throughout *Extraño juguete*; an indication of its structural importance is that the opening scene offers a game of this variety.

As the drama begins, Angélica expresses her dismay over the fact that she has forgotten to turn on her radio soap opera, "Sangre en las venas" [Blood in Their Veins], and she rushes to the set to do so before the program ends. Angélica continues to dialogue with her sister, except that she refers only to events that are happening in her "novela" [soap opera], while Perla talks on about her clothing, cutting the grass, and the fact that she has observed a man watching the house. Clearly, as early as the first scene the sisters do not communicate, but even more importantly, they emphasize that lack of communication and set the stage for future examples of talking at cross-purposes.

Variations on this type of language game may be found throughout *Extraño juguete*. For example, at one point, the sisters deliberately misunderstand Maggi's reference to "la transmisión de los partidos" [broadcast of the games], insisting that he means political parties, when he obviously refers to soccer games. Perla then announces that Maggi must assuredly *play* soccer, although the salesman pointedly speaks only of listening to the game. This leads to the sisters' conclusion that Maggi is deaf, and despite his protests to the contrary, Angélica and Perla will not let the issue rest:

ANGÉLICA. ¿Ud. dónde juega?
   [*Where do you play?*]
MAGGI. No, escucho.
   [*No, I listen.*]
ANGÉLICA (*a Perla*). Háblale más fuerte que no escucha.
   [*(To Perla.) Speak louder; he can't hear.*]
PERLA (*a Angélica*). ¿Es medio sordo?
   [*(To Angélica.) Is he half-deaf?*]
ANGÉLICA. Dijo que no escuchaba.
   [*He said he didn't hear.*]
MAGGI. Disculpen, pero no entiendo. . . .
   [*Excuse me, but I don't understand. . . .*]
PERLA (*a Angélica*). Vocaliza mejor, no te entiende.
   [*(To Angélica.) Speak up; he doesn't understand you.*]

ANGÉLICA. No hay que avergonzarse. El 30 por ciento de la población a su edad, padece de sordera.
[*There's no need to be embarrassed. Thirty percent of the population your age suffers from deafness.*]
MAGGI. Yo sólo dije que no jugaba al fútbol. Que escuchaba nada más.
[*I only said that I didn't play soccer. That I only listened to it.*]
PERLA (*a Angélica*). ¿Qué tiene que ver el fútbol con la sordera?
[*(To Angélica.) What does soccer have to do with deafness?*]
ANGÉLICA (*a Perla*). ¿Habrá recibido un pelotazo en el oído?[27]
[*(To Perla.) Do you think he might have been hit in the ear by a ball?*].

This exchange goes on at great length, with Maggi becoming increasingly upset as the sisters continue their conversation, discussing sports for the deaf and wax buildup in the ears, ignoring his comments completely. He fumbles with his pipe and loudly requests a cigarette, with the result that Perla can then triumphantly exclaim, "No grite que no somos sordas" [Don't shout—we're not deaf]. Interestingly, this verbal game has been accompanied by another type of game throughout the scene: Perla and Angélica play chess while they participate in their verbal game of wits, joining a physical act with linguistic game playing and underscoring the event's ludic symbolism.

In addition, deafness is a theme that complements this type of language game. The characters frequently do not seem to hear what other speakers are saying, and because there is no uptake, there is no communication. By stressing literal deafness, Torres Molina underlines the complex dynamics of the communicative act and the metaphoric deafness occurring onstage. Further, as Eidelberg observes, this scene offers a parody of absurdist theater: "Perla and Angélica's absurd behavior is also a parody of French theater and produces the impression of being improvised, like the dialogue scene about deaf people done in the style of Ionesco."[28] Finally, the language game just described is also used as a power play. At this midpoint in the drama, the women appear to be winning.

The two sisters express that control subtly, as part of a well-executed communicative effort. Indeed, a key technique is the use of two speakers displaying one voice, as the second part of the following example of dialogue illustrates:

PERLA: Puede confiar en nosotras.
[*You can trust us.*]
ANGÉLICA: ¿No nos tiene confianza?
[*He doesn't trust us?*]

PERLA: Claro, somos dos desconocidas. ¿No es cierto?
[*Of course; he doesn't know us at all. Isn't that right?*]
ANGÉLICA: Sin embargo, le abrimos las puertas de nuestra casa.
[*Still, we opened the doors of our house to him.*]
PERLA: Y lo escuchamos atentamente.
[*And we listened to him attentively.*]
ANGÉLICA: Hasta le confiamos algunos secretos.
[*We even confided several secrets in him.*]
PERLA: Porque creíamos en su caballerosidad.
[*Because we believed in his gentlemanly qualities.*]
ANGÉLICA: ¿Y entonces?
[*And then?*]
PERLA: ¿Qué le pasa?
[*What's the matter with him?*]
MAGGI: (*Confundido.*) A mí nada. (51)
[(*Confused.*) *With me? Nothing.*]

The fast pace of this exchange, in which Perla finishes Angélica's remarks, confuses Maggi, who appears to be totally disconcerted by the women's approach and style. The game is clearly verbal, and it highlights the linguistic superiority of the two women.

As the play progresses, however, both the physical and verbal acts of *Extraño juguete* intensify and become more threatening. Maggi assumes greater control, revealing his skill as a magician and alluding to possible violence against the two sisters. A key scene of great physical violence immediately follows a new language game, a series of one-word commands in which Maggi orders the sisters to bring him a number of items—and they hasten to follow his orders: "¡Fuego! ¡Whiskey! ¡Cubitos! ¡Dos! ¡Uno más! ¡Queso! ¡Cuchillo! ¡Galletitas! ¡Servilletas! ¡Escarbadientes! ¡Diario! ¡Radio! ¡Música! ¡Pueden retirarse! ¡En puntas de pie!" [Match! Whiskey! Ice cubes! Two! One more! Cheese! Knife! Crackers! Napkins! Toothpicks! Newspaper! Radio! Music! You may leave! On tiptoes!] (66–67). Maggi's verbal game both humiliates and enrages the sisters, and they finally reach a point where they rebel and try to suffocate their tormentor. Maggi does escape, however, and he returns to the attack with a scene that culminates in the most violent moment of the play, in which he threatens the safety of the women. Again, the cruelty and violence in the physical action of the play have been preceded by linguistic acts that presage and parallel the violence to follow.

These one-word commands, examples of repetition, and plays on words represent some of the many linguistic games that occur throughout *Extraño juguete*. In addition, Torres Molina inundates her drama with an accumulation of linguistically self-conscious references. Silence and deafness have already been mentioned. The nouns *voz* (voice) and *locutor* (speaker) and the verbs *escuchar* (listen) and *hablar* (speak) appear countless times. Early in the play, Maggi ironically observes to Perla and Angélica, "Para qué les voy a mentir. . . . Yo hablo porque he visto mucho, si no, no hablaría" [Why would I lie to you? . . . I speak because I have seen a lot; if not, I wouldn't speak] (33). The character seems to be promoting the value of truth-telling and the importance of effective communication. Nonetheless, dissembling and speaking only to hear one's own voice form the basis of *Extraño juguete*. Multiple references to language, then, emerge as yet another part of the ironic structure of the play, as we gradually learn that the unexpected is the rule in this drama. Language games become a tool for creating that ironic structure.

Torres Molina points to the ironic use of language in the play with the scene that hinges on the appropriate use of the word *también* [also]. Perla asks Maggi a simple question: "¿A usted también le entristecen los atardeceres del domingo?" [Do Sunday afternoons also make you sad?]. This innocent question leads to yet another language game, for Angélica criticizes her sister's use of the word *también* in the context of that question. Angélica drags this discussion on endlessly, with two principal results. First, by underlining the power of a single word to influence meaning so profoundly, this language game foregrounds the power of all discourse. Yet the game also simultaneously subverts that reading, as the endless repetition of banal chatter about such an unimportant detail also points to the ways that too much information can muddle communication and obfuscate clarity. Torres Molina plays with the concept beautifully in this scene. Her characters talk about the value of speaking with clarity in order to communicate well, but they undercut their own message by repeating it to the point of absurdity.

This key scene, like others containing language games, produces another important result. The "*también*" exchange is a model for displaying how characters use language as the medium for assuming control and gaining power. On a surface level, the scene pits Angélica against Perla, as they argue over the semantic and syntactical correctness of "*también*." Yet, before they finish the game, the two sisters join forces to manipulate Maggi, ultimately leaving him a confused victim of their linguistic superiority. The entire scene becomes another power game, revealing the women's ability to control the discourse and the "salesman" whose tools of the trade are supposed to be words.

Like so many other scenes, this scene relies upon abrupt changes in tone and subject matter to create the effects just described. These instant changes are another linguistic strategy used throughout the play, keeping Maggi—and the audience—constantly wondering what is really going on and who is really in control. Toward the end of the play, as Maggi becomes the aggressor, his choice of vocabulary and tone of voice reflect yet another change: "Claro, las nenas se portan mal para que papito les haga cha-chas en la cola, eh. A ver como se bajan las bombachitas. ¡Vamos! ¡Vamos! Rapidito, que las nenas tienen que irse a dormir" [Of course, you little girls are behaving badly so Daddy will have to spank you on your little fannies, right? Let's see you pull down your panties. Come on! Let's go! Quickly, because little girls have to go to sleep] (70). In this new game, Maggi is able to assume control as a father figure and humiliate these grown women completely. Clearly, that control is expressed both in his patronizing tone and in his symbolic choice of words.

Even this abrupt change, however, is no match for the final scene of the play: as we learn that the previous action has been a carefully enacted performance, the dramatic discourse undergoes another major metamorphosis. The character who has just been in control, Maggi, becomes the subservient actor, Sr. Miralles. Perla and Angélica assume their "real" roles as two rich women, Silvia and Mónica. In an ironic, gendered inversion of more traditional trade in human beings, the women have bought a real-live male toy, whom they use in a complicated macro game, complete with scripted dialogue, rules, and multiple interior games. The intense dialogue and verbal games of the interior play give way to the mundane language of economics, as Silvia and Miralles go over his expense account item by item, while Mónica talks on the telephone to a friend. The only echo of past language games is the point/counterpoint of the two completely separate, yet simultaneously occurring conversations. Yet the game is never completely over, since the drama ends with the promise of the characters' next performance. The cycle will continue in future plays.

We have seen an interior play, based on Sr. Miralles's script, from the perspective of its finished performance. This metadrama, however, is presented as part of a series, a yet-incomplete spiral of performances extending into the future. The distance that results from our encounter with the sisters' "strange toy" raises a number of issues concerning the distinctions between a written text and its enactment.

Extraño juguete plays with the nature of improvisation. Torres Molina gives a number of clues indicating that her characters occasionally forget their place in the script or begin to improvise new linguistic games while in the midst of performing Miralles's interior text.[29] Eidelberg notes, "In certain situations, especially when the sisters are dominating the scene, Maggi appears disconcerted, as if those exchanges were unfamiliar, and he even steps out of character."[30] An obvious example of Maggi's failed attempt at improvisation occurs when he interrupts the sisters' attacks on each other with the inappropriate interjection, "¡Y yo soy de Acuario!" [And I'm an Aquarian!] (36). His non sequitur is met by Perla's indignant response:

PERLA: (*Pausa.*) Y eso qué tiene que ver.
   [*(Pause.) And what does that have to do with it?*]
MAGGI: (*Confundido.*) ¿No estaban hablando de . . . astrología?
   [*(Confused.) Weren't you talking about . . . astrology?*]
PERLA: (*Indignada.*) No, señor Maggi, no estábamos hablando de Astrología. (36)
   [*Indignant. No, Mr. Maggi, we were not talking about Astrology.*]

The sisters continue to embarrass Maggi because of his obvious gaffe, to the extent that he begins fumbling in his pockets, presumably for his script. The tone of the scene is tense as Maggi/Miralles, the writer/actor, awkwardly tries to extricate himself from his momentary lapse of memory. The main point of interest, however, is the sisters' complete lack of patience with Miralles's improvisational skills in this situation. They only stop applying pressure after making him suffer, even at the expense of verisimilitude within the interior play. The effect of that example of improvisation and numerous others may be seen in the sisters' review of Maggi's performance and his subsequent self-defense as an actor working under difficult conditions:

ANGÉLICA: Cambió mucho del texto del accidente, ¿no?
   [*You changed the text of the accident quite a bit, didn't you?*]
MAGGI: Era muy largo.
   [*It was very long.*]
PERLA: Yo lo noté un poco distraído.
   [*I also noted you were a bit distracted.*]
MAGGI: ¿Sabe qué pasa? Son muchas horas. (75)
   [*You know how it goes. Such long hours.*]

In a play that focuses upon verbal skill and language games, the relative success of the characters' improvisations must be perceived as noteworthy, not only in the sisters' metacritique, but by the reader/ spectator as well.

The games of *Extraño juguete* offer a series of encounters between the serious and the comic, the frivolous and the cruel, the creative and the subversive use of words. This is a play that gains a great deal of power when examined in retrospect, because once we understand how Torres Molina is playing with the reader/spectator, we can better understand how linguistic game playing complements the physical games we see on stage, which ultimately bears on issues of both social class and gender. The overriding characteristic of the interaction of the verbal and the physical is the deliberateness of all levels of game playing. This textual strategy leaves us with some basic questions about the nature of communication itself—in the theater and in society. Torres Molina plays with words, with gender, with sociocultural issues, and with the theater. In so doing, she asks her audience to participate in the performative act of (re)interpreting reality—and reconsidering the instruments we use to communicate it.

Diana Raznovich's *Casa matriz*[31] offers up a perfect complement to *Extraño juguete* and *El eterno femenino*. Like them, it emphasizes consumerism—with the commodities in question material goods, people, and emotions. By means of its humor, the play employs many of the same metatheatrical techniques and displays a decidedly nonrealistic style. And, like the other dramas discussed in this chapter, *Casa matriz* examines the connections between gender, sexuality, and performance. As Diana Taylor rightly observes, Raznovich problematizes what it means to be a woman, specifically a mother and daughter, in Argentine society.[32] Numerous aspects of gendered stereotyping emerge in the text, but the principal focus of the gender roles is one that distinguishes this play from the others studied in the chapter: the relationship between mothers and daughters.[33]

Casa matriz was composed in 1988 in Buenos Aires as part of what Raznovich calls a memorable series of encounters with nine other women writers.[34] Nora Glickman describes the genesis of the play:

> *Casa matriz* arises from a collective project realized by a group of women writers. . . . The group was self-administered; that is, it functioned without a therapist but within a kind of therapeutic space. No one was forced to follow a specific format, except for one obligation: each participant had to adhere to the same theme—the mother, or the reconstruction of the mother-daughter relationship.[35]

The description of the drama's conception points to the game playing that occurs in *Casa matriz*. Even in the composition of the dramatic text itself, the ludic enters as the workshop of women writers takes a topic each of them knows well and plays with ways to communicate it. The members of the group volunteer to participate, and they establish beforehand the rules of the game, much like the participants of Raznovich's drama.

Casa matriz has, as its central premise, the encounter between a fifty-year-old and a thirty-year-old woman. The younger one, Bárbara, a writer (dramatist) and professor of literature, has given herself a unique birthday present: she hires the older woman, who works for a business that rents out substitute mothers, to come to her home as a kind of live toy. As the initial stage directions spell out, the substitute mother has been trained by the Casa Central (Mother House) to perform over a thousand maternal roles, and she often brags about the quality of her own performance, as when she is able to produce real tears: "Son lágrimas de verdad. Toque. No puede reclamar un efecto más trágico. Soy la mater sufriente por excelencia" [They're real tears. Touch them. You couldn't ask for a more tragic effect. I'm the suffering mater par excellence] (182).[36] The Madre Sustituta (Substitute Mother) interprets several different roles within the play. Her maternal representations include being overbearing and condescending, long-suffering and self-abnegating, critical and guilt-producing, competitive with her own "daughter" for a lesbian lover, and—in a particularly macabre scene—dead. Many of these roles are exaggerated for true comic effect, as in the example of the stereotypical guilt-producing substitute mother, who arrives at the train station in a wheelchair, encased in plaster from head to toe. Although the substitute mother focuses on finding out how her "daughter" is doing in school and whether or not she has been taking her vitamins, the frantic daughter discovers that her mother has been washing windows for years in order to pay for her child's education and that she has broken every bone in her body by falling three stories in a window-washing accident. Still, the mother plans to continue helping her daughter by finding a new job licking stamps in the post office: "Todo ha sido por ti. Yo no tengo importancia" [Everything has been for you. I have no importance] (173). Clichés and hyperbole punctuate the humorous nature of this representation, but the final scene makes a true spectacle of the mother's basic nourishing function. In her last role, the substitute mother dons a giant breast, which Bárbara, climbing onto her lap, begins to suckle. Although their relationship appears to be only a business deal, Raznovich ends the play by highlighting the complexity of an arrangement involving the most basic of human emotions. Bárbara clearly wants the relationship to continue in future performances (much like the end of *Extraño juguete*), and the substitute mother exhibits a twinge of jealousy towards Bárbara's real mother, although she swiftly regains her professional composure. The young woman, however, is left bereft, crying "¡Mamaaaaaaá!" as the spotlights dim.

Casa matriz is inherently metatheatrical, with its game playing deriving in part from numerous plays within the play and constant role-playing within the role. In a key example of the multiple levels of this theatrical game, we learn that the "daughter" is a playwright, and in one of the inset plays the substitute mother, playing the part of an ultramodern sophisticate, asks Bárbara if she has finished writing the play featuring her "mother" as the protagonist. The two discuss the casting of the mother's part (Norma Aleandro), and the substitute mother offers to give the actress a few pointers: "Yo podría enseñarle algunos trucos para parecerse más a mí. No quiero sugerirle que tome el modelo real. Eso es inalcanzable. Es mejor que me reinvente. Pero hay ciertas claves de mi personalidad . . ." [I could teach her some tricks so she'd resemble me more. I don't want to suggest that she capture the real model. That's unattainable. It's better for her to reinvent me. But there are certain keys to my personality . . .] (183). This exchange explicitly calls attention to the fictive nature of the entire enterprise as it emphasizes the role within the role. There is, of course, no "real model," and the entire exterior play is precisely about reinventing oneself.

Even the set and costumes are stylized and self-conscious: the beginning stage directions inform us that the untidiness of the young woman's bedroom is intended to reflect strategic disarray, and she wears colors that match the set, "su espacio creado teatralmente para recibir a la madre sustituta" [its space created theatrically to receive the substitute mother] (160). The substitute mother's constant costume changes illustrate her movement from role to role; the daughter then takes her cues from the new "mother" she encounters. Moreover, as Glickman has observed, linguistic changes also mark the shifting roles within the role, as the women's vocabulary and speech patterns reflect the social group they are representing at that moment.[37] Raznovich plays with performance, with the conflict between illusion and reality, as her two characters continuously interrupt the dramatic fiction by commenting on, questioning, or critiquing their role-playing; the dramatist repeatedly describes the action in the stage directions as "corta el juego" [she cuts the game short] or "rompe el juego" [she breaks off the game]. On some occasions, the substitute mother is the one who stops the play in progress. At other times, Bárbara breaks her role to function as the "director" of their interior plays:

BARBARA: (A la profesional) Dígalo más convencida, señora. Tiene un cierto dejo profesional. Logre que yo me olvide que lo hace por dinero. Pagué muy bien por oír esas deliciosas palabras. Construya mejor las frases. Explícate. (179)[38]
[(To the professional.) Say it more convincingly, madam. You have a certain professional lilt to your words. Make me forget that you're doing it for money. I paid a lot to hear those delicious words. Construct your sentences better. Explain yourself.]

Here, as in virtually all of her interruptions of the dramatic fiction,[39] Bárbara zeros in on the women's financial arrangement, as she discusses her employee's obligations to perform well: "Yo ahorré un año para este momento, junté dólar tras dólar para tenerla aquí conmigo. Usted me pertenece. ¡Y no lo digo en un sentido figurado!" [I saved a year for this moment; I put together one dollar after another to have you here with me. You belong to me. And I'm not saying it in a figurative sense!] (163).

This exchange, focusing on the details of the services provided, occurs in several other manifestations in the course of the drama. It emphasizes Raznovich's satiric take on consumerism, as the quintessential "free" bond, the relationship between a mother and daughter, is prostituted. Indeed, after the substitute mother points out that she normally provides mothering services for eight clients a day, Bárbara replies, "¿Y quién le ha pedido ese dato? ¿No le parece promiscuo decirme qué cantidad de hijos pagan hoy para que usted sea su madre?" [And who has requested that fact? Doesn't it seem promiscuous to tell me how many children are paying today for you to be their mother?] (163).[40] Raznovich turns the mother-daughter bond upside down, transforming this intimate tie into yet another object for sale. In so doing, the dramatist parodies the consumer mentality common in modern society as she pokes fun at human relationships. As the substitute mother explains, the Casa Central trains them to perform their scenes well: "Sabemos cómo comenzar, cómo alcanzar el clímax y cómo cortar a tiempo. Ese es nuestro arte mayor. Una buena ensalada de afectos. Antes la gente sentía naturalmente, ahora se compran sentimientos" [We know how to begin, how to reach the climax, and how to cut it off on time. That's our greatest art. A good salad of affection. It used to be that people felt things naturally; now they buy feelings] (176).

The drama's title suggests several parodic subtexts at work. The most obvious element of the title is "*matriz*," with its associative link to the womb and motherhood, although the word also suggests a "master copy," which, indeed, lies at the center of Raznovich's play: the substitute mother is trained at the Mother Center to emulate the master copies—the stereotypical roles—of Hispanic mothers and perform them for her (double) audience. A "*casa matriz*" is also a mother-house, in the sense of a religious order, or the headquarters of a company, and although the second connotation is the more obvious of the two, both concepts are clearly, if ironically, contained within the drama. The wordplay inherent in the translations of the playtext offers further evidence of the sense of play that permeates *Casa matriz*. Cajiao Salas and Vargas's translation, *Dial-a-Mom*, cleverly captures the humor underlying the Mother Center concept. *MaTRIX, Inc.*, the translated title in Taylor and Martínez's bilingual edition, illuminates yet another level of the ludic in the text, as it deconstructs to allude to the confluence of "Ma" and "tricks" as well as "matrix." Both translations recall the entrepreneurial element of the play, as the fake mother sells the tricks of her trade, learned at the company headquarters, to her client.

Casa matriz is fast-paced and funny, although, as Glickman reminds us, the humor of the play never conceals the sharpness of its criticism. Irony predominates, as in the scene in which the substitute mother feigns death so that her hysterical "daughter" can bemoan her fate and beg her "mother's" forgiveness. Once again, however, the mother interrupts the daughter's emotional harangue countless times to answer her rhetorical questions, criticize the young woman, or complain about her physical abuse. The dramatist has derailed our expectations, transforming the death of a mother into a remarkably entertaining scene; indeed, Glickman concludes that the game is cruel, ferocious, and, at the same time, entertaining.[41]

Glickman's reference to the game points to yet another element of the game playing at work in *Casa matriz*. In this scene, as in so many others, the substitute mother seems unable to stay in role, which often produces anger and frustration in Bárbara, as her emotional expectations are continuously undercut. The women's contract, the rules of their game, spells out what the substitute mother is being paid to do, and it would appear that one of the players is not following the rules.

On one level, the "professional" may simply not be very good at her job, which plays with the theme of consumerism: by having the employee display unprofessional behavior, especially after so many references to her superior training at the Mother Center, Raznovich may be underscoring the ludic and ludicrous nature of the entire enterprise, in which one woman, expected to master over twelve hundred maternal roles, becomes the living toy of another person. On another level, however, Raznovich also seems to suggest that toying with Bárbara's emotions is part of the game, as the mother cleverly and cruelly manipulates the young woman. By hiring a substitute mother, the dramatist also hints, the employer agrees to be treated like a child, which necessarily inverts the traditional employer/employee relationship as the mother dominates in the mother/daughter hierarchy of the new game. The movement shifts throughout the course of the play, in part because the characters' constant interruptions break the dramatic fiction.

A clear example of the complexity of these shifting relationships comes from the substitute mother's original entrance. While waiting for her to arrive, Bárbara is presented in her bedroom, conducting Bach's "Magnificat" with a baton; the play thus begins with the character playing a role. When the doorbell rings, the young woman reacts in anger, apparently at the timing of the interruption, and breaks the baton, although she immediately changes direction and assumes her first role as "daughter": "Te queda fantástico ese traje mamá" [That outfit looks fantastic on you, Mom] (162). This opening action would appear to be insignificant, but Bárbara returns to it later in the play, complaining that her substitute mother should have waited five minutes more, because she had requested a cold, distant mother who would make her "daughter" suffer by forcing her to wait: "Quiero esperarla. Yo pagué por esperar. Yo pagué por padecer. . . . Yo contraté una madre que me hiciera sufrir por sus continuas inasistencias a nuestras citas" [I want to wait for you. I paid to wait. I paid to suffer. . . . I hired a mother who would make me suffer by constantly standing me up] (167). Surprisingly, the substitute mother agrees and, offering to restage the entire entrance scene, she walks out the door. Bárbara picks up a baton and begins to conduct, but she cannot concentrate; speaking to the closed door, she tries to put an end to the charade: "¡Es inútil! ¡La magia de la llegada está rota!" [It's useless! The magic of the arrival is broken!] (168). There is, however, no response, no matter how many times Bárbara opens and closes the door or conducts the music in repeated starts and stops. Finally, she appears to give up:

"Bien, lo admito, lo admito. Me tiene en sus manos. Estoy desesperada. Ha logrado su propósito. Ha sembrado en mí la duda. Admito que me preocupa pensar que ese timbre puede no sonar. . . . Lo ha logrado magistralmente" [Well, I admit it, I admit it. You have me in your hands. I'm desperate. You've achieved your goal. You have sown doubt in me. I admit that it worries me to think that that doorbell may not ring. . . . You've achieved it masterfully.] (168). At that moment, when she appears utterly brokenhearted, the doorbell rings. Bárbara reacts with great satisfaction: "Una demora perfecta, calculada, ni desmedida ni breve." [A perfect, calculated delay, neither too long nor too short] (168). The second entrance clearly meets Bárbara's masochistic expectations, although it is hard to know at times who is really the dominant player in the game.[42]

This multileveled manifestation of game playing is ultimately what Taylor describes as transgressive: Raznovich "rejected the ponderous realistic style so popular among her fellow dramatists. Her sense of humor and love of disruption, inversion, and the unexpected that characterize her work as a cartoonist also characterize her theater. Raznovich's intentions are always revolutionary and transgressive, though not always in the sense that her more openly political colleagues understand or appreciate."[43] The ludic offers Raznovich a perfect way to express that transgression. In her cartoon characters, parodic inversions, humor, and metatheatrical techniques, Raznovich lays bare some of the most sacred universal beliefs. A final example from the play illustrates the extent to which the playwright employs the ludic to challenge traditional gender roles, as Bárbara returns again to conduct her imaginary orchestra in Bach's "Magnificat." At this point, we discover the "true" significance of the recording, the daughter's clothing, and even the color of the room: Bárbara triumphantly exclaims that all were gifts from Lourdes, the "mother's" lover. The mother/daughter relationship has taken yet another twist, as the lesbian relationship becomes an object of competition and contest. In this example of role-playing within the role, however, the substitute mother gives her "daughter" the gift of winning the game. Showing her jealousy, she snatches the young woman's baton and breaks it in half, stating:

Para eso pagó en dólares a la Casa Matriz. Para salir ganadora en algunos juegos. No la dejé con culpa. Se pudo vengar . . . en fin . . . son parte de las satisfacciones que Casa Matriz ofrece a su clientela. (185)

[That's why you paid the Mother House in dollars. To be the winner in some games. I didn't leave you feeling guilty. You could get revenge . . . after all . . . that's part of the fulfillment that the Mother House offers its clientele.]

The "prize" for winning this last game is the enormous breast that the substitute mother offers to Bárbara.[44] And although the "daughter" is so delighted with the scripted ending that she immediately begins to plan their next encounter, perhaps the ultimate game is the "mother's" refusal to play this role again—because, as she hints, she has gotten a bit too close to Bárbara, or because she needs to reestablish the control she has sought to maintain throughout the course of the drama. One more time, however, although the game seems to self-destruct, Raznovich suggests that these two women will continue to use the theater to play games of power.

Once again, games and play are underscored in the living "toys" and games of *Extraño juguete* and *Casa matriz* and in the raffles, contests, and carnival games of *El eterno femenino*. Each of the dramas emphasizes the ludic, interrogating in literal and metaphorical games issues of female identity and analyzing such topics as the relationship between gender and power in child-parent, male-female, and female-female configurations. As all three of the dramas discussed in this chapter make manifest, gender, game, and performance have come together in remarkably similar ways to lay bare the stereotypes and clichés that mark the perception of Spanish American women shared by much of the world. In their texts, Castellanos, Torres Molina, and Raznovich take those stereotypes and stand them on their heads, questioning through the theater the basic issue of female subjectivity: what it means to be a woman. In so doing, those playwrights highlight the games women play and the masks behind which they hide in order to encourage the audience of readers or spectators to see women in a new light. As we laugh at the deconstruction of old clichés, we can begin to understand the new Spanish American woman and her possibilities for the future.

6

Games and/in Spanish American Society in Plays by Myrna Casas, Griselda Gambaro, and Josefina Plá

"Society expresses its interpretation of life and the
world through play."
—Huizinga

IT IS CLEAR THAT EVERY DRAMA ANALYZED IN THIS BOOK IS IN SOME WAY
about Spanish American society. Nonetheless, three plays focus on social issues in unique ways. Myrna Casas's *El gran circo eukraniano*
[The Great USkrainian Circus] uses metatheatrical games within a circus setting to point to a central theme: the nature of social and national identity in her native Puerto Rico. Griselda Gambaro makes a
stark statement about Argentine society in *El despojamiento* [Strip-
tease], as the protagonist is stripped of both her clothing and her dignity in a game of whose rules she knows nothing. Josefina Plá's
contribution, *Historia de un número* [Story of a Number], is about a
real and metaphorical "numbers game" that could apply to Paraguay
or more universally. In each of these plays, the authors explore the
construction of individual and social identities. The game playing in
the dramas is more metaphorical than literally associated with children's play, but the essence of the game is nonetheless a key element
of the playtexts. Calling attention to the "game of life," Casas,
Gambaro, and Plá capture the spirit of the ludic as they explore via
the medium of the theater the cultures and societies from which they
come. Their dramas illustrate what Richard Schechner and Mady
Schuman have described as the connecting action between theater and
social life: the ongoing conversion of relationships into displays, and
the progression of displays as a means of ordering relationships. The
differences between society and the theater, they add, "lie in how con-

117

scious all players are, or can be, of the conventions, the rules, that define the games—and how much these rules can change."[1]

The Puerto Rican dramatist Myrna Casas[2] uses a number of meta-theatrical techniques to explore social issues in the two-act drama, *El gran circo eukraniano*, which was written in 1986 and first performed in 1988.[3] The idea of the ludic enters with the consummate play space, that of the circus, which is reinforced by the playing of circus music, actors who dress as circus animals or trapeze artists, and other allusions to the big top. It is also suggestive of alternative women's performance; referring to the circus tent scene in the second act of *El eterno femenino*, Kirsten Nigro points to the circus's association with the "teatro de carpa" [tent theater], "with its song and dance routines, burlesque, stand-up comedy and irreverent humor, where women have more freedom to perform in ways radically different and more transgressive than on the commercial stage."[4] Still, this circus is much more: it is made clear to the audience on numerous occasions that the circus is equally a theater and that this circus "family" is actually a group of itinerant actors who improvise scenes in each town:

GABRIELA JOSÉ: Señorita, aquí todo es inventado, invento, invención, imaginación. Esto es un teatro.
[*Miss, everything here is made up, invented, an invention imagined. This is a theater.*]
ALINA: Yo creía que era un circo.
[*I thought it was a circus.*]
IGOR: El circo también es un teatro.[5]
[*The circus is also a theater.*]

One of the troupe's members goes into the community to glean information about local citizens, who then will see their own stories dramatized in the theater-circus performance. The actors often refer to the literal and metaphorical mirror that they hold up to society:

(*Música y Nené, Cósima, y Alejandra al público. Sandro e Igor hacen piruetas*)
[*Music and Nené, Cósima, and Alejandra go down to the audience. Sandro and Igor do pirouettes*]
NENÉ: Mire, mírese aquí y luego allí. Verá su retrato, a lo mejor el de un amigo o algún conocido, algún pariente.
[*Shows a mirror. Look, look here and there. You'll see your portrait, maybe you'll see a friend or someone you know, a relative, perhaps.*]

ALEJANDRA: Reconózcase, mírese bien, vea en el fondo del ojo el fondo de su
alma y después quizás podrá verse en mí allí en escenario. (14 [142])
[*Recognize yourself. Take a good look at yourself. Look deep into your
eyes, your soul, and then maybe you'll see yourself in me, there on the
stage.*]

This *theatrum mundi* motif is exploited from a number of angles
throughout the performance, with theatrical illusion constantly put on
display and destabilized. Vicky Unruh describes the group's "singular
approach to theater" as one that "combines a circus framework with
anti-illusionist Brechtian elements and the ambiance of a *creación co-
lectiva* [collective creation]."[6] Ultimately, the theater and the ludic
join forces in Casas's creation of a unique spectacle that will speak to
audiences of all types.

Game playing emerges from the destabilizing of theatrical illusion
as Casas toys with her characters and her audience, employing a wide
variety of metatheatrical techniques. Direct allusions to the circus and
theater *as* theater are many. Characters constantly role-play within
their roles, and the drama is rife with plays within the play.[7] Casas
also intercalates references to other texts (the most theatrically self-
conscious one is Emilio Pasarell's *Desarrollo de la afición teatral*) and
to contemporary Puerto Rican society—its problems, streets, and vocabulary—into her play. In addition, her characters frequently comment self-consciously on their dialogue:

GABRIELA JOSÉ: Qué le vamos a hacer, así somos las madres.
[*What else could I do? That's how we mothers are.*]
SANDRO: Eso me suena a novela de televisión o novela.
[*That sounds like a line in a soap or a play.*]
GABRIELA JOSÉ: A lo mejor sí, a lo mejor se me quedó de alguna obra que he
visto. (3 [129])
[*Maybe I heard it on TV or at the theater.*]

The motif of the soap opera assumes a symbolic function in *El gran
circo eukraniano* through multiple references to the genre, implying
that the lives of these characters, and, by extension, those of the audience members, resemble a soap opera. Casas continuously breaks the
fourth wall, with a supposed audience member, Alina, joining the
actors in their improvisation; we do not know for certain whether she
is "real" or not. The dramatist further plays with theatrical illusion
by incorporating into the onstage dialogue numerous examples of the
actors talking directly to the audience:

ALINA: (*A público.*) ¿No lo recuerdan? Lo ves, ellos lo recuerdan. (23 [162])
[*(To the audience.) Don't you remember? See, they remember.*]

The combined effect of so many metatheatrical techniques produces an awareness on the part of the audience that the theater is like a game and that Casas is playing as much with theatrical conventions as with audience expectations.

Those expectations are turned on their heads as the dramatic action shifts back and forth, often without warning, from drama to inset drama. False starts, interruptions, comments on the acting, and uncompleted scenes self-reflexively mark the performance, and they all take place in front of the audience. Characters sometimes change roles in the middle of an inset play, further muddying the waters. Moreover, some characters' versions of the truth are frequently undermined by other characters. Nené, for example, states that he was discovered by the company's leader standing in front of a café; moments later, we hear that he was really found lying in a gutter. Igor describes his life story as a struggle to escape from abject poverty, but Alejandra interrupts to tell the audience directly that Igor's father was a millionaire who kicked his son out of the house for refusing to study or work in the family business. When Alejandra narrates her autobiography in third person, Alina points out that she is talking about herself, to which the actress replies, "You heard wrong" [155]. Contradictory stories surface throughout the play. Alina, the supposed member of the audience, climbs on stage to voice the effect of so much contradiction:

(*Al público.*) ¿Pero, qué es esto? Qué obra más rara. Yo creía que se trataba de un circo. ¿Ustedes también? ¿Ah? ¿Verdad que sí? ¿Alguno de ustedes creía que era una obra de teatro? Bueno, son actrices y actores. Ay, yo voy a averiguar qué están haciendo allá atrás. (13 [140])
[*(To the audience.) What is this? What a strange play. I thought it was supposed to be a circus. You, too, huh? Am I right? Did any of you think it was a play? Well, they're actors and actresses. I'm going to find out what they're doing back there.*]

Casas is playing a game with her audience, too, as the audience's confusion about the nature of the spectacle is discussed by a woman who seems to be one of them but who is really an actress herself. That contradiction is illuminated even more brightly as Gabriela José, the ring mistress, quickly adds, "Señoras y señores, damas y caballeros, niños y niñas, Bienvenidos al gran circo eucraniano [*sic*]. Casa de Ilusión, y verdad, invento y certeza" [Ladies and gentlemen, boys and girls, welcome to the great USkranian circus. House of illusion and truth, invention and uncertainty] (13 [141]). A ludic spirit infuses the text: the entire play is an enormous game, one in which circus spectators agree to play simply by entering the tent. On this basic level, the audience knowingly suspends disbelief, aware that certain rules—of verisimilitude, for example—will be broken. They don't know, however, that in Casas's version of the circus game (which might be called "What's Really Going On?"), the actors take things one step further.

Although the audience must participate in a game for which the rules are unclear, Casas makes it clear that nothing should be taken too seriously. Alina coughs, and the entire play comes to a halt:

GABRIELA JOSÉ: Ah no, ahora sale con una tosecita. Eso déjelo para el entreacto. Igor, trajo las pastillitas. Déselas a la señorita. . . . Gracias, gracias, Igor. Señorita para su carraspara. Y no haga ruido con el papelito que eso también molesta. (13–14 [141])
[*Oh, no! Now she's coughing. That should be taken care of during intermission. Igor, you brought the cough drops. Give her some . . . Thank you, Igor. And don't make any noise with the wrapper, that's also distracting.*]

In a real sense, stopping the play is part of the macro game, as the actors toy with the members of the audience. In another scene, Casas shows her light comic touch when Alina interrupts an inset play to object to the swearing she hears:

Un momentito, un momentito. (*Todos la miran estupefactos*). Se supone que sea un auto. Un auto es una obra teatral de tema religioso. En España en el siglo dieciséis un auto . . . (32 [172])

[Wait a minute, wait a minute. (Everyone looks at her in amazement.) This is supposed to be a morality play. A morality play or a miracle play is of religious nature. In Spain, in the Sixteenth Century . . .]

The other characters make fun of Alina's pretentious lessons in theater history and pretend that they do not even know the meaning of the words to which Alina objects:

SANDRO: ¿Malo?
  [*Swear?*]
ALEJANDRA: ¿Qué es eso?
  [*What's that?*]
ALINA: Palabrotas. Malas palabras. Dicen malas palabras.

[*Swear. Use bad words. You're all swearing right and left.*]
CÓSIMA: ¿Malas palabras? ¿Nosotros? ¿Quién ha dicho una mala palabra?
[*We're swearing? We? Who swore?*]
ALINA: No empiecen otra vez con el jueguito. Ahora yo soy una de ustedes.
[*Now don't you start playing games with me. I'm one of you.*]
IGOR: ¿Una de quién?
[*One of who?*]
CÓSIMA: ¿Qué tú te has creído? Y que una de nosotros. Ja . . .
[*Who do you think you are? One of us . . . (Bronx cheer.)*]
ALINA: Pero improvisé con ustedes.
[*But I improvised with you.*]
ALEJANDRA: Bastante mal que lo haces. (32–33 [173])
[*And you're pretty lousy at it too.*]

The theater/circus troupe's actors are, indeed, playing games with Alina, and even though she later tries to tell Gabriela José that she was acting in the miracle play, the ring mistress informs Alina that she must leave the group.

Casas ends her drama with more confusion for the audience: Gabriela José, who has narrated various versions of her own life story in the course of the play, yearns for her lost son. At that moment, a young man appears on stage. Casas gives us conflicting clues; he may be the missing son, or he may be Alina's brother, come to "rescue" his sister: "Busco a mi hermana. Cada vez que aparece una compañía por aquí insiste en unirse a ella" [I'm looking for my sister. Every time a circus comes to town, she wants to join it] (40 [182]). Like all the other stories or games of make-believe in *El gran circo eukraniano*, this final one is also unresolved.

The game has a great deal to do with the nature of identity in the theater and in society. Just as each of the characters' life stories shifts and inverts, depending upon who is narrating, Casas seems to suggest that, like her "family" of characters who continuously assume new roles, the members of the larger "family" in Puerto Rican society also wear masks and costumes, playing with their own self-definitions as they interact with others. The actors of this play do, indeed, hold up a mirror to the rest of society, but in this theatrically self-conscious spectacle, the mirror reveals a (play)house: "Casa de Ilusión, y verdad, invento y certeza" [House of illusion and truth, invention and certainty] (13 [141]).

In addition to dealing with the topic of Puerto Rican identity, which surfaces in both the outer frame and the inset plays, Casas examines related aspects of island society. The dramatist plays a game similar to others we have seen as she teases the reader/spectator with the name of the island: it is both unnamed and clearly identifiable. References to specific places—even streets—make it easy to guess the setting, and typical vocabulary, such as *guagua*, adds to our identification of what the characters call a "very complicated country." The drama raises a number of problematic issues for Puerto Rican culture: emigration to the United States, crime, drugs, politics, unemployment, homelessness, transportation, the division between rural and urban areas, and education. In *El gran circo eukraniano*, Casas uses the ludic spirit, incarnated in both the setting of the circus and the play's metatheatrical techniques, to explore her "very complicated country" and the nature of its identity.

A one-act monologue by Griselda Gambaro, *El despojamiento*, examines game playing in complementary ways. Sharon Magnarelli sees *El despojamiento* (1974)[8] as prototypical of the dramatist's works in its use of multiple, interrelated thematic threads or referents: "the historical (tensions leading to the Argentine military crisis of 1976), the socio-political (oppression in all its forms and the complicity of the victim in that oppression), [and] the feminist (the oppression of women in both economic and erotic terms)"; the critic adds to this list of thematic threads the theatrical.[9] In this play, Gambaro uses the victim-victimizer game to great effect: the drama's perverse game functions on social, political, gender, and theatrical levels simultaneously.[10] Furthermore, just as we have seen in so many other playtexts, an understanding of the rules of the game is central to its playing.

El despojamiento has only two characters, a woman and a young man, but only the woman speaks, since whenever the man enters the room, he refuses to respond to her questions and comments. The setting is a waiting room, with a small table covered with magazines, and two chairs. The woman appears to be waiting to audition for a role; she carries a large envelope of photos of herself and is dressed "con una pretensión de elegancia" [with a pretense of elegance], although she gradually reveals that she is past her prime and that her clothing is borrowed and cheaply made.[11] In fact, the woman divulges a great deal about the insecurities of an aging actress. It becomes clear that she is desperate for a job and for the fame that she had as an ingenue. That desperation will lead her to acquiesce to the attacks on her dignity and body that the young man will inflict upon her, as he returns to the room from time to time to take something material from her— her cape, her shoe, an earring he rips from her ear—or a piece of furniture from the room. Gambaro emphasizes that the woman is merely an object to the man, as she notes in her stage direction: "*Entra el muchacho. Su comportamiento es despersonalizado, como si actuara sólo con objetos, incluida la mujer, que le resultaran indiferentes*" [The young man enters. His behavior is depersonalized, as if he were interacting only with objects—including the woman—to which he was completely indifferent] (172). The woman is so determined to cooperate with her potential employers that she allows the molestation to continue. The "despojamiento" of the title alludes to the idea that she has literally been stripped, but it also metaphorically suggests a sense of despoiling, plundering, depriving, or divesting of dignity.[12] Throughout the drama, Gambaro plays with the image and deconstruction of mask/masquerade in the stripping away of the woman's clothing and identity—by the young man, by her husband or lover, by the theater industry, and by society.[13]

Gambaro uses this game of emotional and physical violence as the central structuring device of her work. In the course of the play, however, it becomes clear that the main player has not been informed of the rules of the game. Not knowing how she should respond in order to have a real chance at this acting job, she exhibits a wide range of emotions, alternating between surprise and confusion, self-doubt, anger, and acquiescence. Increasingly, however, her lack of knowledge about the rules of the game combines with her insecurities to produce a level of self-abuse that parallels the abuse perpetrated by the young man: "Idiota, ¿para qué me disculpé? ¿Para qué le di explicaciones? ¡No voy a aprender nunca a callarme! ¡Me cortaría la lengua!" [Idiot, what did I apologize for? Why did I give him explanations? I'll never learn to keep my mouth shut! I should just cut out my tongue!] (173). Gambaro never clarifies whether or not the unseen players of this game even exist, leaving the reader/spectator with the same confusion that the woman experiences. Along with her, we may assume that other players of the game, other off-stage directors of the action, may be waiting on the other side of the door. Desperate for a job, eager to find explanations for the young man's bizarre behavior, the woman neither leaves the room nor demands to speak to his superiors. Instead, she assumes, "Seguro que la pidió el director. Querrá saber cómo estoy vestida" [Surely the director asked him to do it. He must want to know how I'm dressed] (173). It is, of course, equally possible that there is no director who wants to see her clothing and that the young man alone is responsible for this cruel hoax.

The abusive game that the young man plays with the actress on stage is also metatheatrical, in that the game functions like an inset play within the larger play. The woman, not coincidentally an actress, is trying to play the role that she assumes her director wants her to play. The director, whether the young man or other, unnamed figures who never appear on stage, could be trying to manipulate—or at least observe—the woman's reactions and responses, although it is equally possible that the game is simply a gratuitous demonstration of power and subordination. Either way, the actress has not been given a script.

In addition, the drama underscores other metadramatic elements.[14] The actress constantly muses aloud about the nature of the roles she has played in the past and can expect to be given in the future. She speaks of her ability to enrich a script with her imagination and acting ability, and she occasionally plays roles inside her role. Recalling a time when she has acted the role of an ingenue for her lover or husband, she recalls the dialogue:

> Cuando le represento a Pepe, se queda embobado. "Negra, haceme la ingenua."
> (*Baja los ojos, representa*) "No, señor, ¡no, señor! Mamá me prohibió hablar con desconocidos. ¿Cuáles son sus intenciones?" (179)

> [When I do that role for Pepe, he's blown away. "Honey, play the part of the ingenue for me." (*She lowers her eyes, acting the part*). "No, sir, no sir! Momma said I should never talk to strangers. What are your intentions?]

This example of role-playing within the role calls attention to the idea of role-playing in the theater and in society. In their relationship, the actress plays games of seduction with Pepe, with assigned roles and stereotyped dialogue that each understands and expects. Their game will both complement and contrast in a significant way with the one played in the waiting room.

As she ad libs her way through each mini-scene in Gambaro's drama, the actress plays the role that has worked for her in the past: she attempts to seduce, striking smiling, elegant poses and raising her skirt, and she plans her attack carefully and self-consciously: "(*Ríe*) ¡yo tengo la batalla ganada! Todavía dispongo de un par de ojos que. . . . Cuando vuelva ese infeliz, lo miraré así (*con patética coquetería*) seductora y . . . lo dejo duro. 'Mocoso, ¿alguna vez viste una mirada como ésta?' No, mejor no hablo. Ninguna familiaridad." (*She laughs.*) I have the battle won! I still have a pair of eyes at my disposal that . . .

When that sorry guy comes back, I'll look at him like this (*with pathetic flirting*), all seductive and . . . I'll leave him hard. "You little brat, have you ever in your life seen a look like this?" No, it's better not to speak. No familiarity] (174). Yet the woman's game, which we might call "Seduction," is doomed to fail, because her coplayer completely ignores her attempts to use sex to win the "battle." Following Boling's reading of the play, the dominant game in *El despojamiento* could ironically be named "Striptease," combining both the idea of stripping the woman (and again, I want to emphasize here that she is a victim who is stripped, rather than the playful initiator of a an erotic, pleasurable striptease) and the tease—for the woman and for the audience—of not knowing what is to happen next. For the woman, however, this is a violent, manipulative, and deconstructed striptease, and it is much more a game of power than of sex. As Boling suggests, "Gambaro's play deconstructs the connection between female identity and the relation of power in a phallocentric world by representing the divestiture of meaning from the woman by the young man."[15] Gambaro highlights these two adult games in *El despojamiento* in an exploration of gender and power. In each, the woman loses—because the other participant(s) do not follow the rules of the game, because they do not share those rules with all the players, or because the woman, long a victim of abuse and oppression, is incapable of fully apprehending the "real" rules. Indeed, as Magnarelli notes, the woman does not "recognize that she cannot win this perverse game whose rules she has misunderstood by not distinguishing between eroticism and oppression, or perhaps more important, between seer and seen/scene."[16]

In this game of violence, the young man's actions become increasingly hostile. The woman is thrown off balance yet again when he extends his hand toward her as if he were planning to caress her, as the stage directions attest: "*Ella lo mira en suspenso, como ante un imprevisto gesto amistoso. El muchacho mantiene inmóvil la mano y luego, con un gesto brusco, le arranca el pendiente*" [*She looks at him in suspense, as if he had made an unforeseen, friendly, gesture. The young man holds his hand motionless and then, with a brusque gesture, he yanks out her earring*] (175). In this case, as in the others, the woman initially reacts with anger but then quickly talks herself out of standing up for herself, imagining that the director will admire her serenity and cooperation. The woman's inability to defend herself is finally explained in more detailed references to her husband, Pepe, as she reveals that he has hit her:

Me acuerdo aquella vez, cuando Pepe me pegó hasta dejarme de cama, y
las vecinas llamaron a la policía y yo dije: "Aquí no pasó nada, me caí de
la escalera." (*Ríe*) ¡Se quedaron con un cuarto de narices! Y Pepe vino y
me besó. En cambio, si lo hubiera acusado, ¡pobre Pepe!, ¡qué humilla-
ción! Para él, para mí. (*Queda abstraída un segundo*) Para mí, ya humi-
llada por dejarme golpear. (177)

[I remember that time when Pepe beat me so bad I had to take to my bed,
and the neighbors called the police and I said, "Nothing happened here, I
fell down the stairs." *She laughs*. They were out of luck! And Pepe came
and kissed me. However, if I had accused him, poor Pepe! What humiliation! For him, for me. (*She is engrossed for a second in her thoughts.*) For
me, who was already humiliated by letting myself get beaten up.]

The woman's reactions can now be explained as repetitions of a pattern that she knows well and has long practiced: she is the victim of
domestic abuse. The telling realization of her humiliation fits perfectly
with the woman's behavior in the waiting room of *El despojamiento*.
She cannot leave the abusive relationship, she cannot sustain a defense, and she allows herself to continue to be humiliated. Indeed, the
woman is humiliated a final time, when the young man enters yet again,
and tries to rip off her skirt. This time, after her initial negative reaction, which again yields no response from the young man, the woman
simply takes off her skirt and gives it to him: "¡Tome!, se la doy. ¿Ve?
Tan amigos" [Take it, I'm giving it to you. See? Such good friends]
(178). The young man returns several more times to remove the rest
of the furniture, and the woman responds by taking off her stockings,
unbuttoning her blouse in what the stage directions describe as a pathetically provocative gesture, and spreading her legs: "¡Acá espero!"
[I'm here, waiting!] (181). The play ends with her smile frozen and her
head lowered, as the woman breaks into tears and cries out, "¡Pepe!"
The striptease has turned in on itself as the woman reduces herself to
living the role of the prostitute she has predicted might be her future
in the theater. In this game, which she has played countless times before in real life, she is degraded and humiliated so much that she simply takes over the role of victimizer and becomes her own torturer.

El despojamiento uses game playing to analyze the theater, male-
female relationships, and the effects of aging on the realization of one's
dreams, as Gambaro literally and figuratively strips away the masks
and costumes that define social relationships. The Paraguayan Josefina Plá[17] creates a social commentary that also functions as a type

of game in *Historia de un número*.[18] In this one-act drama, subtitled "Farsa trillada y sentimental en once tiempos" [Hackneyed and Sentimental Farce in Eleven Movements],[19] the nameless characters are stereotyped and depersonalized: Él, Ella, Vendedor, Muchacha de trenzas, Sastre, Juez [He, She, Salesman, Girl with pigtails, Tailor, Judge], etc. Influenced, as Teresa Méndez-Faith asserts, by both European postwar theater (Brecht, the Absurdists, and the Existentialist writers), and Spanish American dramatists such as Luisa Josefina Hernández and Osvaldo Dragún, this "hackneyed, sentimental farce" displays numerous ludic characteristics.[20] Plá divides the play into eleven movements or moments that correspond to the life of a person who does not have a number and, hence, an identity. An inversion of the idea that we are "only a number," *Historia de un número* suggests that without that number, we do not exist in society; in a real way, this drama presages the significant role that numbers play in our lives as technology makes the world even more number driven and controlled.

The first two scenes involve the courtship and union of the protagonist's parents. From the beginning, Plá's characters often repeat their onstage movements and dialogue, emphasizing the effect of their actions and making them look like a choreographed game; Plá tellingly uses "Este juego se repite" [This game is repeated] to describe that repetition. The entire courtship is stereotypically scripted. The characters talk about the weather and the natural world surrounding them, until one of them slips up and says the wrong thing:

ÉL:¿Le gustan a usted las nubes? . . .
[*Do you like clouds? . . .*]
ELLA: Horriblemente . . . Oh, disculpe. No quise decir eso. Quise decir. . . .
[*Horribly . . . Oh, pardon me. I didn't mean to say that. I meant to say. . . .*]
ÉL: Sí ya sé cómo pasa eso. Quiere uno decir una cosa y sale otra.
[*Yes, I know how that happens. You mean to say one thing and something else pops out.*]
ELLA: Eso mismo. ¿Y a usted? . . . ¿Le gusta el pasto?
[*That's exactly it. And you? . . . Do you like grass?*]
ÉL: Horrorosamente . . . Oh, disculpe. No quería decir eso.
[*Dreadfully . . . Oh, pardon me. I didn't mean to say that.*]
ELLA: Ya, ya sé cómo sucede eso. Uno piensa una cosa y dice otra. (50)
[*Yeah, I know how that happens. You think one thing and say another.*]

On the one hand, Plá has captured the awkwardness of first encounters—the need to measure every word and action carefully and the clumsy dialogue that often arises out of nervousness. On the other hand, however, the repetitions make the dialogue look artificial, linguistically self-conscious, and preplanned. The game becomes more important than the meaning of the words and the scene, like so many others in the play, resembles a parody of first encounters more than a realistic depiction of them.

Seeing courtship as a game is even more evident in the self-consciousness of other dialogue exchanges. As the man hints at the motivation for his happiness, the woman appears clueless. He finally responds in exasperation:

ÉL: Un motivo . . . Pero usted no me ayuda.
  [*One reason . . . but you aren't helping me.*]
ELLA: ¿Sí? . . . Lo siento . . . ¿Qué debo hacer? . . .
  [*Yes? . . . I'm sorry . . . What should I do?*]
ÉL: Preguntarme el motivo.
  [*Ask me about the reason.*]
ELLA: ¿Es importante que yo lo sepa?
  [*Is it important for me to know it?*]
ÉL: (*Con pasión*). ¡Oh, sí; muy importante! (50–51)
  (With passion.) Oh, yes, very important!]

The characters illustrate in this example both the scripted nature of many social roles and the ways in which we serve as the directors of the scripts of others. The scene emerges, then, as theatrically self-conscious, reminding the audience about the nature of role and identity—in the theater and beyond.

The birth of the couple's child in the third scene continues the repetition of actions, which Plá calls the "juego de dormir" [game of sleeping], as the two take turns, while lying on the bed, one putting his/her head on the other's shoulder, with the other awake and staring at the doorway. The man seems especially afraid of what might enter through the doorway. Gradually, we realize that the terrible monster of his dreams is a child, and the act ends with a grotesque birth, filled with loud noises and darkness, as the two pantomime what Plá describes as "un Nacimiento patéticamente desventurado" [a pathetically wretched Nativity] (54). Immediately thereafter, the man disappears from his family and from the play, and the woman is left to raise her child alone. That child has entered the world, Plá tells us, without a number: "Será un non en todas partes" [He'll be a nobody, the odd man out everywhere he goes] (54). The suggestion is, however, that "name" could also be substituted for "number," as the Celador [official sitting at a desk] tells the baby's mother, "No debió usted haberlo dejado entrar. Son complicaciones para una mujer sola" [You shouldn't have let him enter. They're complications for a woman alone] (54). Here, the lack of a paternal figure and identity combine with the problems of single parenthood to create an even larger social problem. Moreover, Plá's decision not to give her characters specific names also functions to emphasize what Severino João Albuquerque, utilizing Martin Esslin's typology of violence in modern drama, describes as violence against the characters: "The playwright may also do violence to his or her characters by denying them a name and instead using numbers (as does Isaac Chocrón in *Tric-Trac*), personal pronouns such as Él and Ella [He and She] (as does Maruxa Vilalta in *Esta noche amándonos tanto*), and order of entrance such as *Hombre Primero* and *Hombre Segundo* [First Man and Second Man] (as does Virgilio Piñera in *Estudio en blanco y negro*)."[21] Plá further alludes to problems of overpopulation—even with a mother's love and protection, the child is, ironically, just another number in an overpopulated world: "Su hijo figura entre el millón y medio nacido de más este año, y para los cuales el mundo no tiene previsto un lugar en la mesa" [Your son is just one of the many million and a half born this year, for whom the world has not prepared a seat at the table] (55). In *Historia de un número*, the lack of a number is tied intimately to problems of population, poverty, violence, and identity.

From that moment on, the fatherless child is denied an identity and the benefits of society. He grows from childhood to adolescence and adulthood with countless opportunities missed because of his lack of a number. Eight consecutive Ventanilleros [clerks] tell him that he is entitled to nothing: "No hay carta para usted;" "No hay puesto para usted;" "No hay amigos para usted;" "No hay deseos cumplidos para usted" [There's no letter for you; There's no job for you; There are no friends for you; There are no desires fulfilled for you], etc. (56). The young man learns that he cannot find shoes or a suit that fits ("No hay saco a su medida, señor. No hay número" [There's no suit in your size, sir. There's no number]); he cannot play the lottery (and buy a number for himself) without money for the ticket; he cannot get a girlfriend ("Mi mamá no quiere . . . dice que un hombre sin número no me conviene" [My mom won't let me . . . she says a man without a number isn't fitting]); and he cannot get a seat on the train, since the number on his ticket is always one more or less than the train allows. He enlists in the army in order to get a number, but after the war is over, he returns to civilian life as poor and as beaten as ever.

As the play moves towards its conclusion, the man's desperation becomes increasingly apparent, as two individuals offer him a way out:

INDIVIDUO 1: Con dinero hay siempre número.
[*With money there's always a number.*]
INDIVIDUO 2: Con número hay siempre dinero.
[*With a number there's always money.*]
INDIVIDUO 1: Número es dinero.
[*Number is money.*]
INDIVIDUO 2: Dinero es número. (61–62)
[*Money is number.*]

The two individuals hand the man a revolver, and the three leave to commit a crime, which apparently goes awry, because the man is caught and, in the final scene, taken before a judge. Although his lawyer repeatedly offers as his client's excuse "No tenía número" [He didn't have a number], the judge is unmoved and decrees that since all of the crimes the young man has committed are the result of having been born and raised without a number, he will now and forever be given one. The play ends with the guards lifting the black sheet that had covered the man in the courtroom, revealing that he is wearing a prison uniform with an enormous number "131313" emblazoned across the chest. The symbolism is clear and insistent: numberless people have no social identity, are destined to live in poverty and misery, and will ultimately be driven to a life of crime.

Plá's techniques make it impossible to miss her message. Without name or number, her unidimensional characters are truly without a social identity. The repetitions of dialogue and action help to drive home the dramatist's points, but they also establish the play itself as a kind of game of social roles and realities. In *Historia de un número*, a player without a number is marginalized to the extent that he is not even allowed to enter the game. Denied participation, such a frustrated player will ultimately break the rules and be permanently exiled from ever playing the game again. The overt moralizing of this short play is made even more evident in the accumulation of short scenes, the predictable dialogue, and stereotypical actions. Plá's story of a number is ironically the story of a person, but his depersonalization makes him just another number in a game all too familiar in the third world—and, indeed, throughout the entire world.[22]

El despojamiento, Historia de un número, and *El gran circo eukraniano* echo many of the other dramas examined elsewhere in this study—*Extraño juguete* serving as a clear example—in their examination of social roles, employment of role playing within the role, utilization of violence, and ironic endings. In each play, the games are most of all about power relationships, as the characters and conflicts reflect some of the basic elements of the game of life. Those power relationships are made manifest in the nexus of gender and the theater (*El despojamiento*), in the search for personal and social identity (*Historia de un número*), and in the representation of community and national identity by means of the performance idiom (*El gran circo eukraniano*). In the three plays explored in this chapter, we see a clear consciousness of their ludic nature, as their creators use the theater itself (or its stand-in, the circus) to interrogate issues central to human culture and society. Games are played with the characters (both with and without their voluntary participation), who confront the difficulties of not knowing the rules of the games they are playing or of discovering the consequences of rule-breaking. Games are also played with the audience, whose exploration of these sociocultural issues is influenced by the dramatists' tricks of the theatrical trade: like the characters within the plays, we discover that information has been withheld, that narrators can be unreliable, that fellow audience members are really actors/characters, that we have not been fully apprized of the rules of the game. In all three dramas, although the words "game" and "play" appear frequently, the games are more metaphorical than explicit representations of children's play, but they nonetheless highlight what happens when we act "as if," exposing the masks that we choose to wear and those society selects for us.

7

Games and the Historical-Political Realities of Spanish America in Dramas by Griselda Gambaro, Jesusa Rodríguez, and Sabina Berman

Fantasy play can reveal a great deal of material, but any kind of play can be used defensively.

—Anna Freud

A RECENT ESSAY BY NIEVES MARTÍNEZ DE OLCOZ SERVES AS A USEFUL point of departure for the plays discussed in this chapter. In "Decisiones de la máscara neutra: Dramaturgia femenina y fin de siglo en América Latina," Martínez de Olcoz analyzes the complex relationship existing between the feminine body, the nation, and the theater of Latin America:

> Dramaturgy in the 80s works from the confluence of plots dealing with women and the nation, the imperative of rewriting gender (sexual and rhetorical), and History (with a capital "H"). The talent of the end-of-the-century female dramatist in Latin America is formulated in the space where the author/interpreter's gesture of political identity can be a perfect allegory for national identity, by presenting itself as a question of *ownership*, where acquiring signs of identity implies a relatively violent performative act (an unpredictable action, improvised at the bosom of culture). The writer's country is her gender (as Raznovich stated), based on Diana Taylor's insightful assumptions regarding the negotiation of a performance where *there is no nation without gender, nor body without nationality.*[1]

As is the case in so many of the dramas examined in this study, the theatrical, gender, social, and historical/political aspects of much of contemporary Spanish American theater come together in the plays' literal and metaphoric game playing. This blurring of categories suggests, of course, what we already know: the personal is the political, gender issues are central to both the domestic and political spheres, performance is inherent in Spanish American society. The political upheaval, violence, and repression that marked the last half of the twentieth century often found their expression in the theater in games and play. The reasons are many, but fundamentally, games serve as metaphors for the issues defining these countries' historical and sociopolitical realities. Games may mask direct confrontations, making the plays in which they appear more likely to be staged than censored. In addition, the use of the game metaphor may be one more instance of the encoded language that defined the discourse of many of the countries living under repressive conditions. Finally, these games are charged with theatricality: in their self-conscious use of games and play, the dramatists discussed in this chapter explore the nature of theater, representation, and identity—both on a personal level and for their countries. The plays are diverse in the extreme: Griselda Gambaro presents an Argentine horror show in *Información para extranjeros* [Information for Foreigners], Jesusa Rodríguez plays with one of Mexico's best-known historical figures as she deconstructs contemporary politics in *Sor Juana en Almoloya* [Sor Juana in Almoloya], and Sabina Berman examines Mexican politics and corruption in *Krisis*. Each of these dramas offers a unique vision of the playwright's view of historical and political issues. And, although they are separated geographically, Mexican and Argentine theater share the idea of crisis, as Bixler has asserted: just as in Argentina, the word "crisis" is heard frequently in the streets of Mexico, where a political, social, and economic crisis distresses and overwhelms every Mexican on a daily basis.[2]

The subtitle of Gambaro's *Información para extranjeros* (1973)[3] is "Crónica en 20 escenas" [Chronicle in 20 Scenes], and "scenes" is a key word: the play is set in a large, two-story house, with numerous hallways, stairs, and connecting rooms, and the audience, divided into groups, is led through the house to experience the actions occurring in each scene. Reminiscent of Cortázar's *Rayuela*, the order of the action could change depending upon which group an audience member joined, for Gambaro announces in her initial stage directions that Group 1's itinerary describes only one of the scenic possibilities.[4] Each group is led by a guide,[5] and the different groups occasionally meet each other in the hallways or witness the same scene simultaneously. Gambaro's strategy includes the members of her audience in the theatrical game, forcing them to participate by receiving the testimony of the violent acts they will see enacted within the house. She further confounds the definitions of "audience" on yet another level by inserting actors into the audience, just as Casas did in *El gran circo eukraniano*; these actors will, from time to time, interact with the guide or the action of the diverse scenes. This suggests an interesting possibility: although the dramatist does not insist that her audience interact physically with the play—"El público no será nunca forzado a participar de la acción" [The audience will never be forced to participate in the action] (70)—the traditional lines separating text from audience have been so destabilized that it is possible in any given performance that someone will be moved to take part in the dramatic action, just as Gambaro's overarching goal is to move her spectators to action outside the theater.

Información para extranjeros is based on real stories of repression, torture, and disappearance that took place in the years prior to the beginning of the Dirty War. From time to time, the guides offer an "Explanation for foreigners" to contextualize specific events or characters (although Marguerite Feitlowitz avers that the foreigners are really those Argentines who continued to ignore information about the repressive events that were transpiring).[6] These "explicaciones para extranjeros" come from Argentine newspapers of the time; mixing the fictional and the historical, *Información para extranjeros* also draws attention to the fictive nature of some of the actual newspaper accounts of the atrocities that were taking place. And, as the guide warns in his ironic opening words, the scenes will require an adult sensibility: "El espectáculo es prohibido para menores de 18 años. También prohibido para menores de 35 y mayores de 36. El resto puede asistir sin problemas. . . . La pieza responde a nuestro estilo de vida: argentino, occidental y cristiano. Estamos en 1971" [The spectacle is prohibited for those under 18. It's also prohibited for those younger than 35 and older than 36. The rest may attend without a problem. . . . The play responds to our lifestyle: Argentine, Western, and Christian. We're in 1971] (70). It soon becomes clear that the stage has been set to present acts of State-produced atrocity; as Diana Taylor so aptly puts it, "By interweaving fragments of theatrical scenes with acts of criminal violence, Gambaro indicates the degree to which theatre in Latin America is an arena of intense and dangerous ideological conflict."[7]

Virtually all of the scenes depict violence and torture, many of which are interspersed with poetry, songs, or dialogue from plays by

García Lorca and Shakespeare. One couplet ("violín, violón / es la mejor razón") alludes to the reign of Juan Manuel de Rosas, who had violin music played during the decapitations of his enemies.[8] The stage directions sometimes inform us that the acting in a particular scene is supposed to be amateurish or stylized. At times, the guide enters the fiction taking place in a particular room. On other occasions, the realism of a scene is undercut by garish costumes or makeup. The guide often talks directly to the audience, commenting on the comportment of the characters they have seen or on the arrangements for seeing well or sitting comfortably. In the most obvious breaks with the dramatic fiction—which is already broken by the constantly changing episodes inherent in the play's structure—characters remind us that they are actors, as when a guide pokes his head in a door, asking if he can bring his group into a room, and a voice replies, "¿Y a mí qué me importa? ¡Rajen! Estoy ensayando" [And what do I care? Beat it! I'm rehearsing] (71), or when the guide apologizes to the women in the audience for the vulgar language they have heard: "Disculpen señoras. Yo no sabía nada. El teatro moderno es así" [I'm sorry, ladies. I didn't know. Modern theater is like that] (107). Gambaro's metatheatrical techniques—the plays within the play, role-playing within the role, announcements of theatrical process, and literary and real-life allusions—collectively serve to break the tension produced by the horror witnessed on stage.[9]

The horror unfolds in scene after unrelenting scene of violence and human degradation. One entire scene features only a mostly naked man who, when the spotlight hits him, raises his head, looking surprised and afraid; he covers his genitals with his hands. Several times, the group passes by a room from which a death rattle emanates. Later, an "audience member" steps over to the dying woman and smothers her. Another set of scenes focuses on a young girl who has clearly been tortured repeatedly. Different characters, including the guide, offer the girl a loaded gun, encouraging her to use it on herself to end her suffering and even showing her what parts of the body will most effectively produce the desired results. When we hear a shot later in the play, we infer that she has committed suicide. One of Gambaro's central techniques in *Información para extranjeros* is the piling on of violence and sadism in the series of scenes; the cumulative effect of so much torture is the intensification of the experience for the audience, some of whom might even fear that they could become the next victims.

Literal and metaphoric games are crucial elements of the drama. On the most basic level, the entire drama is a game, which Gambaro has devised for her audience members. As noted above, the shifting and fragmented story line (depending upon which group one is assigned) and the possibilities of audience interaction make the game one of endless themes and variations. The theatrical self-consciousness of the staging also contributes to the idea of the game. Eugene L. Moretta's comments on Spanish American theater of the 1950s and 1960s point to such connections:

> Organized and regulated forms of role playing, like acting (professional or *ad hoc*), games (let us remember the presence of both theatre and game in the English word "play"), and ritual all occur within bounded spaces which separate the participants from the larger world and allow for autonomous spheres of activity. As part of the content of a dramatic work, each form represents one self-contained world within another, a single exercise in role playing set inside a conventional role-playing framework.[10]

A clear example of the interaction of games and role-playing is the reenactment of the Milgram experiment, which was first performed in the 1960s in Yale University's psychology department and later repeated at other U.S. universities and in Germany. Although they were told that the researchers were investigating the effects of punishment on learning, the experiment really tested the subjects' willingness to inflict pain or death on total strangers, the "pupils" who were hooked to electrodes and supposedly shocked when they gave incorrect answers in a memory exercise. The subjects, who did not know that the screams they heard were faked, increased the voltage of electric shocks to their "pupils" with every mistake, the majority following their "orders" without question, even when they had been told that doing so would cause the death of the pupil. Gambaro repeats this experiment in one of the scenes of *Información para extranjeros* and has one of the participants describe the statistical results at the end.[11] The guide then ironically adds, "La experiencia se realizó en Alemania y Estados Unidos. Entre nosotros sería completamente absurda" [The experiment took place in Germany and the United States. It would be completely absurd to perform it here] (84). This scene, the third of twenty, is the first to introduce the idea of the game, as the experiment's coordinator explains the rules to the man who will administer the electric shocks: "Acá está la lista de las palabras. Juego limpio: léalas lentamente, con buena pronunciación" [Here is the list of words. Play fair: read them slowly, with good pronunciation] (76). Audience members witnessing what they think is the torture and death of another human being, especially a victim who thinks he is only participating in a harmless experiment to study learning, might well find the words "juego limpio" [play fair] ironic in the extreme. For those who know the details of the experiment, of course, the game is hardly "limpio"; everyone is playing dirty with the real subject. But on still another level, the audience members are also subjects in this theatrical game/ experiment, and much like the subjects in the real Milgram experiment, they are able to allow the infliction of great pain and suffering on another individual without raising even a whisper of protest.

The scene featuring the Milgram experiment functions as a multileveled game. Yet Gambaro's use of the game becomes even more blatant with numerous scenes specifically treating children's themes by way of games, lullabies, fairy tales, and play (such as characters dressed up like dolls or puppets), although it should be noted that adults always play the children's parts. The fourteenth scene begins with one of the "Explanations for foreigners," detailing the abduction and murder in 1971 of Juan Pablo Maestre and his wife, Mirta Elena Misetech, accused of belonging to the Fuerzas Armadas Revolucionarias. Part of the guide's explanation is that Mirta lost a shoe as she was thrown into her abductors' car. The kidnapping is performed onstage, concluding with a group of policemen who, dressed as sweepers with long-handled brooms, dance as if in a musical comedy and sing:

> ¡Venimos a limpiar! [We've come to clean!]
> ¡Venimos a limpiar! [We've come to clean!]
> La mugre de la calle [The filth from the street]
> Venimos a limpiar [We've come to clean]
> Que las madres rueguen [Let the mothers beg]
> que los niños jueguen [Let the children play]
> ¡con felicidad! [merrily!] (112)

The double meaning of the policemen's "clean-up" of the streets is obvious in this bizarre song and dance routine. Even more obvious is the subsequent argument between the guide and a policemen over the owner of the shoe: Snow White or Cinderella. The police ask everyone to try on the shoe and finally find a young girl it will fit: "El príncipe azul se casará contigo" [Prince Charming will marry you] (113). Gambaro has created a morality tale, an allegory of evil that juxtaposes kidnapping and death with children's fairy tales to make a point about the disappearance of a real-life young couple.

Children's games will play an even more significant role in the fifteenth scene, where a group is playing "Martín Pescador, ¿me dejarás pasar?" [Martín Pescador, Will You Let Me Go By?], a game similar to "London Bridges," which lets some children through a bridge and keeps others out, in response to their answers to questions the "bridgemakers" ask. The guide even invites the audience to join in, which Rosalea Postma posits might illustrate Gambaro's desire to test her spectators, to see what effect the punishment of others might have on their participation.[12] As the game continues, a man shouts out, "¡No lo soltés! ¡A éste lo conozco!" [Don't let him loose! I know this one!] (115), and the groups start to push each other in an increasingly violent mob scene while absurdly dressed policemen beat the players and the crowd crushes the "prisoner" caught inside the bridge. In a final note, one of the policemen begins to attack the audience, although the "victims" are really actors mixed in with the spectators. The innocence of this children's game has been subverted and perverted in Gambaro's version of "Martín Pescador" by means of betrayal, mob rule, and police brutality.

The penultimate children's game occurs in the eighteenth scene. A deformed child-monster wearing a long white shirt and heavy makeup enters, along with other adult characters dressed as children; the child-monster sings:

> Antón, Antón Pirulero [Antón, Antón Pirulero]
> Cada cual, cada cual [each one, each one]
> atienda su juego [waiting for their turn]
> y el que no [and the one who doesn't]
> el que no, [the one who doesn't]
> ¡una prenda tendrá! [forfeits!] (120)

The child-monster selects one of the bigger children, gives him a club, and sends him outside the circle that the children have formed. The children play "Antón Pirulero" by singing and pretending to play instruments while the child-monster in the center (Antón Pirulero) turns around and around, his arms extended like wings. The goal of the game is for the children in the circle to pay close attention so that when Antón stops and points at one of them, that child will be moving his/her own arms like Antón; those who lose three times are out. The game is played very quickly, with the children singing.[13] The child with the club begins to knock the other players senseless, until only he and the child-monster are left; at that point, the child-monster aims an imaginary gun at the child wielding the club and kills him. The child-monster plays alone, with increasingly spasmodic gestures, and the song becomes unintelligible as the lights go out. This game is rife with symbolism as the torturing bully attacks the innocent participants while the child-monster, most likely representing the State, provides him with his weapon. Of course, even the executioner must eventually be eliminated.

Once again, a children's game has been transformed to provide a forum for the discussion of political repression. And once again, the game then moves to a different level. This time, the child-monster is ignored while two men and a girl ask each other, "¿Cuál es tu juego?" [What's your game?]; the answer is always "El miedo" [Fear], except in the case of the girl, who says, "El miedo. (*Una pausa*) Y la pregunta. . . . ¿Por qué el miedo?" [Fear. (*A pause.*) And the question. . . . Why fear?] (121). In the verses that follow, the girl encapsulates the essence of the drama:

El tiempo está alterado, los años por venir están alterados [Time is changed, the years yet to come are changed]
Tú sabes dónde me encontrarás [You know where you'll find me]
Yo, el miedo, yo la muerte [I, fear; I, death]
yo, la memoria inasible [I, ungraspable memory]
yo, el recuerdo de la ternura de tus manos [I, the memory of the tenderness of your hands]
yo, la tristeza de nuestra vida fracasada [I, the sadness of our failed life]
Yo asediaré el "eso no me concierne" con mi angustia [I'll lay siege to "that doesn't concern me" with my anguish]
y quebraré el sueño ajeno con fuegos de artificio [and I'll break the strange dream with fires of artifice]
horribles, indecentes [horrible, indecent]
con fusilamientos incontables caeré sobre la indiferencia [with innumerable executions I'll fall on the indifference]
de los que pasan [of those who go by]
hasta que empiecen a preguntar, a preguntarse [until they begin to ask, to question] (121–22)[14]

Gambaro has presented her grotesque game as a segue to a poetic treatise that ties together the fear of the victims and observers of violence and torture. As we will see, the last game of *Información para extranjeros* brings the spectator back to the larger game the dramatist is playing with her audience.

The final scene of the play once again unites torture and game playing. A blindfolded prisoner is brought into a room filled with prostitutes and a chorus, who will be forced to sing and dance as a way of applauding what will happen to the prisoner. The men who have escorted the blindfolded prisoner begin a game similar to "Blindman's Bluff" or "Marco Polo," called "Gallito Ciego" [Blind Cock of the Walk]. They spin the man around to disorient him and move away, calling "¡Cocorocó!" [Cockadoodledoo!] while he feels for them with his hands extended. The prisoner's helplessness leads one of the prostitutes to reach out toward his blindfold, but the men push her away ("¡No te metás! El juego es nuestro. ¡A tu lugar, puta!" [Don't get involved! It's our game. Back to your place, whore!], 126). Noticing that the prisoner is sweating, the men strip him (*"manteniendo un aire ambiguo de juego y violencia"* [*maintaining an ambiguous air of game and violence*], 126) and propose a new game: "Huevo Duro" [Hard-boiled Egg]. The prisoner holds his body rigid while the men attack him, tie him up, hit him on the head, and drag him away, where it becomes obvious that they murder him. Both of the games in this final scene involve violence, humiliation, and torture; they are clearly intended to mirror the terrorism taking place outside the theater, just as they must surely produce terror in the audience. Still, the surprises have not yet ended. Suddenly the action stops, the actors leave, the stage is dismantled, and the guide announces that the play is over, sardonically inviting the audience to applaud:

> El teatro imita la vida [Theater imitates life]
> Si no aplauden [If you don't applaud]
> es que la vida es jodida [it's because life is screwed up]
> Vayamos a la salida. [Let's go to the exit.] (128)

But even as the guide is shepherding the group toward the door, police sirens can be heard in the distance, suggesting that the game may just be beginning for the members of the audience.

Taylor, exploring the theatricality of terrorism in this drama, claims that terrorists capitalize on our deepest fears and infantile fantasies to include the general public in their complicity and guilt: "The hideous intrusion of children's songs and games in Gambaro's *Information* illustrates how terrorism pushes the population to regress to those early areas of experience that prove most overwhelming and hardest to decode. One approaches as an adult and turns away as a frightened child incapable of action."[15] She further states that by creating what the *Nunca más* report on the "disappeared" called "a climate of fear in which subversion would be impossible," state terrorists, "as those who orchestrated Argentina's Dirty War knew, destabilize the population and make it easier for the government to maintain power."[16] The children's games of *Información para extranjeros* provide an ironic doubling of the display of adult violence and torture that permeates the drama. Perverting innocence, they show the adult world as even darker in retrospect, illustrating the deep fears that immobilize the general population and permit repressive governments to assume and maintain control.

With Jesusa Rodríguez's *Sor Juana en Almoloya (Pastorela virtual)* (1995),[17] the historical and political game is turned on its head. Rodríguez wears many hats and performs many roles—actor, director, dramatist, and performance artist—in the theater that she co-owns with Liliana Felipe, the independent Teatro de la Capilla.[18] Her works—often sketches—are characterized by their daring, humorous, and mordant look at Mexican society, politics and history. Rodríguez, often writing with Felipe, loves to parody the images and texts of the sacred literary and historical icons of her country, and she particularly appears to enjoy skewering its politicians. "*Sor Juana en Almoloya*," states Amalia Gladhart, "reflects many of the concerns raised in Rodríguez's other works, in which political satire, a destabilization of gender roles, lesbian desire, and a resistant recuperation of history all figure prominently."[19] The play exploits kitsch and "camp," subverting conventions as it exposes political corruption and the pomposity of literary criticism. Although Rodríguez does not directly employ children's games, the playful tone perfectly expresses a ludic spirit standing in sharp contrast to Gambaro's powerful investigations of violence and torture. Moreover, it could easily be sustained that the entire drama is a game in its pastiche, wordplay, and parody. This singular type of drama, performed for a cabaret audience, expresses game playing in an assuredly distinct and distinctive manner. Rodríguez is having fun with her subject matter; as she tells us early on in the play, any similarity to real life is virtual (395). In a 1997 interview with Mark and Blanca Kelty, Rodríguez discusses the experience of writing a metaphor that could represent the state of her country and its current crises: "You have to touch the essence of what is happening [in the country], because if not, it won't interest anyone. And if not, what you're doing is making jokes."[20] This union of game, metaphor, and political crisis—real and virtual—lies at the center of *Sor Juana en Almoloya*.

Rodríguez sets up her play to look simultaneously back at the past and forward to the future. Produced and published in 1995, the dramatic action takes place in the year 2000. Presaging the future, Rodríguez's stage direction slyly thanks God that the PAN (or, as she calls it, the Partido reAcción Nacional) has gained power in Mexico and reestablished morality. The protagonist, however, is the seventeenth-century nun, Sor Juana Inés de la Cruz, a prisoner in Almoloya, the high-security prison constructed outside Mexico City where the "big fish"—Raúl Salinas de Gortari, the major drug traffickers—are incarcerated. Sor Juana, transported to the first year of the new millennium, still finds herself in a cell, although of a slightly different type: combining the past, present, and future, her books, ancient geometry instruments, inkwell, and quill pen sit next to an old-model Apple computer, and a large video screen can be seen at the back. As the play begins, Sor Juana is cackling over a copy of the letter of self-defense that ex-President Carlos Salinas de Gortari had sent to the media in 1995.[21] Concurrent with Rodríguez's creation of the play, this letter now "reappears" five years later, allowing the dramatist to comment on its contents from the perspective of the future—but via the game that brings the letter's reader back from her three-hundred-year-old grave:

Juar juar, juar, ¡qué bárbaro!, qué hábil era este sujeto, una sola carta escrita desde su exilio virtual movilizaba a políticos e intelectuales . . . y con eso logró que no lo culparan de nada, ni lo trajeron a declarar sobre los asesinatos y el derrumbe del país, ni devolvió un quinto de todo lo que se robó, vaya, ni siquiera lo expulsaron del PRI. No cabe duda: o este tipo era un genio, o sus contemporáneos unos pendejos. (395–96).

[Har dee har har, fantastic! How skillful this guy was; one little letter, written from his virtual exile, motivated politicos and intellectuals . . . and with all that, he managed not to be blamed for anything; they didn't even bring him in to make a statement on the assassinations and the collapse of the country, and he didn't even return a fifth of everything he robbed; why, they didn't even expel him from the PRI. There's no doubt: either this guy was a genius, or his contemporaries were a bunch of idiots.]

Sor Juana declares that the best aspect of Salinas's letter is the renovation of the epistolary genre, and she vows to imitate his model and answer the letter as a means of getting out of prison. She calls it "La Respuesta Zopilotea" [The Buzzardly Reply] and begins with a list of the "buzzard" Salinas's "honorifics" that illustrates the playwright's wordplay for the "in" crowd: "Ex-celentísimo, Ex-señor, Ex-presidente CSG: Carlos Sinvergüenza y Góngora, Salinas de Gortari, Familia de la Cerda Portorratero de Cárdenas, Conde de Sanborn's. . . ." [Ex-cellency, ex-sir, Ex-president GSG: Carlos Shameless and Góngora, Salinas de Gortari, Family of the Ratport of Cárdenas, Count of Sanborn's. . . .] (396). What follows is a brilliant parody of Sor Juana's "Respuesta a Sor Filotea," although this Sor Juana lays it on the line, directly verbalizing her indignation at having been brought to the prison to write speeches and public relations copy for the Panistas ("loas a sus fundamentalismos, arcos triunfales a Fox y a Fernández de Cevallos" [works in praise of their fundamentalist beliefs, triumphal arches to Fox and to Fernández de Cevallos]) when Raúl Salinas is about to be released: "Y aunque hizo cosas buenas que parecieron malas no hizo cosas malas que parecieron peores. En cambio a mí pretenden castigarme y humillarme severamente sólo por ser mujer e inclinarme a la cogitación" [And although he did good things that seemed bad, he didn't do bad things that seemed even worse. On the other hand, they're trying to punish and humiliate me solely because I'm a woman inclined to cogitation] (396, 397).

While Sor Juana is reading Salinas's letter, its text is projected onto the screen, as is a photo of Salinas dressed as Sor Filotea. All of this produces a multileveled game: the colonial nun talks via cyberspace to the man who thwarted her attempts at free expression and thought, but like the Bishop of Puebla who hid under the pseudonym of Sor Filotea, Salinas will also hide behind "her" disguise in a comic inversion of the Golden Age convention of the *mujer vestida de hombre* (woman dressed as a man).[22] And, like so many of the other intertextual references of *Sor Juana en Almoloya*, the deceptive photo of Salinas in drag becomes a campy play on the nun's sonnet "Este, que ves, engaño colorido" [This colored deception that you see].

Rodríguez cleverly follows this image with yet another from the repertoire of Sor Juana. Claiming that she has hit the wrong button on her computer, Sor Juana materializes her lawyer, who, she avers, is really a dupe of the Panistas. Repeating the previous image, the lawyer also wears women's clothing, echoing and parodying the *gracioso* (servant) Castaño's famous speech in *Los empeños de una casa* when he dons women's clothes and speaks directly to the women in the audience. The attorney claims that the Vicereine paid him off in new pesos to trade clothing so that she will be able to slip past the prison guards and visit Sor Juana ("Por suerte," he adds, "que hoy no me puse el *jogging* color marrón" [Luckily, I didn't put on my brown sweatsuit today], 398). The parody reveals the lawyer's ties with corruption:

No hay ladrón que tanto encubra [There's no thief who covers up more]
ni paje que tanto mienta [nor page who lies as much]
ni gitano que así engañe [nor gypsy who deceives in this way]
soy licenciado panista [I'm a PAN party lawyer]
y nunca fui Salinista. [and I never was for Salinas.]

(399)

The licenciado does such a good job imitating a woman that he worries
at the end that he might be politically seduced: "Temor llevo de que
algún otro partido me enamore" [I'm afraid that some other party
might fall in love with me] (400).

The games of seduction and disguise continue with the arrival of
another cross-dressed character, the Condesa [Countess] de Paredes,
Sor Juana's benefactor, dressed as the Licenciado. Juana's play on
names illuminates the gender bending: "¡Licen, Lili, Lysi-Filis! Eres
tú" [Law-, Lili, Lysi-Filis! It's you] (400–401). Using typical pseud-
onyms of sixteenth- and seventeenth-century poetry, "Lysi" has come
to beg Sor Juana to give in to her oppressors and allow her books to
be burned; by turning her back on her intellectual pursuits, the
woman argues, Sor Juana might be able to avoid more prison time.
Showing the pressures women writers face, Rodríguez takes the game
a step further by bringing in Octavio Paz—whose opinions from *Sor
Juana y las trampas de la fe* are conveyed by a voice off stage—to
critique Sor Juana's writing and talk about the supposed sexual relationship between the two women. Rodríguez presents Paz (here, the
patriarchal "powerful Oz," invisible, but nonetheless able to control
the opinions and behavior of others) as the epitome of academic/intel-
lectual arrogance. The focus of the selections from Paz's book on Sor
Juana is, of course, his controversial biographical exegesis of the nun's
writing in terms of her sexuality. Rodríguez plays with the concept by
having the Condesa de Paredes (dressed as a man) and Sor Juana engage in the very behavior that the voice representing Paz describes:

La mayoría de los biógrafos de Sor Juana darían el monto total de las becas
y premios que han ganado por tener la oportunidad de atisbar desde lejos
lo que vosotros tenéis ante vuestras narices. . . . A continuación tendremos
la oportunidad de entender con toda claridad el verdadero significado de
los términos que utiliza el pristino erudito para explicar esta amistad. (*Las
dos mujeres se acercan peligrosamente.*) Nótese el safismo sublimado.
(*Ahora se besan apasionadamente.*) Vedlas entregadas a las silenciosas
orgías de la meditación. Una monja, la otra casada. ¿Qué podrían hacer

juntas? (*Sor Juana salta encima de la virreina y ambas se repantigan a sus anchas.*) (402)

[The majority of Sor Juana's biographers would give the sum total of all the scholarships and prizes they have ever won to have the opportunity to observe from afar what you have right in front of your eyes. . . . Following this, we will have the opportunity to understand with total clarity the true significance of the terms that the erudite PRI party member is using to explain this friendship. *The two women get dangerously close to each other.* Note the sublimated sapphism. *Now they kiss passionately.* See them falling into silent orgies of meditation. One, a nun; the other, a married woman. What might they do together? (*Sor Juana jumps on top of the Vicereine and both sprawl around.*)]

Rodríguez creates a multilayered, gender-bending parody in this scene. Playing with the highly theatrical concepts of role-playing, disguise, and cross dressing, she has carefully led us from Salinas as Sor Filotea to Castaño's famous scene, and now, to the Condesa-as-male frolicking with the nun. Still, Rodríguez leaves a measure of ambiguity inherent in the presentation of the two women, both because the Condesa is "male" and because the women's actions are so exaggerated and parodic that we are left in doubt about their relationship. Gladhart observes, "Same sex desire is stressed, but always with a playful uncertainty: is it all a joke on Paz, or is it the 'true' relationship between the two women we see on stage? . . . I want here to underline the ambiguity. Lysi and Sor Juana are openly and physically affectionate, but are at the same time clearly toying with the critic's—and the spectator's—assumptions."[23] Disguise and dissimulation are the means by which the games are played in *Sor Juana en Almoloya*, and the layering of levels adds to the game as it also creates additional irony.

Rodríguez not only allows Sor Juana to toy with Paz's assumptions as he "rewrites" her work from his male, twentieth-century perspective, but she also adds Sor Juana's rewriting of her own texts as an additional layer of self-conscious play. After rewriting Sonnet 165 (now, the satiric "Detente sombra de Virrey esquivo" [Halt, shadow of disdainful Viceroy]), she asks her audience to judge the result: "Creo que no quedó tan mal, / opinad amigos míos, os suplico intervengáis / pues un público pasivo / no cumple con el reclamo / de un soneto interactivo" [I think it didn't turn out too bad; / tell me what you think, my friends, I beg you to take a stand / since a passive audience / doesn't answer the call / of an interactive sonnet] (400). Sor Juana playfully brings the reader/spectator actively into the discussion of literary criticism here, but we also realize that we have been included throughout the play, because every intertextual reference—literary or real-life— asks us to decipher or remove the disguise, to make connections, to recall the text being parodied or the person being caricatured. In yet another structural parallel reminiscent of Sor Juana's answer to Salinas's/Sor Filotea's letter, the nun now responds to Paz's *Las trampas de la fe* (and Paz's quest for the Nobel prize for literature) with a rewriting of her own well-known "sátira filosófica" [philosophical satire], one that cleverly attacks Paz while simultaneously defending her gender:

> Hombres necios que acusáis a la mujer sin razón [Foolish men who accuse woman without any grounds]
> sin ver que también las hay, que sí tenemos razón. [without seeing that there are plenty of us, and we are right.]
> Si con ansia sin igual solicitáis el Nobel [If you solicit the Nobel with equal yearning]
> ¿Por qué queréis que hablen bien si seleccionáis a Paz? [why do you want them to speak well if you choose Paz?]
>   . . .
> ¿Cuál mayor culpa ha tenido en una pasión errada: [Who has been more to blame in a mistaken passion:]
> la que premia ser rogada o el que ruega ser premiado? [she who prizes being asked or he who asks to be prized?] (403)

As Gladhart states, the institutional entrapment that Sor Juana has suffered leaves parody (rewriting) as her only means of resistance and escape.[24]

With her parodic rewritings, Rodríguez shows that she understands not only the conceptual underpinnings of Sor Juana's—and Paz's— arguments but also the stylistic ones—the wordplay, parallelisms, and conventions of rhyme and meter. In an ingenious example, Sor Juana tells Filis/Lysi that as an *esdrújula* (word with the stress on the third-to-last syllable), she has inspired a decasyllabic *romance* (ballad):

> Lámina sirva el cielo al retrato, Lísida, de su angélica forma, [May your angelical form serve heaven as a portrait plate, Lísida,]
> Cálamos forme el sol de sus luces, sílabas las estrellas componga. [May the sun form pens from the light you radiate, may the stars compose syllables.]
> Cúmulo de primores tu talle, dóricas esculturas asombra, [Your figure a concurrence of fine things, it astounds Doric sculptures,]

Jónicos lineamientos desprecia, émula su labor de sí propia. [Disdain Ionic
lines, their emulous labor of themselves.] (402)

The accumulation of rewritten texts in *Sor Juana en Almoloya* calls
attention to rewriting in general—to issues of adaptation and censorship and to the impact of contemporary criticism and theory on classical literary texts—just as it illuminates the role of gender in critical
approaches to Sor Juana's works and, by extension, all literature.
Moreover, the play's metapoetic games and metatheatrical strategies
work together to bash establishment figures like Paz and the politicians from both major parties, whose conservative agendas and scan-
dalous behavior have made them what Rodríguez considers fitting
targets for her satire.

The rewriting taking place—of Sor Juana, of Mexican history, of
literature—is made all the more intense by means of the fusion of the
seventeenth, twentieth, and twenty-first centuries, which is exempli-
fied by the transformation of antique writing instruments into computers, albeit old, unreliable Apples. Hypertext and cyberspace become
the means of bringing Sor Juana out (and in Rodríguez's playful version, "out" would have multiple connotations) of her time and space
and into a new, virtual reality. Rodríguez's game is to play with the
disjunction of time and space, with modern-day computers and long-
dead writers, as when Sor Juana tells Lysi (disguised as the Licenciado) that she looks divine—in fact, even better than ever: "Te ves como
corregida en Page Maker" [You look like you were corrected in Page
Maker] (401).

When the cellphone-carrying Procuradora (at once a nun and a pol-
itician's henchwoman) comes in to judge Sor Juana, she announces
that Sor Juana's *pastorela virtual* (virtual pastourelle) (itself a de
facto composite of past and present) has been banned for its lack of
decency. Rodríguez immediately brings us back to the subtitle of the
play, as we suspect that the very drama we are seeing staged is the
subject of the Procuradora's and the Panistas's censorship: "Hemos
descubierto que su pastorela es desestabilizadora . . . eso provoca la
subversión" [We have discovered that your pastourelle is destabilizing
. . . that provokes subversion] (406).[25] The Condesa de Paredes/Lysi is
hauled away to a mental hospital and Sor Juana is condemned to rot
in Almoloya as the official edict of the Sacred Tribunal (the Partido
reAcción Nacional) is read aloud:

Queda prohibida *In Totum* la comedia denominada "Pastorela virtual" de
la monja jerónima Sor Juana Inés de la Cruz. O mejor se prohíbe la obra
In Totototum Piarum Aurium de la mencionada monja. . . . (410)[26]

[The play titled "Virtual Pastourelle," by the Hieronymus nun Sor Juana Inés de la Cruz is prohibited *In Totum*. Or, even better, the work of the aforementioned nun is prohibited *In Totototototum Piarum Aurium*. . . .]

Sor Juana is left distraught, bemoaning the "democratic change" that took her country from the *dinosaurios priístas* (PRI dinosaurs) to the *trilobites fundamentalistas* (fundamentalist trilobites). Left without hope, she writes her epitaph, which is, naturally, yet another example of rewriting:

Yo Juana Inés de la Cruz ratifico mi versión y firmo con mi sangre, ojalá toda se derramara en beneficio de la verdad. Suplico a mis amadas hermanas se apiaden de este país y no voten por el PAN ni por el PRI. Yo, la peor del mundo, Juana Inés de la Cruz. (410)

[I, Juana Inés de la Cruz, ratify my version and sign with my blood, which I hope will be spilled in support of the truth. I beg my beloved sisters to take pity on this country and vote for neither the PAN nor the PRI. I, the most wretched of the world, Juana Inés de la Cruz.]

As the play ends, we are reminded that although Rodríguez's Sor Juana ended her days in Almoloya prison, Raúl Salinas and Mario Aburto were freed ("al demostrar su inocencia" [upon proving their innocence], 410), and the nun's prophecy came true: the PAN did win the elections in 2000, and Vicente Fox became president of Mexico. The last words—if not the last laugh—of the play go to a group of denunciatory politicians and businessmen, who offer comments like those of Carlos Salinas ("Ya se los había dicho, esa monja es una corrupta" [I told you already—that nun is corrupt]) and Emilio Azcárraga[27] ("Todas son iguales, pinches viejas" [They're all the same, those old bags], 411).

The game is over, and Sor Juana appears to have lost, although Rodríguez's larger game, encompassing the entire play, inverts the equation and transforms the supposed winners into losers. In her playful critique of Mexican politics and culture, Rodríguez has taken on establishment figures and sacred icons by fusing time and space and by infusing her text with mordant wit and humor. As Bixler avers, "As America's first feminist and an icon of liberal thought, Sor Juana serves as an effective metaphor through which Jesusa is able to critique the repressive and regressive mentality of the PRI as well as that of the rising PAN."[28] The game at work in this play has a lot to do with winning and losing, but it also emphasizes the rules of game playing.

Sor Juana, ever the breaker of rules (in terms of social and religious expectations for women's social behavior and intellectual engagement), is forced via her high-tech, anachronistic, and postmodern encounter with the twenty-first century to confront the rules governing the game for women and, even more, women writers. *Sor Juana en Almoloya*, in its game playing, asks us to confront those rules as well.

Sabina Berman's *Krisis*[29] offers yet another type of game playing. Here, as in Rodríguez's piece, the entire play is a game, and it is also a game of political power. The players, a group of five childhood friends who have grown up to assume the highest political offices in the land, constantly refer to the rules of the game. In this game, winning and losing are everything, for the winners have the opportunity to lead Mexico and become billionaires, while the losers will literally lose their lives. In addition to the metaphor that the game and its players represent, Berman also includes a children's game, although in the only instance examined in this book, the children's roles are actually played by children rather than adults disguised as children (as, for example, was the case in . . . *y a otra cosa mariposa*, *Juegos a la hora de la siesta*, or *Información para extranjeros*). The play—and its games—also expose their own theatrical nature, which, in turn, emphasizes the innate theatricality of politics. *Krisis* is a brilliant exposé of political chicanery and corruption whose messages are made even more manifest in the games the characters play.

The crisis to which the title refers is really a series of crises. At the heart of the drama is the profound economic crisis that made a few corrupt politicians in Mexico extremely wealthy. The crisis of corruption then led to crises of confidence and credibility for the Mexican people and those representing them.[30] Numerous other related national crises—drug trafficking, the destruction of the environment, problems with the petroleum industry—are part and parcel of the story that unfolds.[31] As Bixler explains, *Krisis* "makes a mockery of the characteristics most commonly associated with Mexico's Partido Revolucionario Institucional: cronyism, 'el dedazo,' corruption, graft, demagoguery, fraud, elitism, and violent political assassinations followed by cover-up. No one in Mexican theatre has ever dared to portray the PRI in such a blatant, realist, and violent fashion as Sabina Berman."[32] The specific crisis for the characters in *Krisis*—apart from their many personal crises (sexual, ethical, professional)—has to do with controlling who will be given the PRI's presidential nomination; the assassination of possible opponents reflects real events in Mexican history (the death of Luis Donaldo Colosio, for example) and forms the basis of much of the conflict in the play.[33]

Berman's characters often underscore the impact of the current political situation on the country's history as, for example, when one character asks another to get involved for the sake of the country: "La crisis se volverá insoportable, y entonces usted esta gente pura—no nosotros los políticos—ustedes cambiarán la Historia de este país" [The crisis will become unbearable, and then you, this pure people—not us politicians—you will change the History of this country].[34] The man, however, refuses to implicate himself: "A mí la Historia de este país ya no me interesa; por qué me va a interesar si cada seis años este país ha destrozado mi historia personal. . . . este país convertido en un pantano de influencia y corrupción" [The History of this country doesn't interest me; why should it interest me if every six years this country has destroyed my personal history. . . . this country, converted into a swamp of influence and corruption] (56). The crises destroying Mexico are all about power games, and everyone wants to win. One of the women warns her lover that he displays too much respect and not enough drive: "Lo que te sobra es respeto. Respeto a las reglas. Respeto a los amigos" [You have too much respect. Respect for the rules. Respect for your friends] (74). Certainly, in the events portrayed in *Krisis*, the characters who have respect—for others, for the rules—lose the game. Although the lover suggests by means of a game metaphor that a slower, more conciliatory approach will ultimately win out ("Hay que moverse sobre el tablero de juego y repetar las reglas. Negociar. Medir, mediar, concertar. Hacer malabarismos. Lo importante es no caerse del tablero, aunque estés en el rincón") [You have to move across the game board and respect the rules. Negotiate. Measure, mediate, agree on things. Juggle. What's important is not to fall off the game board, even if you're in a corner], the woman replies, "Hay que botar el tablero, coger todo y correr" [You have to knock over the game board, grab everything, and run] (74).

From the perspective of the ludic, the opening scene of *Krisis* is of vital importance. Projected on the back wall of the stage is a video (described by those who saw the play staged as a film in black and white, with the jerky feeling of a home movie), set in the house of the rich and powerful Pedrero family in 1960, in which five children are playing Monopoly—the Mexican version—the perfect symbolic manifestation of their later appropriation of property and wealth.[35] The layering of media (video inside the theatrical representation) serves as a temporal distancing technique, since every scene that follows will take place thirty-six years later, although Berman does include flashbacks and flash forwards in those later scenes to illustrate the simultaneity of actions taking place in several different settings.[36] The children, as we will soon discover, are versions in miniature of their future personalities. In a move exemplifying this parallel, the stage directions state that the children dress and act as gangsters: "De hecho la escena podría ser perfectamente alguna de un episodio de Los Intocables, excepto que los protagonistas tienen 12 años" [In fact, the scene could perfectly be one from an episode of The Untouchables, except that the protagonists are 12 years old] (52). What is more, just like the "games" they will play as adults, the Monopoly game will include cheating, manipulation, and rule-breaking, and it will end in murder.[37]

From the opening words of the play, "Compro Petróleos Mexicanos" [I'll Buy Mexican Petroleum], Berman begins her attack on the privileged politicians who took advantage of Mexico's financial crisis to feather their own nests. Pedrero, the most aristocratic member of the group, tries from the outset to break whatever rules he wants in order to win the game:

PEDRERO: Te compro Teléfonos, ahora que estás en apuros.
[*I'll buy the Telephone Company from you, now that you're hard up.*]
SEIJAS: Tienes que caer en Teléfonos para comprarla.
[*You have to land on the Telephone Company to buy it.*]
PEDRERO. Me vale. Te ofrezco mil pesos, ahora que estás en apuros.
[*It's worth something to me. I'm offering you a thousand pesos, now that you're short of money.*]
JESÚS: Tienes que caer en la casilla.
[*You have to land on the space.*]
PEDRERO: Me vale dije. Te ofrezco dos mil.
[*I said it's worth something to me. I'll offer you two thousand.*]
SEIJAS: 'tas loco. Tienes que seguir las reglas.
[*You're crazy. You have to follow the rules.*]
PEDRERO: Es mi Monopolio, es mi casa y son mis dados. Dos mil quinientos, Polito bonito: yo hago las reglas. (53)
[*It's my Monopoly game, it's my house, and they're my dice. Two thousand five hundred, my nice little Polito: I make the rules.*]

The game presents in microcosm the crisis in corruption and leadership that was inundating the country. Pedrero, ever the one to take advantage of a situation that might benefit him, literally and figuratively holds the dice; he owns the game and he makes the rules. Pedrero must win, and when he does not, he becomes furious. On his next turn, Pedrero lands in jail, which leads everyone but him to laugh at his misfortune. Seijas, who previously had been the voice of reason, the rule follower, feels free to make fun of Pedrero's "fall": "La cárcel. El castigo divino."; "Todo se paga en esta vida"; "Hay justicia en el mundo" [Jail. The divine punishment; What goes around, comes around in this life; There's justice in the world] (54). Pedrero's brother, Jesús, de-escalates the rising tension between the two by pointing out to his brother that he has cheated the bank, and the game now becomes yet another means by which Pedrero reveals his lack of ethics:

POLO: Siempre tienes que tranzar un poco, ¿verdad?
   [*You always have to cheat just a little, right?*]
PEDRERO: Si uno juega es para ganar, pendejo. (54)
   [*If you play, it's to win, idiot.*]

The game changes, as the "gangster" Pedrero turns his anger on an innocent victim, the young indigenous servant whom he has alternately bullied, ignored, and disobeyed since she appeared onstage to send the boy off to bed. When the maid enters with a vanilla malt instead of a chocolate one for Pedrero, he takes a pistol from the collection hanging on the wall next to a picture of General Obregón and shoots her in the face, adding the chilling words, "Te dije de chocolate" [I said, "chocolate"] (54). Bixler explains the real-life referent of the scene: "This video recreates a little known, and less publicized, aspect of the life of the Salinas brothers, who, as children, killed their maid.[38] The scene ends with the horrified reactions of the other boys and Seijas's suggestion that they put her body in the refrigerator; the exact details of what follows will appear later in the reminiscences of several characters.

Berman makes the symbolism of her grotesque game blatantly obvious. Like every children's game we have seen, the game functions as a metaphor for more serious and deadly actions in society. All resemblance to childhood innocence is lost, replaced by calculating, win-at-all-costs collusion and violent behavior, and in this case, the fact that children and not adults are performing the scene makes the event even more chilling. The innocent victim, the maid—poor, female, indigenous—is the scapegoat. Punished for the sins of the rich and powerful, she will be used and discarded.[39]

Still, in Berman's farce the incident is not quite forgotten. As a grown man, Seijas, an ethics professor cum ghostwriter of political speeches, has capitulated to Pedrero and his gang to a humiliating degree. His power-hungry wife, Patricia, is sleeping with several of his cronies, and Seijas, seeming not to care, has been transformed into a Prozac-popping psychotic who echoes Pedrero's murder of the maid by shooting his own wife in the face. Even more, Seijas's Bible-quoting, judgmental sister is completely transformed: wielding an electric carving knife, she dismembers her sister-in-law in the bathtub—all while wearing a bath cap and rubber gloves—and kills Patricia's lover with the electric knife. Just as in the case of the murder of the maid, Seijas plans to stuff the body in a refrigerator. Betrayal and murder work on even more levels, however, as a package bomb sent from Pedrero arrives at the house minutes later, ironically taking care of the problem for him once again. Furthermore, because Pedrero has previously arranged the assassination of another member of the group, he appears to have won again.

The female characters in *Krisis* receive harsh treatment from the men in their lives. In a variation of Monopoly, Patricia trades sex for the favors of money and power, but she also seems to delight in rubbing her husband's nose in the game she is playing. Her game is seduction, and she is an expert at playing it, as the stage directions explain: *"Patricia de pronto se vuelve amigable; es una seductora insistente, irresistible cuando necesita algo de alguien"* [Patricia suddenly becomes quite friendly; she's an insistent seductress, irresistible when she needs something from someone] (58). Seijas's sister, the religious zealot, murders and dismembers her victims, and in a clear example of the drama's black humor, she complains that using the electric knife to accomplish the job is a lot more difficult than cutting up a chicken. The maid, of course, is victimized from the beginning. All three women in the play are murdered; two of the three are shot in the face and the other is blown to pieces by a bomb, raising a number of implications regarding the erasure of identity in the deliberate destruction of the female body.[40]

If the female characters are presented as bizarre and exaggerated, so, too, are the male characters, who categorize themselves as life-long friends, but who continually betray one another via sex and assassination. Still, tied together by the blood spilled so long ago in the Pedrero's house, they literally wear the symbol of their union: "El anillo de la mafia de los cinco. Todavía lo usamos todos" [The Mafia ring of the five. We all still wear it] (68). The group includes the power-hungry Pedrero, who is ready to "inherit" the presidency from his brother,

Jesús, as another *sexenio* (election every six years) approaches; the psychotic Seijas, who has prostituted his ethics and writes empty political speeches for his friends; Benetton and Polo, United States-educated politicians (Polo is the Secretary of State who has secretly been told by Pedrero's brother that he—rather than Jesús's own brother—will be the new presidential nominee, and Benetton is his Under Secretary) who try to influence the others to turn their backs on corruption but who also have their own history of impropriety; and Coco, the narco-politician and murderer who will literally do anything to win power, influence, and the next nomination for the presidency. The picture they paint of the political realities of mid-1990s Mexico is powerful, despite their occasionally cartoonish characterization. Patricia links herself sexually to several members of the group because she sees them as godlike winners in their games of power: "En la Biblia los elegidos de Dios hacen sus propias reglas no porque sean elegidos de Dios sino al visré, porque trascienden las leyes humanas se vuelven como dioses. Todo es política. Juego de poder. Arriba en el Cielo como en la Tierra. Todo" [In the Bible, God's chosen people make their own laws not because they are elected by God but the opposite: because they transcend human laws they become like gods. Everything is politics. Game of power. Up in Heaven just like on Earth. Everything] (60). Coco describes the men as modern Caesars who will take turns ruling the country every six years until well into the twenty-first century. Yet the five are so embroiled in games of intrigue that each sells out the other in a plot so complicated that it resembles the union of soap opera and farce.

As if the real-life power games involving the characters of *Krisis* were not enough, Berman injects a fantasy sequence into the play. Polo has been having visions in which the ghost of Benito Juárez guides him to reject corruption and return Mexico to a time of real democracy and ethics. In their "appointment with History," Polo and Benetton meet a winged Juárez, who flies in the window surrounded by a blaze of light. Juárez fills the room with his theories ("El poder emana de la Ley, no de los hombres" [Power emanates from the Law, not from men] 83), but when Polo objects that things don't work that way in Mexico anymore or that building consensus is better than starting a revolution, Juárez hits him with a bound copy of the Constitution. Their encounter is comical, especially because Juárez's wing falls off and he keeps jumping up on a table:

POLO: No seas rígido Benito. Seguro tú también robaste un poquito.
[*Don't be so inflexible, Benito. Surely you also robbed just a little.*]

Benito le suelta un librazo.
  [*Benito belts him with the book.*]
POLO: Es un poquito de ilegalidad.
  [*It's a tiny bit of illegality.*]
Benito le suelta un librazo.
  [*Benito belts him with the book.*]
POLO: La Constitución no es la Sacrada Escritura, Benito.
  [*The Constitution isn't the Holy Book, Benito.*]
BENITO: (*Alza otra vez el libro.*) ¡Lo es! (84)
  [*He raises the book again. It is!*]

With a final, prophetic warning and marvelous *coup de théâtre*, Juárez tells Polo that their next meeting will take place in the Heaven of History, flies out the window in a blaze of light, and ascends, while the sound of flapping wings is transformed into the sound of applause. This fantasy sequence, a type of play within the play, is both ludic and highly theatrical in nature. Its flying national hero/guardian angel highlights Berman's creation of farce while simultaneously reminding her audience of the ideals that once defined the country.[41]

Juárez's prediction is accurate, and Polo is assassinated, leading to the deaths of virtually all of the remaining characters at the hands of Pedrero. The winner of the game of power is the person who, as a child, cheated at Monopoly and calmly murdered another human being; as an adult, he continues to accumulate "Monopoly" properties and eliminates those who stand in his way by means of the monopoly on politics that the PRI held for so many years. Berman concludes that the game will live on in infinite permutations. The drama does have one final game, however: the game Berman plays with her audience. In structuring her text, the playwright constantly keeps us guessing. The complicated plot and the endless intrigues and betrayals are complemented by a combination of flashbacks and flash forwards that express the simultaneity of much of the dramatic action but that also complicate the experience of determining what is going on. The dramatist leaves us clues, at the time apparently innocuous, that will acquire great importance in future events. The best example is the box delivered to Patricia's apartment early in the play, which is subsequently revealed to contain the bomb that will explode in the final scene. In effect, the playwright does not inform us of all the rules of her game, although the end results are much less disastrous: instead of finding ourselves part of a life-and-death experience, we simply have to work harder to decipher the layers of intrigue. By playing with the sequence of events and the distribution of information, Berman includes us in a game of her own, one that playfully parallels the power games seen throughout the play.[42]

Información para extranjeros, *Sor Juana en Almoloya*, and *Krisis* offer three distinct views of political and historical issues. The two Mexican plays discuss many of the same events, although the styles and techniques used to explore them are markedly different, ranging from the transgressive representation found in Rodríguez's cabaret piece to the expression of state-encouraged violence and corruption presented in *Krisis*'s non-linear exposé. *Información* and *Krisis* employ significant examples of children's games, and in both examples, the games illuminate adult actions that are much more sinister in nature. In essence, however, all three dramas use games to talk about the game of political power and the players—winners and losers— involved. Whether the dramatists employ graphic sex and violent torture or intercalate a flying-angel Juárez or Sor Juana coping with a malfunctioning computer, the games played onstage ultimately guide us to understand the historical-political problems that have plagued the countries involved.[43] The ludic and the theatrical fuse to expose the dark side of politics and to encourage the audience to really see the game for what it is.

8
Conclusions: Only a Game or
More than a Game?

"Play is itself a complex system that no one now fully understands, and it will remain a mystery deserving inquiry for decades to come."
>   —Joseph W. Meeker (*The Comedy of Survival*)

ÉL: ¿Qué es lo que estás haciendo conmigo?
  [*What is it you're doing with me?*]
ELLA: Jugar.
  [*Playing.*]
ÉL: ¿Jugar? ¿Llamas a esto jugar?
  [*Playing? You call this playing?*]
>   —Maritza Wilde (*Adjetivos*)

THE SEVENTEEN PLAYS EXPLORED IN THIS BOOK OFFER, BOTH INDIVIDU-ally and in unison, more than a mere sampling of the types of game playing that Spanish American women have produced in the last fifty years. Each representative example is significant by itself, but it ac-quires additional weight when seen in conjunction with so many other dramas in which the game is a central metaphor. There is great variety in the game playing: we have seen plays with games featuring both chil-dren and adult actors, dramas that overtly involve children's games, others that portray violent psychological or physical games of power, those that use the game metaphor as the overarching thematic or structural element of the playtext, and still others that present games the author plays with the reader or spectator. These examples of games and play fall into at least one of three categories: they highlight sociopolitical problems, the domestic sphere (with an emphasis on gen-der issues), or the theater itself. The means of presenting the games are varied, as well: the dramatic representations of the ludic range from the expression of a playful spirit to the utilization of game play-

158

ing to illustrate the depths of human depravity. In the end, however, the games are either a contest *for* or a representation *of* something,[1] thus underlining the significance of power and/or (meta)-theatricality in the dramas in which they appear.

The strategy often seems to work as a way of speaking about the unspeakable: their metaphoric treatment of human life as one enormous game allows dramatists living in repressive conditions to convey messages that they otherwise might not be able to express. This can help avoid censorship, and, in societies that use coded discourse on a regular basis—for example, Argentina during the Dirty War—it can provide audiences with information and ammunition for future action. Ann Witte has affirmed that "Resistance to dictatorship and the treatment of women's issues are increasingly linked in the most recent work of some of the contemporary Argentine women playwrights;"[2] her point is directly applicable to the vast majority of the dramas discussed in this book. By destabilizing the discourses of power, these texts illuminate the tension between following rules and breaking them, between freedom and figurative or literal captivity. Ironically, although perhaps not surprisingly, a great majority of the games we have seen here are far from innocent, and virtually all of them are unsettling. The women who have created these dramas about games and play challenge the myth that play is an innocent social impulse. The cultural and ideological significance of their texts ultimately derives from the dramatists' appropriation, revision, and subversion of a commonplace historically associated less with the serious realities of adulthood than with the playfulness of childhood. Their dramas utilize games to both mirror and sabotage social values and attitudes, treating topics as far ranging as the maintenance of social control and the relationship between play and aggression, socialization, and creativity, in plays as diverse as Gambaro's *Los siameses*, Plá's *Historia de un número*, Casas's *El gran circo eukraniano*, and Rodríguez's *Sor Juana en Almoloya*. In dramas that violate boundaries, expose risk taking, and celebrate transgression, these playwrights are serious about play.

Game playing in these dramas often serves to intensify the theatrical experience while calling the reader or spectator to observe the connections between games and the theater. First, the game is inherently a type of play within a play, inviting the audience to participate in deciphering its relationship to the outer frame. In theatrical terms, a number of the games seen in this book appear to function as rehearsals for future enactment. Wilde's *Adjetivos* emphasizes the theatrical self-consciousness of act and rehearsal, while Mahieu's *Juegos a la hora de la siesta* and Berman's *Krisis* predict future incarnations of violent actions. On an affective level, the games we have seen may make the events they represent appear stronger, more violent, or more chilling in contrast to the presumed innocence of children at play. That contrast comes in part from the fact that play often speaks to our deepest and oldest memories. The games we see onstage transport us back to a time when our realities, contests, and assumption of new roles were singularly different events than those depicted onstage.

In their self-conscious theatricality, the games played out in these dramas focus on issues of human identity and existence, emerging as sites of self-reflection as well as self-representation. Gene Koppel, who based his approach to literary analysis on Gadamer's idea that art is a game set apart from real life but also vitally related to actual existence, asserts that games and play have great existential and epistemological implications: "The result is an increase in knowledge, an Aristotelian 'recognition' which has significant relationships to the reader's life," as we are forced to take a "hard look at the shallowness of rules and roles demanded of those who play."[3] A related element of many of those dramas is that of ritual—sacred and profane. Both play and the theater have deep cultural links to ritual, and we have seen numerous examples of ritualized violence masquerading as play in these dramas. The ceremonies within several of the texts in this book return us to the cathartic function of both ritual and theater. In addition, they point to essential questions regarding the nature of role, identity, and social script in the "identity laboratory" of the theater. The games themselves make visible the performance and performative aspects—the theatricality—of numerous aspects of human interactions in the areas of gender, of politics, of torture. Role playing within the role emerges as a central strategy of many of these games, and the idea of performance is compounded in texts as varied as Garro's *Felipe Ángeles*, Gambaro's *Información para extranjeros*, and Raznovich's *Casa matriz*. Frequently, we see what game theorists call joint pretense, in which characters play the dual roles of director (planning roles, themes, and settings) and actor,[4] a phenomenon common in much self-reflexive theater.

Stylistically, the plays in this study share a number of key characteristics. Ruth E. Burke's *The Games of Poetics*, while focusing on narrative, nonetheless highlights many of the elements of the ludic spirit we have seen in the dramatic texts examined in this book. Ludic strategies such as radical juxtaposition, systematic exploration of the forms and the terms of the medium, and subversion of conventions at every level are part of an all-encompassing "rage to be free." The play principle is manifested in irony, in a sense of the theatrical, in linguistic interplay and parody, and in exaggeration and distortion.[5] Many of the dramas exhibit verbal dueling, ritualized insults, and play language. Even in the darkest plays, these elements are pervasive, and they may be seen in great numbers in the dramas that function as macrogames between the reader or spectator and the dramatist, with Garro's *La dama boba* and Rodríguez's *Sor Juana en Almoloya* offering clear examples. Games within the text and between the text and the audience can allow the dramatist to question textual authority and interrogate art itself.

It is useful at this point to return to the issue of gender, as this book focuses on game playing in dramas by women. Knowing that a number of male writers have created remarkably similar examples of game playing, what is it about these plays that suggests a gendered reading? I would submit that one aspect of the answer to that question has to do with the sheer quantity of plays that use game playing as an essential element of their design. Certainly, given the percentage of women in Spanish America writing for the stage—much less being produced and published—the numbers are high, and the seventeen plays of this study constitute only a partial list. Individually, these dramas are powerful, but collectively, they enable us to see what might not be as obvious in a less global investigation. Moreover, it appears that the playwrights have found a textual strategy that works across time and changing theatrical trends, as game playing remains a common metaphor in women-authored dramas well into the late 1990s—and there is no indication that the trend will end any time soon.

Why would so many women write plays using this metaphor? The possibilities are many, but ultimately, they have to do with women's understanding of participating in a game in which they do not know the rules, or for which they have been socialized to follow the rules in order to achieve their goals. Many of the dramas in this book explore the connections between male fantasies (of pleasure and of power) and games or contests. The display of power over others relates, of course, to gender relationships as much as to those in the political sphere; as Witte avers, "Latin American feminism has never really existed in clear separation from broader political concerns."[6] Certainly, dramas such as Berman's *Krisis*, Wilde's *Adjetivos*, and Gambaro's *El campo* and *Información para extranjeros* illustrate the union of politics and feminism. From a less confrontational perspective, women may, by virtue of their traditional association with domestic space and child rearing, be more attuned to the world of game playing, and their writing may well reflect that experience. Many dramas speak to specifically female spaces, relationships, or activities. The game—at least in dramas such as Raznovich's *Casa matriz*—also works well to treat a topic long ignored in the theater of male authors: the relationship between mothers and daughters. Other games take place in traditionally female settings—for example, the beauty parlor of Castellanos's *El eterno femenino* or the convent "cell" of Rodríguez's *Sor Juana en Almoloya*—or utilize experiences more often associated with women—the striptease of Gambaro's *El despojamiento* comes to mind as a clear example. Play often involves the negotiation of space, which fits well into examinations of gender and power. As marginalized members of their societies, women may find that filtering their experiences through game playing is safer than more overt attempts to protest or present the conditions that define their personal, social, and political lives. In many of the examples in this book, the playwrights dramatize games of power and authority. In the final analysis, games and play seem to allow women the opportunity to explore issues that might otherwise be taboo or politically or socially dangerous.

Moreover, the games use as their structural bases terms and concepts that appear often in discussions of gender: the binary oppositions of winner/loser, rule follower/rule breaker, all or nothing, winner-take-all, etc. are emblematic of an essentially gendered way of seeing the world, in which nuances, alternative visions, or multiple or shared experiences give way to the univocal readings more associated with males than with females. When free play becomes rule bound and competitive, the game also becomes more allied with the patriarchy. Many of the women dramatists of this book appear to recognize the ways in which certain games imitate the power structures governing the relationships between men and women as they play with the concept in their works. The women of Romero's *El juego*, for example, support this idea, as their interpersonal games echo those that will most likely take place with the arrival of El Viejo. Susana Torres Molina explores the issue in both *Extraño juguete* and . . . *y a otra cosa mariposa*. And although male writers have employed games as well, something special characterizes the game playing in female-authored texts precisely because of the social, cultural, and political implications inherent in competition.

A strong measure of ambiguity defines this game playing. Allied with freedom and a spirit of play, the games nonetheless often illustrate authoritarian repression and violence. As a result, the types of games that appear perform contradictory functions at the same moment. In *Disappearing Acts*, Diana Taylor described public spectacles during Argentina's Dirty War as simultaneously building and dismantling a sense of community, forging and erasing images of national and gender identity, allowing a population insight into events and blinding it to the meaning of its situation.[7] I would submit that play and games in the theater of Spanish American women of the last fifty years could also be characterized in this manner. I would add that these women writers play with product and process: the games in their dramas emphasize both the end results of game playing and the steps taken to reach those results.

The texts and their contexts—the games and their theatrical, social, psychological and political correlates—illuminate significant trends in recent, woman-authored Spanish American drama, and they do so in a quantitatively and qualitatively distinct manner. Whether their games are literal or metaphoric, representative of the status quo or subversive/transgressive, focus on the personal or the political, the dramas on display here illuminate an aspect of women's theater in Spanish America that seems to defy national boundaries. This group of playwrights raises questions and challenges audiences as they play with the idea that life is both an imitation of and infinitely more than a game.

Notes

CHAPTER 1: INTRODUCTION

1. I have tried to give information on the performance of these plays wherever possible and relevant, but this study focuses on the dramatic text rather than on the theatrical spectacle or text of performance.

2. Patricia W. O'Connor argues a similar point with regard to Spanish women dramatists, observing that the devaluation of their domestic contributions, their words, their likes and interests, and their culture, has decisively influenced their absence in the most verbal and public sector of the literary arts: the theater (my translation, *Dramaturgas españolas de hoy: Una introducción* [Madrid: Espiral/Fundamentos, 1988], 12).

In *Feminist Theories for Dramatic Criticism*, Gayle Austin echoes this analysis, noting that "The writing of plays requires mastering to some degree a male-dominated, public production machinery, something that relatively few women have been able to do over the long history of the form, and consequently there is not as large a body of extant plays by women as there is of novels. Only a handful of plays by women have entered the canon of 'approved' works" (*Feminist Theories for Dramatic Criticism* [Ann Arbor: University of Michigan Press, 1990], 2). Because Spanish American theater has reflected a similar state of affairs, the situation has prompted recent anthologies of women-authored plays (such as editions by Nora Eidelberg and María Mercedes Jaramillo, *Voces en escena: Antología de dramaturgas latinoamericanas.* [Medellín, Colombia: Universidad de Antioquia, 1991] and Elba Andrade and Hilde F. Cramsie, *Dramaturgas latinoamericanas contemporáneas: Antología crítica* [Madrid: Verbum, 1991], as well as the translations of *Women Writing Women: An Anthology of Spanish-American Theater of the 1980s*, ed. Teresa Cajiao Salas and Margarita Vargas [Albany: SUNY Press, 1997], and critical anthologies such as *Latin American Women Dramatists: Theater, Texts, and Theories*, ed. Catherine Larson and Margarita Vargas [Bloomington: Indiana University Press, 1988]). Many of these works were motivated by the sense, expressed above by O'Connor and Austin, that Spanish American women dramatists had been marginalized and the female voice muted throughout theater history.

3. Catherine M. Boyle, "Griselda Gambaro and the Female Dramatist: The Audacious Trespasser," in *Knives and Angels: Women Writers in Latin America*, ed. Susan Bassnett (London: Zed, 1990), 145–46.

4. Boyle sees the emergence of women-authored drama in Spanish America as uniquely powerful: "To write and produce theatre is to hold a certain power, to have power over the word not as the poet or the novelist has, but within a medium that has an immediate, dynamic and potentially subversive interaction with the society in which it is created and staged" (Boyle, "Griselda Gambaro," 146).

5. As a medium for expressing social realities (even in countries in which censorship continues to exist), the theater often reflects an extremist stance: it serves either as a tool for challenging authority or it supports the status quo, the latter being the case with much Cuban theater written by women after the Revolution. This type of theater fulfills the role of reinforcing social and ideological values through the presentation of overtly moralistic plays inside the factories or farm cooperatives. Spanish American women dramatists are now writing plays that illustrate both of these social functions; whichever the authors' ideological position, their dramatic texts often exhibit a uniquely female perspective on the political, social, and cultural realities of their lives.

6. My analysis of the varying percentages of dramas that Spanish American men and women have written about game playing is based on the observation of the generations writing for the stage in the last half of the twentieth century; the plays discussed here offer a representative survey of the dramas that have appeared during that fifty-year period.

7. Jacqueline Eyring Bixler, "Games and Reality on the Latin American Stage," *Latin American Literary Review* 12 (1984): 22.

8. Catherine Larson, "Playwrights of Passage: Women and Game-Playing on the Stage," *Latin American Literary Review* 19 (1991): 77–89.

9. Johan Huizinga, *Homo Ludens: A Study of the Play Element in Culture* (Boston: Beacon, 1962). The first edition of the book was published (in Dutch) in 1938.

10. Huizinga observes:

The spirit of playful competition is, as a social impulse, older than culture itself and pervades all life like a veritable ferment. Ritual grew up in sacred play; poetry was born in play and nourished on play; music and dancing were pure play. Wisdom and philosophy found expression in words and form derived from religious contests. The rules of warfare, the conventions of noble living were built up on play patterns. We have to conclude, therefore, that civilisation in its earliest phases played. It does not come from play like a babe detaching itself from the womb; it arises in, and as, play and never leaves it. (Huizinga, *Homo Ludens*, 173)

11. Nora Eidelberg begins her discussion of ludic theater with the following linguistic analysis of the terms "theater" and "game":

The Germanic languages employ the same word to designate both: *Spiel* in German, *spelletje* in Dutch, and *play* in English. The Greeks did not have a generic word to encompass all the stages of the game; the closest was the word *agon* (competition). The word *drama* (dramatic work) originated in Dionysian competitions in the 6th century B.C. The Romans, on the other hand, did have a word related to *game*, including drama. They had *lares ludentes* (dances) and *ludiones*, which were the predecessors of mimodramas and Roman *satura* (farce).
    . . . At some time in the past the word *ludio* or *ludión* must have been used in Spanish with regard to theatrical representation, to justify the words *preludio* [prelude], that which precedes a play, and *interludio* [interlude], cultured derivations of *ludus*, game, representation. The word *game*, from the Latin *iocus*, has replaced the word *ludus* in the Romance languages, being used in all types of manifestations of the ludic. One speaks of *jugar un papel* [playing a role] or a *rol* [role] as referring to any type of acting in the theater. People also talk of *juegos en escena* [staged plays], and in French they say *jouer une comédie* [to stage a play]. In the Middle Ages, in France as well as in Spain, there were representations that had the name "dramatic games," which were brief compositions, with little action, performed by minstrels and troubadours. (my translation, *Teatro experimental hispanoamericano 1960–1980: La re-*

alidad social como manipulación [Minneapolis, Minn.: Institute for the Study of Ideologies and Literature, 1985], 12–13).

12. See Clifford Geertz, "Deep Play: Notes on the Balinese Cockfight," in *The Interpretation of Cultures* (New York: Basic Books, 1973), especially pp. 449–50.

13. For a discussion of the oppositions that typify women's role in the "reigning binary system of meaning," see Ann Rosalind Jones's "Writing the Body: Toward an Understanding of *l'écriture féminine*," in *The New Feminist Criticism: Essays on Women, Literature, and Theory*, ed. Elaine Showalter (New York: Pantheon, 1985), 366.

14. Turner states, "Performative reflexivity is a condition in which a sociocultural group, or its most perceptive members acting representatively, turn, bend or reflect back on themselves, upon the relations, actions, symbols, meanings, codes, roles, statuses, social structures, ethical and legal rules, and other sociocultural components that make up their public 'selves' " (Victor Turner, *The Anthropology of Performance* [New York: Performing Arts Journal Publications, 1986], 24).

15. Amalia Gladhart, *The Leper in Blue: Coercive Performance in Contemporary Latin American Theater* (Chapel Hill: University of North Carolina Press, 2000), 75.

16. Ibid., 23.

17. As chapter 2 will discuss more thoroughly, many ludic scholars view "game" and "play" as synonymous concepts (Huizinga even talked about war in terms of games and play), although others perceive play as an umbrella term encompassing subcategories such as games, competitions, sports, etc. Even investigations of the ludic in literary studies range from analyses of discrete examples of games and play within a text, to discussions of games that the writer plays on/with the reader. The terms blur for a number of reasons, including the evolution of the study of the ludic and the appropriation of the terminology and concepts by such a diverse number of fields. Perhaps the most difficult aspect of any attempt to differentiate the two terms is linguistic: we may say that we are playing a game, which certainly can be viewed in either positive or negative terms, and we may also comment that someone is playing a game (or playing games) with us, an observation that generally connotes a more negative perspective. In the plays written by the women dramatists examined in this book, games and play are utilized virtually universally to critique or subvert more innocent incarnations of the ludic spirit. Indeed, the subversive or ironic representation of innocent, childhood play appears to be one of the playwrights' principal strategies for producing audience reaction and response.

18. Sandra Messinger Cypess makes an important point in her study of Mexican women dramatists that merits discussion here in the larger context of this examination of game playing in the theater of Spanish American women: "The white critic in the United States working on Mexican texts must realize that like the writer, she or he cannot detach her or himself from the historical circumstances in which she or he writes. Just as every text 'encodes within itself its own ideology of how, by whom, and for whom it was produced' [quoting Terry Eagleton], the critic also writes from a particular perspective that influences her perception of the text. . . . However, acknowledging that the reading involves issues of race, class, sex and culture does not mean that a reader must mirror the writer's identity or socio-historical situation in order to read the text" ("From Colonial Construct to Feminist Figures: Re/visions by Mexican Women Dramatists," *Theatre Journal* 41 [1989]: 493). Emulating Cypess, I feel that it is important to stress that although I may not share racial, class, or cultural experi-

ences with all of the women writers treated in this book, my readings need not result from a shared history.

19. In this book, I follow Huizinga's general description of play as "a stepping out of 'real' life into a temporary sphere of activity with a disposition all of its own" (Huizinga, *Homo Ludens*, 8), and, continuing his ideas, many of the games I examine foreground either contest or representation. Performance and "make-believe" are central to my understanding of the ludic, although I contend that in a number of the examples of play and games found in this study, all players do not enter the game freely or voluntarily (or, at least, they do not appear to understand the implications of entering the game), which allows the dramatist to explore such serious topics as human depravity and torture, political manipulation, and ritualized violence. Consequently, the ludic spirit is most frequently ironized, with game playing the means for these women writers to bring dangerous or taboo issues to the attention of their audiences.

20. Richard Hornby, *Drama, Metadrama, and Perception* (Lewisburg, Pa.: Bucknell University Press, 1986).

21. Games have also emerged as key strategies in Spanish American films in recent years, from the Academy Award-winning *La historia oficial* (1985, directed by the Argentine Luis Puenzo, screenplay by Puenzo and the dramatist Aída Bortnik) to *My House is on Fire*, a 1997 film by the Chilean father-son team of Ariel Dorfman and Rodrigo Fidel Dorfman, based on a text that the elder Dorfman (Ariel) wrote while in exile in Amsterdam and adapted by relocating the setting of the story to the United States. See also the English translation of the text in the collection *My House is on Fire* (1990).

22. For more detailed examinations of performance theory and the ways in which critical reaction to performance has changed through the years, see Elin Diamond (intro. and ed., *Performance and Cultural Politics* [London: Routledge, 1996]), Amalia Gladhart (*The Leper in Blue*), Philip Auslander (*From Acting to Performance: Essays in Modernism and Postmodernism* [London: Routledge, 1997]), Herbert Blau (*The Audience* [Baltimore: Johns Hopkins University Press, 1990] and "Universals of Performance; or, Amortizing Play," in *The Eye of Prey: Subversions of the Postmodern* [Bloomington: Indiana University Press, 1987]), Marvin Carlson (*Performance: A Critical Introduction* [London: Routledge, 1996]), David George ("On Ambiguity: Towards a Post-Modern Performance Theory," *Theatre Research International* 14, no. 1 [1989]), Richard Schechner (*Essays on Performance Theory: 1970–1976* [New York: Drama Book Specialists, 1977]), and Bert O. States ("Performance as Metaphor," *Theatre Journal* 48, no. 1 [1996]). Gladhart's comments on performance are particularly relevant to this study of games in the theater:

> Within a dramatic text, an emphasis on performance may function as a means of questioning that text, displacing its authority and highlighting the manner of its construction. Performance may be evoked, in ways often similar to the play within the play of self-referential theater, as a site of negotiation between dramatic text and social context or as a means of questioning the viability of the theater itself. (Gladhart, *Leper*, 21)

23. Bixler, "Games and Reality," 22.

24. Sandra M. Gilbert, "What Do Feminist Critics Want? A Postcard from the Volcano," in *The New Feminist Criticism: Essays on Women, Literature, and Theory*, ed. Elaine Showalter (New York: Pantheon, 1985), 31.

25. Gayle Greene and Coppélia Kahn, "Feminist Scholarship and the Social Con-

struction of Woman," in *Making a Difference: Feminist Literary Criticism*, ed. Gayle Green and Coppélia Kahn (London: Methuen, 1985), 1. Although Greene and Kahn make this point in their discussion of feminist literary *scholarship*, I would contend that their point is equally applicable to feminist creative writing.

26. Huizinga, *Homo Ludens*, 1, 5, 46.

27. Helene Keyssar, *Feminist Theatre: An Introduction to Plays of Contemporary British and American Women* (New York: Grove, 1986), 3.

28. Huizinga, *Homo Ludens*, 10.

CHAPTER 2: LUDIC THEORY

1. Joseph W. Meeker, *The Comedy of Survival: Literary Ecology and a Play Ethic*, 3rd ed. (Tucson: University of Arizona Press, 1997), 104.

2. Jack Maguire, *Hopscotch, Hangman, Hot Potato, & Ha Ha Ha: A Rulebook of Children's Games* (New York: Simon and Schuster, 1990), 2.

3. Known by different names in other countries, "Musical Chairs," notes Maguire, can be traced back to the First Crusade,

> when long-distance travelers playfully spoofed their desperate scurry for coach seats. "London Bridge" dates back to the eleventh-century destruction of the major bridge in that city—along with the Britons standing on it—by Norway's King Olaf and his troops.
>
> One of the grimmest stories of the origin of a game involves the apparently sweet, innocent game now called "Ring-Around-the-Rosy." The first line of this verse, originally "Ring-a-ring o' roses," refers to the circular body rash which killed more than 70,000 people between 1664 and 1665. The healthy attempted to thwart the disease by carrying herbs ("A pocket full of posies"). In the final stages of the disease, the victim would start sneezing violently ("A-tishoo! A-tishoo!," later corrupted to "Ashes! Ashes!"). Death followed quickly ("We all fall down").
> (Maguire, *Hopscotch*, 3–4)

4. Maguire, *Hopscotch*, 2–5. In the foreword to *Hopscotch, Hangman, Hot Potato, & Ha Ha Ha: A Rulebook of Children's Games*, Bob ("Captain Kangaroo") Keeshan underscores these social functions:

> On the playground of life, game playing equips each of us with the "rules of the game." As youngsters, games taught us how to work together, to accommodate, and to help one another. Through playful moments, children can act out real-life situations. In imagined contexts, they can learn how to solve problems, look for options, and resolve conflicts.
>
> By winning or losing at games, children experience the real world but in a less harsh fashion. Children learn about their environment and how to relate to other children, as well as grown-ups. They learn about healthy competition and about trying to do their best. And, because most games have winners and losers, children learn to accept positive and negative outcomes. Game playing offers opportunities for children to build self-confidence and enhance self-esteem. (Keeshan, *Hopscotch*, xi)

5. Maguire, *Hopscotch*, 4–5.

6. Ibid., 5.

7. Johan Huizinga, *Homo Ludens*, 13.

8. Ruth E. Burke, *The Games of Poetics: Ludic Criticism and Postmodern Fiction* (New York: Peter Lang, 1994), 1–3.

9. Ibid., 1.

10. Although I have been profoundly influenced by Huizinga, Caillois, and Turner, my research has also been informed by what David Cohen terms the three traditions of the literature on play: Piaget, who focused on the relationship between play and exploration; psychoanalysts such as Susan Isaacs, Anna Freud, and Melanie Klein, who investigated the emotions expressed in play and the use of play to heal; and educators (including Montessori and Froebel) who explored what play could be used for (David Cohen, *The Development of Play* [New York: New York University Press, 1987], 6–7).

11. Huizinga, *Homo Ludens*, 28.

12. Jacques Ehrmann, "Homo Ludens Revisited," in *Game, Play, Literature*, ed. Jacques Ehrmann. (Boston: Beacon, 1968), 31.

13. Roger Caillois, *Man, Play, and Games*, trans. Meyer Barash (New York: Free Press of Glencoe, 1961).

14. Burke, *Games of Poetics*, 17.

15. Ibid., 18.

16. See Gordana Yovanovich's study of play in the early poetry of Nicolás Guillén ("Play as a Mode of Empowerment for Women and as a Model for Poetics in the Early Poetry of Nicolás Guillén," *Hispanic Review* 68 [2001]), Jacques Ehrmann's contrastive analysis of Caillois and Huizinga ("Homo Ludens Revisited," in *Game, Play, Literature*), and Victor Turner's critique ("Carnival, Ritual, and Play in Rio de Janeiro," *Time out of Time: Essays on the Festival*, ed. Alessandro Falassi [Albuquerque: University of New Mexico Press, 1987]) for more detailed discussions of the positive and negative aspects of Caillois's taxonomy.

17. Edward Norbeck, "Anthropological Views of Play," *American Zoologist* 14 (1974): 260.

18. Burke, *Games of Poetics*, 32.

19. Ibid., 34.

20. Victor Turner, *Dramas, Fields, and Metaphors*, 32.

21. Ibid., 33, 33, 37–40.

22. Victor Turner, *From Ritual to Theatre: The Human Seriousness of Play*, with a preface by Richard Schechner (New York: Performing Arts Journal Publications, 1982), 11. Turner adds:

There is, therefore, in theatre something of the investigative, judgmental, and even punitive character of law-in-action, and something of the sacred, mythic, numinous, even "supernatural" character of religious action—sometimes to the point of sacrifice. Grotowski hit off this aspect well with his terms, "holy actor," and "secular sacrum." (12)

23. Ibid., 13.

24. Ibid., 104.

25. Ibid., 118.

26. Richard Schechner, "Victor Turner's Last Adventure," preface to *The Anthropology of Performance*, by Victor Turner (New York: Performing Arts Journal Publications, 1986), 7.

27. Turner, *Ritual to Theatre*, 113, 114, 116.

28. Schechner, "Last Adventure," 8. Schechner, like Turner, emphasizes the work of Grotowski, as well as the practitioners of the Theater of the Absurd and the Theater of Cruelty. Schechner's tribute to Turner, "Victor Turner's Last Adventure," was

published after the latter's death as the preface to Turner's *The Anthropology of Performance* (1986).

29. Turner, cited in Schechner, "Last Adventure," 17.

30. Schechner, "Last Adventure," 17.

31. In the United States, the reemergence of critical interest in the topic led to the 1974 founding of the TAASP (The Association for the Anthropological Study of Play), whose conference proceedings form the basis of much of the research publication in the discipline in the last twenty-five years.

32. Burke notes that historically, "Much of the early work in play theory addressed the study of children and their physical, psychological and social development" (*Games of Poetics*, 7), tracing those theories from Plato and Aristotle through Lance Olsen's discussion of Postmodernism and Derrida's work in *Glas*. See the work of Iona Archibald Opie and Peter Opie for concrete examples of children's games.

33. Helen Schwartzman, *Transformations: The Anthropology of Children's Play* (New York: Plenum, 1978), 4.

34. Garry E. Chick, "Play in Games and Sports," in *The Many Faces of Play*, ed. Kendall Blanchard (Champaign, Ill.: Human Kinetics, 1986), 189.

35. Brian Vandenberg, "Mere Child's Play," in *The Many Faces of Play*, ed. Kendall Blanchard (Champaign, Ill.: Human Kinetics, 1986), 116, 119.

36. Huizinga, *Homo Ludens*, 10. Gabriel Weisz reminds us that dramatic structure consists of breaking a state of order and then reestablishing it, adding that the place where order is ruptured is the site of tension, conflict, and free play (Weisz, *El juego viviente: Indagación sobre las partes ocultas del objeto lúdico* [Mexico City: Siglo Veintiuno, 1986], 47).

37. Huizinga, *Homo Ludens*, 11.

38. J. C. Harris observes that there is "considerable diversity of opinion regarding the salient characteristics of play which distinguish it from other behaviors or activities" ("Beyond Huizinga: Relationships between Play and Culture," in *Play as Context*, ed. A. T. Cheska [West Point, N.Y.: Leisure, 1981], 27). See also pp. 276–77 ("The Interchangeability of 'Play' and 'Game'") in Klaus V. Meier's "Play and Paradigmatic Integration" (*The Many Faces of Play*, ed. Kendall Blanchard [Champaign, Ill.: Human Kinetics, 1986]).

39. Meier, "Play and Paradigmatic Integration," 272.

40. Ibid., 272–73.

41. Ibid., 280.

42. Schwartman, *Transformations*, 328.

43. Meier, "Play and Paradigmatic Integration," 275.

44. Hans-Georg Gadamer, *Truth and Method* (New York: Crossroad, 1988), 86.

45. Huizinga, *Homo Ludens*, 28.

46. Burke, *Games of Poetics*, 8.

47. Garry E. Chick, "Play in Literature," in *The Many Faces of Play*, ed. Kendall Blanchard (Champaign, Ill.: Human Kinetics, 1986), 122.

Also of note are the contributions of language philosophers such as Ludwig Wittgenstein to the general topic. Wittgenstein left a relatively brief, but influential, legacy in his observations on the nature of language—specifically, with regard to the language game—that have subsequently been used to examine literary texts. Keir Elam, a semiotician of the theater, appropriated and extended Wittgenstein's notion of the language game to describe the dynamics of the theatrical experience in his insightful

Shakespeare's Universe of Discourse: Language-Games in the Comedies (1984), observing that discourse in the theater is an especially rich area for exploring language games, precisely because dramatic discourse "is always destined, if not on the page then at least potentially on the stage, to interact with its physical and behavioural surroundings, and especially with the body and its movements, in the production of meaning" (Keir Elam, *Shakespeare's Universe of Discourse: Language-Games in the Comedies* [Cambridge: Cambridge University Press, 1984], 12).

Elam's study of Shakespeare's comedies presents five general categories of language games. The first category, *theatrical games,* has to do with putting performances on stage within the drama. Theatrical games deal with indicating or describing objects, using and referring to stage properties, etc. The second category, that of *world-creating games,* concerns deixis, exposition, and reference within the possible world created onstage. *Semantic games* describe the relationships between signs, while *pragmatic games* pertain to the realities of language in use, such as issues of sincerity and appropriateness in speaking, turn-taking, etc. Finally, the fifth category, that of *figural games,* has to do with the nonliteral links between saying and doing, including such tropes and figures as repetition, irony, hyperbole, metaphor, and metonymy, and the use of proverbs or neologisms. The dramatic discourse of all plays contains multiple examples of these five kinds of language games, but different dramatic works contain different numbers or emphasize different types. Elam views Shakespeare's comedies as highly self-conscious in their language use as frames are placed around the games. He concludes that the game-frame dialectic exploits language as activity and as object, lending Shakespearean comedy much of its discursive momentum and depth (Elam, *Shakespeare's Universe,* 21).

48. Nancy A. Benson, "Play Theory and an Elizabethan Sonnet Sequence," in *The Many Faces of Play,* ed. Kendall Blanchard (Champaign, Ill.: Human Kinetics, 1986), 150.

49. Gene Koppel, "Maggie Moran, Anne Tyler's Madcap Heroine: A Game Approach to *Breathing Lessons,*" *Essays in Literature* 18, no. 2 (1991): 283.

50. Ibid., 285–86.

51. Catherine Bellver, "Game-playing and Reading *Ultraísta* Poetry," *Hispanófila* 118 (1996): 26 n. 2, 25.

52. Yovanovich, "Play as a Mode of Empowerment," 16, 25.

53. Pilar V. Rotella, "Games People Play: Oppressors and Oppressed in Three Plays by Latin American Women Writers (Castellanos, Hernández, Gambaro)" (paper presented at the annual meeting of the Midwest Modern Language Association, Chicago, November 1991), 2.

54. Nora Eidelberg, *Teatro experimental hispanoamericano 1960–1980. La realidad social como manipulación* (Minneapolis, Minn.: Institute for the Study of Ideologies and Literature, 1985), 3.

55. I will explore these two elements in greater detail in the chapter analyzing metatheatrical games.

56. Eidelberg, *Teatro experimental,* 4, 15.

57. Gladhart, *Leper,* 97.

58. Jacqueline Eyring Bixler, "The Game of Reading and the Creation of Meaning in *El amasijo,*" *Revista Canadiense de Estudios Hispánicos* 12, no.1 (1987): 13.

59. Bixler, "Games and Reality," 22.

60. Ibid., 23.

61. Ibid.

62. See Eugene L. Moretta's "Spanish-American Theatre of the 50's and 60's: Critical Perspectives on Role Playing" (*Latin American Theatre Review* 13, no. 2 [1980]) for a discussion of metatheatrical role-playing within the role. See also Gerald Wade, "The 'Comedia' as Play" (in *Studies in Honor of Everett W. Hesse*, ed. William C. McCrary and José A. Madrigal [Lincoln, Neb.: Society of Spanish and Spanish American Studies, 1981]) for an analysis of the impact of the work of Huizinga and D. W. Winnicott on Golden Age theater.

63. Bixler, "Game of Reading," 32–33.

64. Edward Norbeck, ed., *The Anthropological Study of Human Play*, Rice University Studies 60, no. 3 (Summer 1974): 5–8.

CHAPTER 3: GAMES IN THE THEATER

1. David William Foster, *Violence in Argentine Literature: Cultural Responses to Tyranny* (Columbia, Mo.: University of Missouri Press, 1995), 145. In this discussion, Foster is referring specifically to Argentina and to Torres Molina's *Extraño juguete*. He adds, "It would be superfluous to say that such a relationship [that existing between metatheatrical elements and the sociocultural role of the spectacle] assumes greater emphasis in a society experiencing a protracted period of national life when official ideologies have sought to conceal the basic sense of the forces of power, thereby forcing cultural artifacts to assume a demystifying and oppositional posture" (145).

2. I have included two plays by Garro in this chapter, because each presents so clearly different—and key—metatheatrical elements as textual strategies.

3. Richard Hornby, *Drama, Metadrama, and Perception* (Lewisburg, Pa.: Bucknell University Press, 1986), 32.

4. Susana Torres Molina, *Extraño juguete* (Buenos Aires: Apex, 1978), 11. My translation; unless otherwise indicated, all translations in this book are mine. Subsequent quotations from *Extraño juguete* are cited parenthetically in the text.

5. Lionel Abel, *Metatheatre: A New View of Dramatic Form* (New York: Hill and Wang, 1963), 60.

6. Keir Elam, *The Semiotics of Theatre and Drama* (London: Methuen, 1980), 90.

7. Manfred Schmeling, *Métathéâtre et intertexte: Aspects du théâtre dans le théâtre* (Paris: Lettres Modernes, 1982), 3, 9–10.

8. Hornby, *Drama*, 31, 32.

9. Daniel Zalacaín, "Circularidad y metateatro en la escena hispanoamericana: algunas piezas representativas," *Hispanófila* 86 (1986): 53.

10. The exact details of the publication and staging history of *Felipe Ángeles* are unclear. In "Feminism in Elena Garro's Recent Works" (in *A Different Reality: Studies on the Work of Elena Garro*, ed. Anita K. Stoll [Lewisburg, Pa.: Bucknell University Press, 1990]), Delia Galván states that the 1967 version of the play published in *Coatl* differs from that of the UNAM in 1979, although she gives no details as to the extent of revision; almost nothing is known about that early version, nor about whether it was modified from its original 1954 form. Interestingly, Galván sees the play—here, she utilizes the 1979 edition—as the link between Garro's two literary

stages (the first works, from the 1950s and 1960s, exhibiting "spontaneity and freshness" and the second, from the early 1980s, illustrating "an angry voice exposing injustices committed by society on its weak members, especially women") (Galván, "Feminism," 136). In her interview with Michèle Muncy, Garro does not mention revision, simply stating that the drama was published in a provincial journal called *Coatl* (Muncy, "The Author Speaks. . . . ," in *A Different Reality*, ed. Anita K. Stoll, 24). There is a further bit of confusion regarding the first staging of the play. Galván asserts that "The National University of Mexico published it one year after its staging in Spain on the opening night of the Sitges Theater Festival, in 1978" (Galván, "Feminism," 137); yet, in *"Felipe Angeles* de Elena Garro," Galván states that it was performed at the 1979 Sitges Festival (29). The UNAM's 1979 edition of the play gives the list of actors and other details of what it describes as the first performance—in Mexico City—including the statement that the play premiered the 13th of October, 1978 in the Ciudad Universitaria Theater in a production directed by Hugo Galarza (Garro, *Felipe Ángeles*, 7). I use the UNAM's 1979 edition; subsequent quotations from this work are cited parenthetically in the text.

11. Elena Garro, cited in Michèle Muncy, "Encuentro con Elena Garro," Interview, *Hispanic Journal* 7, no. 2 (1986): 71, my translation.

12. Sandra Messinger Cypess, "Dramaturgia femenina y transposición histórica," *Alba de América* 7, no. 12–13 (1989): 287.

13. Galván (*"Felipe Angeles"* de Elena Garro: Sacrificio heroico," *Latin American Theatre Review* 20, no. 2 [1987]: 30–33) links Ángeles to Prometheus and, indirectly, to Christ as scapegoat, martyr, and redeemer, and to the Aztec sacrificial victim.

14. Galván, "Feminism," 138.

15. Hornby, *Drama*, 32.

16. Galván, *"Felipe Angeles,"* 31, 33.

17. See studies by John Kronik ("Usigli's *El gesticulador* and the Fiction of Truth," *Latin American Theatre Review* 11, no. 1 [1977]: 5–16) and Catherine Larson ("El juego de la historia en *Felipe Ángeles,"* in *Baúl de recuerdos: Homenaje a Elena Garro*, ed. Robert K. Anderson and Mara L. García [Tlaxcala, México: Universidad Autónoma de Tlaxcala Press, 1999], 73–84) for more detailed descriptions of Usigli's use of metatheater in *El gesticulador*.

18. Cypess, "Dramaturgia femenina," 286, 290.

19. Willy O. Muñoz states that Wilde founded and directed two companies, Amalilef Teatro and Le Rideau, beginning in the 1980s. Her groups have explored the confusion that exists in contemporary society, oppression and dictatorship, and gender issues, winning a number of national theater prizes for their productions ("El juego de las máscaras," in *Antología crítica del teatro breve hispanoamericano: 1948–1993*, ed. María Mercedes Jaramillo and Mario Yepes [Medellín, Colombia: Editorial Universidad de Antioquia, 1997], 530).

20. Ibid., 531. The title alludes to the human propensity to label and attack others with derogatory adjectives, attempting to capture their essence—their identity—in a word or two. Wilde relates the concept to the theater and to history, as her actors struggle with their roles and with the Ceausescus's inability to come to terms with their acts of genocide.

21. Maritze Wilde, *Adjetivos*, in *Antología crítica del teatro breve hispanoamericano: 1948–1993*, ed. María Mercedes Jaramillo and Mario Yepes (Medellín, Colombia: Editorial Universidad de Antioquia, 1997), 516. Subsequent quotations from this work are cited parenthetically in the text.

22. In addition to their discussion of how to interpret their respective roles, the actors also analyze the work of the director. Wilde includes numerous examples of the play within the play to complement this exploration of role-playing within the role. The drama begins in the middle of a rehearsal, is set in a theater, and discusses the theater throughout, and the sado-erotic games that Él and Ella play with one another function as yet other theatrically self-conscious elements of *Adjetivos*. Always, however, we are reminded of the theatricality of the Ceausescus's reign of terror, as well as their trial and execution. Ironically, the real-life Ceausescus stand in stark contrast to the nameless actors who portray them; Wilde's decision to deny her actors specific names both universalizes them and, in a real sense, renders them impotent.

23. Cited in Muñoz, "El juego de las máscaras," 531.

24. Ibid., 533.

25. The seasonal contrast is even more pronounced in that the inset play (the trial and execution of the Ceausescus) takes place at Christmas; "Silent Night" is played immediately before the dictators are executed.

26. See Muñoz:

> These subversions of social rules outside the theater have their corresponding element inside it, in the tyrannical acts of the Ceausescus, who altered the social order of an entire country, and in the actions of the actors, who themselves transgressed norms of morality. The carnivalesque communal insanity is the product of the madness of each individual who acts out his or her fantasies supported by an appropriate mask; in like manner, Ella acts out her sado-erotic fantasy dressed in a pair of red shoes, which constitutes her disguise. (My translation, "El juego de las máscaras," 533)

27. As Muñoz observes, *Adjetivos* shows that either sex is capable of committing violent acts, as was the case with the real-life Ceausescus ("El juego de las máscaras," 532).

28. Garro's text and its relationship to that of Lope have been the subject of four complementary articles. In 1983, Gabriela Mora authored "*La dama boba* de Elena Garro: Verdad y ficción, teatro y metateatro" (*Latin American Theatre Review* 16, no. 2 [1983]: 5–30), which uses Abel, principally, to look at the play within the play as a vehicle for communicating Garro's social concerns, specifically the revelation of certain problems in Mexican society, ranging from the extreme separation of the sexes and races to the Mexican government's general abandonment of such marginal groups as its Indian population ("Verdad y ficción," 21). Anita K. Stoll's "Elena Garro's/Lope de Vega's *La dama boba*: Seventeenth-Century Inspiration for a Twentieth-Century Dramatist" [*Latin American Theatre Review* 23, no. 2 [1990]: 21–31) discusses the cultural chasm separating the disparate groups in Garro's play, concluding that although Lope's text served to promote cultural unity in its time, Garro uses Lope ironically to illustrate just the opposite: that the two cultures are still worlds apart ("Seventeenth-Century Inspiration," 29). Also published in 1990, Denise M. DiPuccio's "The Merging of *La(s) dama(s) boba(s)*" (*Gestos* 9 [1990]: 53–63) sees Garro's text as presenting "three levels of conflicts in which a dominant ideology threatens to absorb a subordinate one: Eurocentric norms overshadow New World traditions; the middle class urban white subjugates the poor rural Indian; patriarchal tradition imposes standards on the female" ("Merging," 53). Unlike Stoll, however, DiPuccio concludes that ultimately, Garro offers a positive reading, suggesting that these different cultures can engage in a mutually enriching exchange. Finally, my 1991 essay, "Lope

de Vega and Elena Garro: The Doubling of *La dama boba*" (*Hispania* 74 [1991]: 15–25), uses a number of theories on the topic of metatheater to examine both the evolving critical discussion of self-conscious theater and issues of adaptation and literary influence. A revised version of that article forms the basis of my discussion of Garro's play in this chapter.

29. Abel, *Metatheatre*, 49; Hornby, *Drama*, 72, 68.

30. Herbert Weisinger, "*Theatrum Mundi*: Illusion as Reality," in *The Agony and the Triumph: Papers on the Use and Abuse of Myth* (East Lansing: Michigan State University Press, 1964), 67–68.

31. Diana Raznovich's *Jardín de otoño*, in which two female soap opera fans kidnap the TV star of their dreams, offers a remarkably similar central premise. The play is translated as *Inner Gardens* in *Defiant Acts*.

32. Elena Garro, *La dama boba*, in *Un hogar sólido* (Xalapa: Universidad Veracruzana, 1983), 177. Subsequent quotations from this work are cited parenthetically in the text.

33. Hornby describes self-reference, which occurs relatively rarely in the theater, as "the most extreme, intense form of metadrama," because it collapses audience identification with the characters and challenges the complacencies of the audience's world view" (*Drama*, 114–17).

34. See Gustavo Pérez-Firmat, Julia Kristeva, and Roland Barthes for three key views of intertextuality. This concept corresponds to Hornby's notion of literary citation or reference.

35. Hornby, *Drama*, 94.

36. In Lope's original, Finea tells her father that her lover has gone to Toledo, but he is actually hiding in her attic. When her father discovers the ruse, the now clever daughter tells him that since she had named the attic "Toledo," she had not really lied.

37. Mora, "*La dama boba* de Elena Garro," 16–18.

38. It might be further argued that by naming her Finea "Lupe," Garro invites identification between her character and Lope: the pairing of Lupe with Lope reminds the reader/spectator of the connection between the two plays. At the same time, the name Lupe, from Guadalupe, serves as another type of subliminal reminder—that this is not just an adaptation of a Spanish Golden Age classic but also a play intended to highlight the specifically Mexican experience.

39. Ironically, Francisco uses the opposite ploy at the end of the drama, when he is not sure that he wants to leave:

¡Soy yo, Francisco Aguilar, el maestro de Tepan! (244)
[It's me, Francisco Aguilar, the teacher of Tepan!]

. . .

Te juro que soy el maestro de Tepan. . . . (245)
[I swear to you that I'm the teacher of Tepan. . . .]

40. Weisinger, "*Theatrum Mundi*," 68.

41. In an interview in 2000, Torres Molina discussed her evolution as an actress and director:

I had acted in Spain, in my play *Extraño juguete*, directed by Norma Aleandro, together with Tato Pavlovsky and Zulema Katz. And before my exile I had starred in *El baño de los pájaros*, a play by the North American Leonard Melfi, that Beatriz Matar directed. Later, when I returned in '81, I began to direct. I premiered my play . . . y a otra cosa mariposa. I wanted this text to be directed by a woman because of its themes, but really at that time there weren't a lot of female theatrical directors, so I planned on directing it myself. So it was that I began to direct for the theater, and at the same time, I stopped acting. Lately, I direct less and I find myself turning more to writing. (My translation, María Claudia André, "Conversaciones sobre vida y teatro con Susana Torres Molina," *Latin American Theatre Review* 35, no. 2 [2002]: 90)

42. Eduardo Pavlovsky, introduction to *Extraño juguete*, by Susana Torres Molina (Buenos Aires: Apex, 1978), 10.

43. Jacqueline Bixler notes that in its initial run, the play "ended rather abruptly when its savage demythification of the Argentine *macho* coincided too closely with the Malvinas fiasco and the extratextual deflation of the Argentine male ego" ("For Women Only? The Theater of Susana Torres Molina," in *Latin American Women Dramatists: Theater, Texts, and Theories*, ed. Catherine Larson and Margarita Vargas [Bloomington: Indiana University Press, 1998], 215–16). Jean Graham-Jones ("Myths, Masks, and Machismo: *Un trabajo fabuloso* by Ricardo Halac and . . . *y a otra cosa mariposa* by Susana Torres Molina" *Gestos* 20 [1995]: 103) assigns more of the blame to bad timing, claiming that although the play was well received by both critics and spectators, its run was interrupted by the summer heat and then never resumed because of the outbreak of the Malvinas/Falklands war." She adds, however, that "Said debacle [was] ironically an acting-out, at the (inter)national level, of the very *machismo* the text sought to expose" ("Myth," 103). In *Exorcising History: Argentine Theater Under Dictatorship*, Graham-Jones again emphasizes the connections between the myth of machismo and politics in the drama, including the play in her description of "Proceso Argentine theater's first steps toward a critical self-distancing and critique of its own participation and complicity in the perpetuation of the authoritarian state" (*Exorcising History* [Lewisburg, Pa.: Bucknell University Press, 2000], 57).

44. See Bixler ("For Women Only?," 223) for a discussion of the parodic subversion of the coming-of-age convention.

45. Laurietz Seda adds yet another dimension to the discussion of sexuality in the play, stating that Torres Molina makes use of the theatricality of transvestism to express a critique of Argentine machismo, to display alternative sexual relationships, to call attention to the construction of gender, to establish a critique of patriarchal society, to avoid censorship, and to establish a commentary on lesbian relationships ("El hábito no hace al monje: Travestismo, homosexualidad y lesbianismo en . . . y a otra cosa mariposa de Susana Torres Molina," *Latin American Theatre Review* 30, no. 2 [1997]: 104). She concludes:

. . . y a otra cosa mariposa is innovative and revolutionary because it explores themes that are taboo within Argentine society. Through the technique of transvestism, gender—that is, the concept that certain standards exist that define or categorize human beings—is concealed, confronted, and challenged. As a result, the existence of an ambiguous space between the genders is suggested. This can attempt to erase the dividing lines between the binary opposition of the sexes and destabilize the absolute values of masculine and feminine, transforming them and establishing other alternatives to human sexual behavior. (My translation, "El hábito," 112)

For a related discussion of homosexual desire in the play, see Yolanda Flores, *The Drama of Gender: Feminist Theater by Women of the Americas* (New York: Peter Lang, 2000).

46. Susana Torres Molina, *. . . y a otra cosa mariposa* (Buenos Aires: Búsqueda, 1988), 14. Subsequent quotations from this work are cited parenthetically in the text. I translate the title as *Moving On*, in the sense of "on to the next thing," although the Spanish captures both that sense and the inherent resonance of the rhyme, reminiscent of the English "After while, crocodile" and typical of children's wordplay.

47. Torres Molina plays ironically with the idea of change throughout the course of the drama, as her male characters appear incapable of experiencing any real maturation, despite their advancing years. Perla Zayas de Lima examines the title of the play in its relationship to development and transformation:

> From the title, taken from a popular everyday phrase, rupture and change are proposed—but also a kind of take-off, which implies the difficult transit from one state to another: in order to be able to fly, the butterfly must abandon its secure contact with the earth. (My translation, "Susana Torres Molina, la mujer y el mito," in *Dramas de mujeres*, ed. Halima Tahan [Buenos Aires: Ediciones Ciudad Argentina, 1998], 334)

48. See also Jean Graham-Jones's argument about the representation of Woman in the drama, which I present in part: "The reading, and appreciation, of this play lies in the fact that *both* sexes are present throughout the performance, thus providing a constant humanization to counter the dehumanizing process of sexist mythologizing. Woman dominates the conversations of the four characters, but always as an imaginary object. . . . All representations of Woman are stand-ins, mediated by a masculine vision of Woman" ("Myths, Masks, and Machismo," 100).

49. Nora Eidelberg and María Mercedes Jaramillo, eds., *Voces en escena: Antología de dramaturgas latinoamericanas* (Medellín, Colombia: Universidad de Antioquia, 1991), 334.

50. Sue-Ellen Case, *Feminism and Theatre* (New York: Methuen, 1988), 121.

51. Hornby, *Drama*, 71–72.

52. Helene Keyssar, *Feminist Theatre: An Introduction to Plays of Contemporary British and American Women* (New York: Grove, 1986), 3.

CHAPTER 4: VIOLENT GAMES

1. Nora Eidelberg, "La ritualización de la violencia en cuatro obras teatrales hispanoamericanas," *Latin American Theatre Review* 13, no. 1 (1979): 37.

2. Ibid.

3. Severino João Albuquerque, *Violent Acts: A Study of Contemporary Latin American Theatre.* (Detroit: Wayne State University Press, 1991), 23.

4. Ibid.

5. Mahieu establishes a tension between having children play at being adults and having adult actors playing the children's roles. Constantly reminding us of the ways in which children imitate adult behaviors through play, she emphasizes the reciprocal aspects of such actions and interactions: adults often act like children, a fact that accentuates the political reading of the text. Moreover, when children murder other children onstage, the horrific effect is underscored by the audience's recognition that

the adult act, committed by an "innocent child," is represented visually by a grown-up.

6. Mahieu was born in Wloclawek, Poland in 1940, the daughter of a Jewish mother and a Catholic father. She spent the war years in Poland and the Ukraine and moved to Argentina when she was ten years old.

7. Martha Martínez, "Tres nuevas dramaturgas argentinas: Roma Mahieu, Hebe Uhart y Diana Raznovich," *Latin American Theatre Review* 13, no. 2 (1980): 40, my translation.

8. Ibid., 43, 47. *Juegos a la hora de la siesta* appeared in English translation in 1977 in *Two Plays*, and it was performed in Santiago de Chile, Montevideo, São Paulo, and several other Brazilian cities. Still, the closing of its performance and the prohibition against publishing the play in Argentina mark a decisive moment in the history of Argentine theater. Ironically, as Charles B. Driskell describes, in 1976 the theater in Buenos Aires had flourished, "to some extent, because black lists in television and cinema were in force, few Argentine films were being made, and many actors . . . returned to making theatre; and, in part, because cinema choices were not up to par" ("Theatre in Buenos Aires: 1976–77," *Latin American Theatre Review* 11, no. 2 [1978]: 103).

9. Roma Mahieu, cited in Martha Martínez, "Seis estrenos del teatro argentino en 1976," *Latin American Theatre Review* 11, no. 2 (1978): 100.

10. Driskell, "Theatre in Buenos Aires," 105.

11. Driskell accurately comments that "The play also manifests the erroneous, idyllic view some of us hold of the child's world, where one finds the greatest of extremes" (ibid.). For a discussion of the verbal or physical violence that often appears in children's play, see *Play Fighting* by Owen Aldis (New York: Academic, 1975).

12. Jacqueline Bixler suggests that their play involves contests (one of Huizinga's categories) as the children struggle for leadership of the group ("Games and Reality, 30), although I would submit that Andrés is always the clear leader of every game, with the result that Mahieu establishes even more strongly his links to despotism and dictatorship. Bixler makes a valid point, however, when she reminds us of the ritualized nature of the material for imitation in the play: Andrés leads the children through the rites of marriage, death, and burial (ibid.). In so doing, I would add, Mahieu again underscores the children's numerous ritualized violent acts and begins to prepare the audience for the death scene at the end, as the children remove their "society's" scapegoat from their midst.

13. Experts in the study and prevention of childhood violence often point to the torture and mutilation of animals as the precursor of violent acts against humans.

14. Roma Mahieu, *Juegos a la hora de la siesta*, TS. (1976), 23. Subsequent citations from this work are cited parenthetically in the text.

15. Mahieu creates a larger game out of the wedding scene, as Andrés moves back and forth between ordering the other children to participate in his scripted performance—and the orders are often accompanied by great physical violence and cruel threats—and using the formulaic language of the Church in his game, a metatheatrical ceremony within the play. The oscillating movement between wedding vows and abusive threats is chilling.

16. Julito, the youth with Down Syndrome, seems to function as a bridge between the children and the adult world. Possessing the body of an adult, he joins the children's erotic game (in the stage directions, Mahieu explains that after the wedding

game, their hugs and kisses take on an erotic tone) but cannot control himself and masturbates, which the children do not understand at all. Nonetheless, Julito's mental and emotional development is quite childlike; whenever Andrés pretends to be a mummy and walks toward him with outstretched hands, the young man is paralyzed with terror. The man-child therefore fits in both worlds—and in neither one.

17. Driskell, "Theatre in Buenos Aires," 105.

18. Ibid.

19. *El juego* received first prize in the 1976 Ministry of Culture's Concurso Literario de Obras de Teatro de la Prevención del Delito [Literary Contest of Theatrical Works for the Prevention of Crime] and was subsequently staged in the Caracas Sala Rajatabla del Ateneo, with Romero herself playing one of the roles. Describing the positive critical reaction, Isaac Chocrón states in the introduction to the first edition of the play:

> Everyone agreed that the work not only represented a good example of theater from a young woman known principally for her work as an actress, but it also expressed a vision of today's omnipresent violence—but tinged with elements of humor and tenderness, which gave it a certain attractiveness. Mariela Romero became the great theatrical surprise of 1976. (My translation, introduction to *El juego* [Caracas: Monte Ávila, 1977], 7)

Chocrón posits three currents or tendencies of Venezuelan theater that may be seen in this work: the fact that Romero is a person of the theater (she is an actress) who also writes for the theater; the fact that she belongs to a group of women writers who have written theater with similar themes and techniques; and the author's concise writing style, which forces the audience to participate in the "co-creation" of the text, since it must use its imagination to fill in the blanks (7–9).

20. Bixler observes that "The wheelchair, frequently used by the submissive character, becomes symbolic of their overall paralysis and powerlessness" ("Games and Reality," 4). Amalia Gladhart, in her extended analysis of the topic, postulates that because *El juego* centers on a need to reach or occupy the chair, rather than on moving around once seated, "The wheelchair remains more icon of paralysis than potential for movement" (*Leper*, 87). Of course, the wheelchair later becomes the seat of power, as it is transformed into the "queen's" throne (see *Leper*, 90–91).

21. Mariela Romero, *El juego*. Caracas: Monte Ávila, 1977, 20. Subsequent quotations from this work are cited parenthetically in the text.

22. Gladhart, *Leper*, 78.

23. See Gladhart, *Leper* 89. I would add that her lie about the romantic dream is actually Ana I's *second* major example of rule breaking in this act; the first is her feigned paralysis, revealed when she jumps out of the wheelchair.

24. Ibid., 75, note 5. Gladhart submits that the treatment of paralysis in *El juego* "demands a consideration of the female body as at once a site of violation and resistance. Ana I and Ana II use their bodies to represent in games the vulnerability of those same bodies in another context" (99). She further notes that in "a wider social context, 'paralysis' is the real condition of women, like Ana I and Ana II, dominated by forces that prevent them from moving" (99).

25. Susan D. Castillo, "*El juego*: texto dramático y montaje," *Latin American Theatre Review* 14, no. 1 [1980]: 28–29. Castillo adds that it is no coincidence that the two exploited Anas are women (29).

26. Martin Esslin classifies five types of violence. The first and second categories,

"violence among characters" and "violence of the playwright or directors toward the characters," are particularly relevant here ("Violence in Modern Drama," in *Brief Chronicles: Essays on Modern Theatre* [London: Temple Smith, 1970], 199–200). The undifferentiated names Romero uses in *El juego* point to the second category, and the violence between Ana I and Ana II—paralleling the violence associated with El Viejo, which never takes place on stage—occurs throughout the play. See also Albuquerque, *Violent Acts*, 24–25.

27. Romero never reveals the actual identities, ages, and relationships of Ana I and Ana II; for the sake of consistency, I will refer to them as "women." Chocrón describes both the female characters and their existential game: "The two protagonists, who constantly waver between being friends, twins, or one single person, carry out a rather painful investigation of 'to have and have not," which is a variation of the fundamental 'to be or not to be.' Both Anas 'are,' but their problem is not having the same characteristics but rather inevitably complementing each other" (my translation, introduction to *El juego*, 10). Still, as part of the game she plays with her audience, Romero also hints that both Anas are one and the same person. On more than one occasion, Ana II proclaims that she has intimate knowledge of Ana I's mind: "Sé muy bien lo que vas a preguntarme. Antes de que lo pienses sé exactamente lo que me vas a decir" [I know very well what you're going to ask me. Before you think of it, I know exactly what you're going to say] (18). Bixler agrees, noting that the fact that they share the same name points to their equality and inseparability ("Games and Reality," 24). Albuquerque sees the play as an example of the "violent double," in which the two individuals are "complementary selves [who] therefore cannot exist apart from each other" (*Violent Acts*, 229). Castillo compares Romero's characters to those of Jean Genet in *The Maids*, viewing their changing personalities as the result of not existing in reality as individuals ("*El juego*," 26). Romero's range of possibilities for the identity of Ana I and Ana II is typical of the Theater of the Absurd. As Joseph Chrzanowski remarks, "Indications of a lack of individuality are the exclusive use of first names, the omission of almost all biographical data, and the absolute lack of details related to costuming. Such characterization comes to be consistent with the vision of the isolated, rootless, and dehumanized man [*sic*] who so populates the literature of this century" (my translation, "El teatro de Mariela Romero," *Revista Canadiense de Estudios Hispánicos* 7, no. 1 [1982]: 207).

28. Albuquerque, *Violent Acts*, 267.

29. John Fraser, *Violence in the Arts* (Cambridge: Cambridge University Press, 1974), 118–19.

30. Albuquerque, *Violent Acts*, 267.

31. Bixler, "Games and Reality," 26.

32. Ibid., 24.

33. Chrzanowski suggests that the dramatist's techniques have their roots in the works of the U.S. playwrights Romero has said she admires (Tennessee Williams, Eugene O'Neill, Arthur Miller, and Edward Albee) and in the anti-theater tradition that derives from Artaud, Ionesco, and Beckett ("El teatro," 207).

34. My translation, Castillo, "*El juego*," 32.

35. Becky Boling, "Reenacting Politics: The Theater of Griselda Gambaro," in *Latin American Women Dramatists: Theater, Texts, and Theories*, ed. Catherine Larson and Margarita Vargas (Bloomington: Indiana University Press, 1998), 8.

36. Marguerite Feitlowitz, "The Theater of Griselda Gambaro," in *Information for*

Foreigners: Three Plays by Griselda Gambaro, ed. and trans. Marguerite Feitlowitz (Evanston, Ill.: Northwestern University Press, 1992), 2.

37. Griselda Gambaro, *Los siameses*, in *9 dramaturgos hispanoamericanos: Antología del teatro hispanoamericano del siglo xx*, ed. Frank Dauster, Leon Lyday, and George Woodyard, 93–143. Vol. 2 (Ottawa: Girol, 1979).

38. Sandra Messinger Cypess, "The Plays of Griselda Gambaro (Argentina)," in *Dramatists in Revolt*, ed. Leon F. Lyday and George W. Woodyard (Austin: University of Texas Press, 1976), 101.

39. Cypess notes that the two main characters are tied together not by blood, but by situation, like the pair in *Waiting for Godot* ("The Plays," 100).

40. Diana Taylor's reading of *Los siameses* illuminates the working of its violence on the individual and society:

> The violence associated with sociopolitical crisis, then, attacks outer and inner: it suspends boundaries, annuls ties, it simultaneously destroys the body, the house, and the society. . . . Whether we see the conflict between the two men as an intrapsychic conflict between parts of one whole, or as an interpsychic confrontation between two men who are somehow joined or related, or as a symbol of fratricial violence through which the powerful self persecutes and kills its (br)others, the violence associated with crisis must be understood to operate concomitantly in the social and personal spheres. (*Theatre of Crisis: Drama and Politics in Latin America* [Lexington: University Press of Kentucky, 1991], 113)

41. Catherine M. Boyle, "Griselda Gambaro and the Female Dramatist: The Audacious Trespasser," in *Knives and Angels: Women Writers in Latin America*, ed. Susan Bassnett (London: Zed, 1990), 150.

42. Ibid.

43. *El campo* was first performed in October, 1968 in Buenos Aires and first published in 1967.

44. Nina L. Molinaro reminds us ("Discipline and Drama: Panoptic Theatre and Griselda Gambaro's *El campo*," *Latin American Theatre Review* 29, no. 2 [1996]: 40 n. 8) of Jean Franco's argument ("Self-Destructing Heroines," *The Minnesota Review* 22–23 [1984]: 108) that the stigmatized female body is a *topos* that runs through much of Latin American literature.

45. Griselda Gambaro, *El campo* (Buenos Aires: Insurrexit, 1967), 28. Subsequent quotations from this work are cited parenthetically in the text.

46. Molinaro, applying Foucault's work in *Discipline and Punish: The Birth of the Prison* to *El campo*, states that the play "turns on the dynamics between the theatricality of power and the power of theatricality" ("Discipline and Drama," 29). She makes a valid point about the simultaneously diffuse and specific nature of the historical referent of the play:

> *El campo* exceeds any local geopolitical reality by implicating the totalitarian regimes of Nazi Germany, Vietnam, Spain, and the former Soviet Union. At the same time, the *absence* of any direct references to Peronist Argentina actively draws attention to the political situation from which the play derives; spectators may extrapolate from the general to the particular in order to allow for the possibility that the environment of *El campo* parallels the atmosphere of Argentina in the 1960s. ("Discipline and Drama," 34)

47. Diana Taylor, "Violent Displays: Griselda Gambaro and Argentina's Drama of Disappearance," in *Information for Foreigners: Three Plays by Griselda Gambaro*,

ed. and trans. Marguerite Feitlowitz (Evanston, Ill.: Northwestern University Press, 1992), 166. Gambaro's play makes frequent and obvious references to the Nazis and to the concentration camps of World War II, but it also clearly presages the events that would soon overwhelm Argentina. As Taylor observes, "Gambaro, throughout her career, incessantly calls attention to the fascistic elements in Argentine government and discourse. Fascism has a long history in Argentina. . . . Gambaro's portrayal of fascism, however, is also directed toward the present, explicitly expressing her alarm at the new wave of authoritarianism in Argentina and the country's ongoing, and intensifying, fascination with fascism" ("Griselda Gambaro," 166). Molinaro further suggests that Gambaro's new discourse on fascism "increasingly comes to characterize the later work of the Argentine dramatist and Latin American theatre generally. Gambaro's early theater has in fact become synonymous with a call to political awareness and responsibility" ("Discipline and Drama," 29).

48. Tamara Holzapfel adds yet another nuance, proposing that *El campo* is an allegory about the pressures exerted by political dictatorships on the arts ("Griselda Gambaro's Theatre of the Absurd," *Latin American Theatre Review* 3, no. 1 [1970]: 11). See also Miguel Angel Giella's analysis of *Los siameses* ("El victimario como víctima en *Los siameses* de Griselda Gambaro: Notas para el análisis." *Gestos* 2 [1987]) and Kirsten Nigro's "Discurso feminino y el teatro de Griselda Gambaro" (in *Ensayos críticos sobre Griselda Gambaro y José Triana*, ed. Diana Taylor [Ottawa: Girol, 1989]), which puts a gendered spin on the discussion of victimization.

49. Franco, "Self-Destructing Heroines," 110.

50. Gladhart, *Leper*, 121.

51. Kathleen Betsko and Rachel Koenig, eds., *Interviews with Contemporary Women Playwrights* (New York: Beech Tree, 1987), 195, 191.

52. Taylor, *Theatre of Crisis*, 145.

CHAPTER 5: GAMES AND GENDER ISSUES

1. Laurence Senelick, ed. *Gender in Performance: The Presentation of Difference in the Performing Arts*, (Hanover, N.H.: Tufts University Press, 1992), ix.

2. Nieves Martínez de Olcoz, "Decisiones de la máscara neutra: Dramaturgia femenina y fin de siglo en América Latina," *Latin American Theatre Review* 31, no. 2 (1998): 7.

3. Griselda Gambaro, who has often eschewed her depiction as a feminist, describes a generalized view of feminist literature that is particularly applicable to this chapter:

As a rule, a work is considered to touch on the theme of feminism when its leading characters are women and are repressed or in rebellion. As far as I am concerned, a work is feminist insofar as it attempts to explain the mechanics of cruelty, oppression, and violence through a story that is developed in a world in which men and women exist. (Quoted in Debra A. Castillo, *Talking Back: Strategies for a Latin American Feminist Literary Criticism* [Ithaca: Cornell University Press, 1992], 30)

4. Kirsten Nigro, "Rosario Castellanos' Debunking of the *Eternal Feminine*," *Journal of Spanish Studies: Twentieth Century* 8, no. 1–2 (1980): 92.

5. Rosario Castellanos, *El eterno femenino* (Mexico City: Fondo de Cultura Eco-

nómica, 1986), 21–22. Subsequent quotations from this work are cited parenthetically in the text. Nigro describes the multitude of episodes as "Cartoon-like frames that are strung together with no regard to the traditional three unities"; she further notes the interpolation of poetry, sung *corridos*, film strips, projected slides, televised sequences, and tape recordings into the playtext ("Debunking," 92). I maintain that the "cartoon-like frames" and the integration of multiple examples of intertextual allusions and elements of popular culture all serve to spotlight the ludic nature of *El eterno femenino*.

6. Lucía Fox Lockert, "El eterno femenino en la obra de Rosario Castellanos," in *Actas del 7° Congreso de la AIH*, ed. Giuseppe Bellini, Vol. 1 (Rome: Bulzoni, 1982), 465.

7. Gladhart, *Leper*, 111. Gladhart's chapter, "Playing Gender," which deals with *El eterno femenino*, was also published previously.

8. See Jill Dolan's "Geographies of Learning: Theatre Studies, Performance, and the 'Performative,'" *Theatre Journal* 45, no. 4 (1993), and Gladhart's *Leper*.

9. In her 1992 study, "Breaking [It] Up is [Not] Hard to Do: Writing Histories and Women Theatre Artists in Latin America," Nigro returns to *El eterno femenino*, suggesting that Castellanos "seems to have anticipated the need to transgress dominant definitions of theatre in her very metatheatrical *The Eternal Feminine*. Although by placing the play's action in a bourgeois beauty parlor Castellanos is poking fun at women of her class and their obsession with their physical appearance, this is also a space where women are made up, in a theatrical sense, where they get into their roles. More significantly, *this* beauty parlor is one where women perform for other women" ("Breaking [It] Up is [Not] Hard to Do: Writing Histories and Women Theatre Artists in Latin America," *Gestos* 14 (1992): 129). Her discussion of alternative kinds of performance space for women continues with examples of the second act's circus tent scene and Sor Juana's inset play (which takes place in the drawing room of a colonial house) and the third act's mixture of parlor and classroom.

10. Although Gladhart suggests that "Castellanos posits women as forced performers, interpreters of an assigned script" (*Leper*, 127), she also observes that "Feminine roles are not mandated solely by a disembodied patriarchal order but fostered and reproduced by women as well, as is evident when Lupita's mother transforms her into the suffering, self-sacrificing mother-to-be or when Lupita counsels her daughter (Lupita II) on the ways of respectable women" (126). The female version of the patriarchal order may be seen, for example, when Lupita's mother induces vomiting in her pregnant daughter and deliberately and jubilantly destroys her physical appearance. Gladhart comments, "Here the artist unpaints her canvas, so that the creation of the ideal woman is explicitly a process of erasure" (126).

11. Sandra Messinger Cypess analyzes the play by turning to the work of anthropologist Victor Turner:

> The mundane element of the act [a woman getting her hair done in preparation for her wedding day] is transformed by being related to a liminal period considered a rite of passage for patriarchal woman, the marriage ceremony. I use liminal in the sense that Victor Turner employs the term, as a complex and dramatic period in which one passes from one stage to another in accordance with a cultural script. Turner's discussion of the liminal phases suggests that the marriage ceremony is a liminal moment in which the woman undergoes a change in status that incorporates her into the appropriate and well-defined position in the patriarchy. I believe that Castellanos makes use of the liminal period to point out another alternative.

During the liminal period of transition, it is possible to generate "new myths, symbols, paradigms, and political structures," which Castellanos attempts to do by first deconstructing the institutionalized myths and paradigms associated with marriage and its corollary roles for women in the patriarchal hierarchy. ("From Colonial Constructs to Feminist Figures: Re/visions by Mexican Women Dramatists," *Theatre Journal* 41 [1989]: 496)

For a more detailed discussion of Turner's contributions to ludic theory, see chapter 2.

12. The *alternativa* and other bullfighting terms are explained by Diane E. Marting in the translation of the play (*The Eternal Feminine*, in *A Rosario Castellanos Reader*, ed. Maureen Ahern and trans. Diane E. Marting and Betty Tyree Osiek (Austin: University of Texas Press, 1988), 262 n. 3).

13. Sieber specifically mentions the "stereotypical ugliness of curlers and mud packs, make-up, costume, and other theatrical accoutrements" ("The Deconstruction of Gender as Archetype in Rosario Castellanos' *El eterno femenino*," *Feministas Unidas* 17, no. 2 [1997]: 6).

14. The day, fittingly and *ironically*, is Mother's Day. When Lupita asks, "¿Gané el concurso de la mejor madre mexicana?" [Did I win the contest for best Mexican mother?], the announcer replies, "No, Lupita. Eso habría sido imposible. ¡Todas, absolutamente todas y cada una de las madres mexicanas son mejores!" [No, Lupita. That would have been impossible. All of them, absolutely each and every Mexican mother is the best!] (67).

15. Sieber adds yet another reference to the ludic. Noting that the electric power in the beauty shop keeps going off, which she calls "a representation of the female struggle to negotiate power," Sieber adds, "It also has the effect of making the everyday reality of the beauty shop even more bizarre: a male colleague perhaps best summed up the situation with the observation that 'the hair dryer wins'" ("The Deconstruction of Gender as Archetype," 8).

16. Cypess, "Colonial Contructs," 496.

17. Nigro, "Debunking," 91.

18. Maureen Ahern, introduction to *A Rosario Castellanos Reader* (Austin: University of Texas Press, 1988), 55.

19. D. J. R. Bruckner, "Woman's Many Lives in 'El Eterno Femenino,'" *New York Times*, 25 March 1990, 63.

20. Bixler notes that "With *Extraño juguete*, which ran for more than one hundred performances during its premiere in 1977, Torres Molina established her place in the Buenos Aires theater scene" ("For Women Only? The Theater of Susana Torres Molina," in *Latin American Women Dramatists: Theater, Texts, and Theories*, ed. Catherine Larson and Margarita Vargas [Bloomington: Indiana University Press, 1998], 215). It was, Bixler tells us, "later re-staged in Madrid in 1979, New York in 1983, and Washington, D.C. in 1986" (231 n. 2). Perla Zayas de Lima describes the *reestreno* (new premiere) of the play in Buenos Aires in 1994, in which the director, Luis Salado, offered a reading that emphasized the humor of the work, which led the strong dose of violence seemingly present in the text to be effectively neutralized ("Susana Torres Molina, la mujer y el mito," in *Dramas de mujeres*, ed. Halima Tahan [Buenos Aires: Ediciones Ciudad Argentina, 1998], 333).

21. Bixler ("For Women Only?," 217, and "Games and Reality," 26) points to the connection between the salesman's name, Maggi, and magic. In that sense, his real and metaphorical magic tricks are yet another manifestation of the ludic.

22. In a move that combines the central premises of *Extraño juguete, Casa matriz,* and *Waiting for Godot,* the Venezuelan Mariela Romero's *Esperando al italiano* has four middle-aged women await the arrival of the lover they have hired (*Esperando al italiano,* in *Las risas de nuestras medusas,* ed. Susana Castillo. Caracas: Fundarte, 1992).

23. For the theoretical implications of these actions, see Derrida's discussion of violent hierarchies in *Of Grammatology* (trans. Gayatri C. Spivak [Baltimore: Johns Hopkins University Press, 1976]) and his analysis of the Theater of Cruelty in "The Theater of Cruelty and the Closure of Representation" (in *Writing and Difference* [Chicago: University of Chicago Press, 1978]). In complementary readings of the play, see Denise M. DiPuccio's "Radical and Materialist Relationships in Torres Molina's *Extraño juguete*" (*Letras femeninas* 11, no. 1–2 [1995]) and Kevin Bauman's "Metatexts, Women, and Sexuality: The Facts and (Ph)allacies in Torres Molina's *Extraño juguete*" (*Romance Languages Annual* 2 [1990]).

24. Bixler, "Games and Reality," 22.

25. Although my work in other contexts has been profoundly influenced by Wittgenstein's discussion of language games, in the context of this chapter, I see the games as conscious manifestations of the ludic, which parallel the physical games also present in the text. The players (at least the female players) seem to understand perfectly how to manipulate language to toy with the traveling salesman. When they break the rules—the conventions governing successful communication, explored by countless speech act theorists including John Austin (*How to Do Things with Words,* ed. J. O. Urmson and Marina Sbisà., 2nd ed. [Cambridge: Harvard University Press, 1975]), John R. Searle (*Speech Acts: An Essay in the Philosophy of Language* [London: Cambridge University Press, 1969]), and H. Paul Grice ("Logic and Conversation," in *Syntax and Semantics. Vol. III: Speech Acts,* ed. Peter Cole and Jerry L. Morgan [New York: Academic Press, 1975])—they know exactly what effect their linguistic actions will have on their interlocutor(s).

26. Bixler, "Games and Reality," 29.

27. Susana Torres Molina, *Extraño juguete* (Buenos Aires: Apex, 1978), 57–58. Subsequent quotations from this work are cited parenthetically in the text.

28. My translation, Nora Eidelberg, *Teatro experimental,* 28.

29. David William Foster suggests that the dialogue presages the "surprise" ending. He observes that even when the spectators don't realize the true nature of the game, they sense that what they are hearing is much more than the conversation of two bored spinsters and a traveling salesman whose sales talk is turning increasingly into a macabre threat (my translation, "Identidades polimórficas y planteo metateatral en *Extraño juguete* de Susana Torres Molina," *Alba de América* 7, no. 12–13 [1989]: 82–83.

Foster indicates several places in which the characters appear to break the dramatic fiction to speak from the perspective of the outer frame. A key example is this exchange, when the salesman, frustrated by the women's apparent lack of interest, stops the interior play and storms out of the apartment:

MAGGI: [. . .] ¿Quiere que les diga una cosa? ¡Estoy harto! Buenas tardes. (*Cierra la puerta y se va.*)

[*Do you want me to tell you something? I'm fed up! Good afternoon! (He closes the door and leaves.)*]

ANGÉLICA: (*A Perla.*) ¡Te felicito! Cada día lo hacés mejor.

[(*To Perla.*) *I congratulate you! You do it better each day.*]
PERLA: Gracias, querida. Tu compañía me inspira. (27)
[*Thanks, dear. Your company inspires me.*]

30. Eidelberg, *Teatro experimental*, 27–28.

31. The multiple scripts and translations of *Casa matriz* raise interesting questions of textual authority. It was first published in *Salirse de madre* (Buenos Aires: Croqui-ñol) in 1989, but it was revised several times before and after. In 1981, Raznovich returned to Argentina from her exile in Spain to participate in the staging of "El desconcierto" at the Teatro Abierto festival, which "brought together dramatists, directors, actors and technicians—all of them black-listed and fearing for their safety—to produce a cycle of one-act plays that demonstrated that Argentina's artists had not succumbed to the dictatorship's silencing tactics" (Diana Taylor, "The Theater of Diana Raznovich and Perceptitide in *El desconcierto*," in *Latin American Women Dramatists*, ed. Catherine Larson and Margarita Vargas [Bloomington: Indiana University Press, 1998], 114). The play was performed in the Teatro Bauen in Buenos Aires in 1993, but translations had been performed earlier in Rome ("Madre Affit-tasi," 1986), Nuremberg (1992), and Stockholm (1992). A translation into English ("Dial-a-Mom") by Teresa Cajiao Salas and Margarita Vargas was published in 1997 in *Women Writing Women*; the translation was based on one of the 1980 versions of *Casa matriz*. Cajiao Salas and Vargas graciously provided me with a typescript version of the play (a version very close to what would ultimately become the "official" second version), which differs significantly from their translation. The text appeared as *Casa matriz* "Segunda versión" in *Antología crítica del teatro breve hispanoam-ericano: 1948–93*, ed. María Mercedes Jaramillo and Mario Yepes (Medellín, Colom-bia: Universidad de Antioquia, 1997); this is the variant form that I use in my study. In her acknowledgments for the second version, Raznovich states that the Italian di-rector Saviana Scalfi and lighting specialist Eugenia Archett, working with the drama-tist prior to the staging of her play at the Spazio Uno theater in Rome, made several suggestions that she would ultimately assimilate (151). Finally, the drama was pub-lished in 2001 in *Jardín de otoño, Casa matriz y De atrás para adelante*. (Prologue by Diana Taylor. Madrid: Consorcio Casa de América), and appeared in 2002 as *Ma-TRIX, Inc.* in a bilingual edition, *Defiant Acts: Four Plays by Diana Raznovich/Actos desafiantes: cuatro obras de Diana Raznovich*, ed. Diana Taylor and Victoria Martí-nez (Lewisburg, Pa.: Bucknell University Press).

32. Diana Taylor, "Negotiating Performance," *Latin American Theatre Review* 26, no. 2 (1993): 54. See also Margo Milleret's examination of the mother-daughter bond in "Daughters *vs.* Mothers on Latin American Stages." Milleret asserts that relations between mothers and daughters are "one of the least explored areas of familial life in Latin America from either on—or off—stage," adding that "Even with the advent of a feminist movement, there are risks involved for women playwrights who stage plays about mothers and daughters" given the hallowed space mothers occupy in Latin American society ("Daughters *vs.* Mothers on Latin American Stages," in *Todo ese fuego [Homenaje a Merlin H. Forster] / All that fire [Studies in honor of Merlin H. Forster]*, ed. Mara L. García and Douglas Weatherford [Mexico City: Universidad Au-tónoma de Tlaxcala, 1999], 136, 137).

33. The Venezuelan Elisa Lerner's *Vida con mamá* (first staged by "El Nuevo Grupo" in May, 1975, first published in 1976) is probably the best example of another play combining ludic elements with mother and daughter characters. *Vida con mamá*

is described by Isaac Chocrón as "una averiguación basada en juegos surgidos de recuerdos" [an examination based on games that arise from memories] ("Prologue," *Vida con mamá* [Caracas: Fundarte, 1981], 7). In the text, a mother and daughter rock away the hours (and, according to Chocrón, commit the crime of wasting their lives), talking about their memories of the past and their views of present-day Latin America. The games become more overt—and even more obviously linked to politics—at the end of the play:

HIJA: *Intimando: ¿Jugamos ludo? La Hija toma de la cómoda el cartón donde van las fichas y se lo entrega a la Madre.*
[*In a friendly manner. Shall we play Ludo? The daughter takes the box of game tokens out of the chest of drawers and gives it to the Mother.*]

MADRE: Prefiero el dominó. Es una institución de la democracia. *La Madre vuelve a poner el cartón en su lugar. De seguida, toma de la cómoda algunas piezas de dómino y las entrega a la Hija.*
[*I prefer Dominoes. They're a democratic institution. The Mother puts the box back in its place. She then takes some dominoes out of the chest of drawers and hands them to the Daughter.*]

HIJA: ¿Y el ludo? *La Hija vuelve a colocar las piezas en su lugar.*
[*And Ludo? The Daughter keeps on putting the playing pieces in their place.*]

MADRE: Un juego que ya no se juega. Lo jugaban en . . . tés dictatoriales.
[*A game that's not played any more. They used to play it in . . . dictatorial teas.*]

HIJA: ¿Tiránico ludo? ¿Democrático ludo?
[*Tyrannical Ludo? Democratic Ludo?*]

MADRE: El país es un juego.
[*The country is a game.*]

HIJA: Juguemos a las claves.
[*Let's play Clues.*]

MADRE: ¡Juguemos a las claves y no seremos esclavos!
[*Let's play Clues and we won't be slaves!*]

HIJA: ¡A las claves y seremos ricos en clavos!
[*Clues and we'll be rich in cloves!*]

MADRE: ¡A las claves y tendremos frescura de claveles!
[*Clues and we'll have carnation freshness!*]

HIJA: ¡Al juego! Una solitaria pero feliz palabra.
[*The game! A lonely but happy word.*]

MADRE: Carabela.
[*Caravel.*]

HIJA: Sigue.
[*Continue.*]

MADRE: Anillo.
[*Ring.*]

HIJA: Prosigue.
[*Go on.*]

MADRE: Pasión.
[*Passion.*]

HIJA: ¡Amante de la literatura!
[*Lover of literature!*]

MADRE: ¡Al juego! Un secreto, ensimismado vocablo.
[*To the game! A secret, engrossing word.*]

HIJA: Coartada. (43)
[*Alibi.*]

Clearly influenced by the Absurdists, *Vida con mamá* emerges as a theatrical game about Venezuela and all of Latin America, about mothers and daughters, and about the search for self. Literally using games, Lerner mines them for their metaphorical richness, creating a playtext that spoke so clearly to Venezuelan audiences and critics of 1975 that it won a number of major prizes; as Chocrón proclaimed, Elisa Lerner was a complete triumph (my translation, 7).

34. Diana Raznovich, *Casa matriz* (Segunda versión), in *Antología crítica del teatro breve hispanoamericano: 1948–1993*, ed. María Mercedes Jaramillo and Mario Yepes (Medellín, Colombia: Universidad de Antioquia, 1997), 159. Subsequent quotations from this work are cited parenthetically in the text.

35. My translation. Nora Glickman, "Parodia y desmitificación del rol femenino en el teatro de Diana Raznovich," *Latin American Theatre Review* 28, no. 1 (1994): 95.

36. The stage directions allude hyperbolically to more than 1200 possible roles, *all* of which each substitute mother has been trained to perform, from which the client will choose five to seven "mothers."

37. Glickman, "Parodia," 96.

38. Inge Bretherton, in her analysis of the interaction of reality and fantasy in symbolic play, refers to the technique as "prompting": one player instructs his or her partner on how to act or what to say, temporarily abandoning the play identity in order to clarify or "improve" the joint performance ("Representing the Social World in Symbolic Play: Reality and Fantasy," in *Symbolic Play: The Development of Social Understanding*, ed. Inge Bretherton [London: Academic Press, 1984], 28).

39. The breaking of the fiction occurs as often as the inset plays themselves, in a dizzying movement back and forth between "illusion" and "reality."

40. Nora Glickman states, "*Casa matriz* presents the extreme, the *non plus ultra* of consumerism: not only can one rent sexual partners, companions for the elderly, maids by the hour, dog walkers, but also mothers. You can rent the kind of intense, primary emotions that you normally don't experience if you have only one mother and are tied to the feelings that your single mother has provoked" (my translation, "Parodia y desmitificación," 97).

41. Ibid.

42. As they wrestle for superior position, Bárbara and her mother illustrate many of the characteristics of the play-fear stimulus—high intensity, strangeness, sudden movement, close distance—that Owen Aldis discusses in *Play Fighting* ([New York: Academic, 1975], 262).

43. Taylor, "The Theater of Diana Raznovich," 114.

44. In the stage directions, Raznovich states that the breast exudes a rich cream that completely covers Bárbara, who is so overjoyed that she clings to her "mother's" neck and exclaims, "Es un final operístico. La voy a contratar para la semana que viene" [It's an operatic ending. I'm going to hire you for next week] (40).

CHAPTER 6: GAMES AND/IN SPANISH AMERICAN SOCIETY

1. Richard Schechner and Mady Schuman, eds. *Ritual, Play, and Performance: Readings in the Social Sciences/Theatre* (New York: Seabury Press, 1976), 79.

2. Myrna Casas is, as Vicky Unruh notes, "one of the principal theater innovators in the generation of Puerto Rican writers who began producing in the early 1960s"

("A Moveable Space: The Problem of Puerto Rico in Myrna Casas's Theater," in *Latin American Women Dramatists: Theater, Texts, and Theories*, ed. Catherine Larson and Margarita Vargas [Bloomington: Indiana University Press, 1998], 126). A writer of poetry, short stories, and opera and *zarzuela* librettos in addition to dramatic texts, Casas has worked in virtually all areas of theater production and has founded her own company, *Producciones Cisne*, which is still active today (127).

3. The play has not been published in Spanish (I am working from a typescript graciously provided by Vicky Unruh), but it appears in English as "The Great USkrainian Circus" in *Women Writing Women: An Anthology of Spanish-American Theater of the 1980s*, ed. and trans. Teresa Cajiao Salas and Margarita Vargas (Albany: SUNY Press, 1997). Camilla Stevens notes, too, that in the 1989 Festival Latino production, the play was called "The Great US Cranial Circus" ("Traveling Troupes: The Performance of Puerto Rican Identity in Plays by Luis Rafael Sánchez and Myrna Casas," *Hispania* 85 no. 2 (2002): 246). The ambiguity and wordplay inherent in the neologism "EUkraniano"/"USkrainian" are typical of Casas's other games in the drama, but also suggest the presence of the United States in Puerto Rican history, society, and culture.

4. Nigro, "Breaking [It] Up," 129. See also Stevens for a discussion of the connections between the circus and the theater: "Just as there are never pure textual beginnings in the sense that we never know when the show is 'on,' this constant shifting of masks makes it impossible to discern the characters' true identities. This brand of circus, in opposition to traditional illusionist theater, seems particularly apt for exploring identity as a flexible construct" ("Traveling Troupes," 245). Finally, see Juan Villegas's "La irrupción del circo en el teatro" for further consideration of the points of contact between the theater and the circus in contemporary Spanish American drama ("La irrupción del circo en el teatro," in *Propuestas escénicas de fin de siglo: FIT 1998*, ed. Juan Villegas [Irvine, Calif.: Gestos, 1999]).

5. Myrna Casas, *El gran circo eukraniano*, typescript, 1988, 9. *The Great USkranian Circus*, in *Women Writing Women: An Anthology of Spanish-American Theater of the 1980s*, ed. and trans. Teresa Cajiao Salas and Margarita Vargas (Albany: SUNY Press, 1997), 136. I use this translation for all subsequent quotations in the chapter.

6. Unruh, "A Moveable Space," 137.

7. Unruh describes these plays within the play:

> The actual performance, initiated with a circus-style parade, combines two kinds of acts. In the first, an actor assumes the character of a local inhabitant and, addressing the audience, improvises a tale of personal experience. In the second, groups of actors, employing the region's vernacular language, perform satirical skits that expose the locale's social problems. The latter include Casas's own *Eran tres y ahora son cuatro* (from the collection *Tres*) and the "Auto de la Providencia Sacramental metropolitano entre Carolina y Cangrejos," portraying several couples as they travel the metropolitan area in fast-moving cars. (Ibid.)

The dramatist incorporates multiple metatheatrical elements: role-playing within the role, the play within the play, literary and real-life references, and an emphasis—via the circus and its opening parade—on spectacle, on theatricality, and on the process of creating them. See also Camilla Stevens's study of the play, which emphasizes the ways in which "The self-conscious use of performance as a method to explore subjectivity exposes the instability of the national family paradigm as a foundation for collective identity" ("Traveling Troupes," 240).

8. *El despojamiento* was first published in 1981 in *Tramoya* (no. 21 and 22: 119–27) and has been published since in slightly amended versions (1983, *Escandalar* 6: 17–22, and the 1989 version I use in this study, published in *Teatro 3*). Diana Taylor comments that "In the early 1970s Gambaro pushes the 'drama of disappearance' further. Her plays of this period, notably *Saying Yes (Decir sí,* 1972), *Strip (El despojamiento,* 1972) and *Information for Foreigners (Información para extranjeros,* 1973) eliminate any remaining vestiges of rationality or coherence from the onstage world" ("Violent Displays: Griselda Gambaro and Argentina's Drama of Disappearance," in *Information for Foreigners: Three Plays by Griselda Gambaro,* ed. Marguerite Feitlowitz [Evanston, Ill.: Northwestern University Press, 1992], 167). I note the discrepancy between Taylor's 1972 dating of the play and that of Sharon Magnarelli, who follows the date (1974) suggested in the 1989 collection, *Teatro 3* ("Acting/Seeing Woman: Griselda Gambaro's *El despojamiento,*" in *Latin American Women's Writing: Feminist Readings in Theory and Crisis,* ed. Anny Brooksbank Jones and Catherine Davies [Oxford: Clarendon, 1996]).

9. Magnarelli, "Acting/Seeing Woman," 11.

10. Ann Witte unites gender and theater in her reading of the play, observing, "*El despojamiento* can be read as an ironic takeoff on a one-woman show, in that it places the actress centerstage only to divest her of the power commonly associated with such a public position. The protagonist turns from the aspiring actress, anxiously waiting for an audition, into the displayed object, without ever assuming the active role she seeks" (*Guiding the Plot: Politics and Feminism in the Work of Women Playwrights from Spain and Argentina, 1960–1990* [New York: Peter Lang, 1996], 127).

11. Griselda Gambaro, *El despojamiento,* in *Teatro 3* (Buenos Aires: Ediciones de la Flor, 1989), 172. Subsequent quotations from this work are cited parenthetically in the text.

12. Becky Boling ("From Pin-Ups to Striptease in Gambaro's *El despojamiento,*" *Latin American Theatre Review* 20, no. 2 [1987]) sees the play as an elaborate erotic and theatrical striptease, while Sharon Magnarelli moves away from the idea of striptease to emphasize a more dehumanizing reading of the play: "Although 'despojamiento' might be translated several ways (stripping, robbing, plundering, despoliation, dispossession), I shall emphasize the latter because of the etymological implications of the term. . . . etymologically the verb implies a far more serious loss than that of clothing, indeed a mortal loss" ("Acting/Seeing Woman," 11 n. 3).

13. Boling observes, "The clothes worn underscore the concept of 'representation' in that there is an effort both to disclose and disguise the socio-economic condition of the woman" ("From Pin-Ups to Striptease," 60).

14. Magnarelli discusses the ways in which audience recognition of the metatheatrical elements of *El despojamiento* could manifest themselves:

> . . . spectators are reminded not to be completely credulous but to seek a contradictory subtext, to look beneath the would-be mirrors of art and discourse (and beyond their artistic frames) in search of the gaps or slippage. Or, perhaps better expressed, spectators are encouraged to ask why the mirrors of art and discourse reflect and frame what and as they do? Whose master(ing) eye/I benefits? . . . We are encouraged to consider how much of our own role playing is created by someone else's discourse of oppression, disguised as eroticism. ("Acting/Seeing Woman," 19–20)

Boling, who stresses the metatheatricality associated with the dismantling of the actual set, notes that this removal of the stage properties "implies that both the objects on the set and the woman herself are only props" ("From Pin-Ups to Striptease," 64).

15. Boling, "From Pin-Ups to Striptease," 62.

16. Magnarelli, "Acting/Seeing Woman," 23.

17. Although she was born in the Canary Islands, Plá has spent nearly her entire life in Paraguay. She is well known in Paraguayan letters as a poet, art critic, essayist, and dramatist and has written dozens of works for the theater, most of which have not been published.

18. The play first appeared in *Teatro breve hispanoamericano contemporáneo* (1967), where the editor, Carlos Solórzano, noted that *Historia de un número* was written in 1949 and until the publication of *Teatro breve* had neither been performed nor published (*Teatro breve hispanoamericano contemporáneo* [Madrid: Aguilar, 1967], 46). However, in Teresa Méndez-Faith's discussion of *Historia de un número* in the Jaramillo-Yepes anthology mentioned below, the author asserts that Plá's drama was written in 1948 and was first staged in 1968 in Mexico. It was not performed in Paraguay until 1971, by which time it had attracted interest in several other countries ("*Historia de número* de Josefina Plá: ¿Farsa trivial en XI tiempos o alegoría teatral para todos los tiempos . . . ?," in *Antología crítica del teatro breve hispanoamericano*, ed. María Mercedes Jaramillo and Mario Yepes [Medellín: Universidad of Antioquia, 1997], 16). In 1978, Joan Rea Boorman stated that Plá "has published and seen performed a large number of plays written in both Guaraní and Spanish," with themes ranging from "realistic portrayals of the materialism, egotism and acquisitiveness of Paraguay's 'haves,' . . . symbolic *autos* (allegories) dealing with Indian superstition on a mythic plane, . . . reworkings of Greek tragedies . . . and absurdist-expressionistic theater depicting the dehumanization of contemporary man in complicated bureaucratic societies" ("Contemporary Latin American Women Dramatists," *Rice University Studies* 64, no. 1 (1978): 75). Reprinted in *Antología crítica del teatro breve hispanoamericano (1948–1993)* (ed. María Mercedes Jaramillo and Mario Yepes [Medellín, Colombia: Universidad de Antioquia, 1997]), *Historia de un número* receives special mention in Laurietz Seda's review of the anthology. Although the other dramas in the collection were written considerably later—much the same as the texts studied in this volume—Seda, echoing the editors, avers that *Historia de un número* merits inclusion because it so profoundly influenced Dragún's *Historias para ser contadas* [Stories to Be Told], among others: "The editors decided to include the text in spite of the chronological distance separating it from other contemporary plays, because it is a work that sets an important precedent in terms of theme [abortion, lack of communication, collective indifference toward the individual] and theatrical techniques [epic theater, theater of the absurd] that began their development later in Latin America" (my translation, *Latin American Theatre Review* 35, no. 1 [2001], 182). Seda's comments reflect my own decision to include Plá's drama in this examination of game playing, as I maintain that the themes and techniques that Plá employed earlier in the twentieth century are also relevant to the topic of this study.

19. Méndez-Faith states that the author calls the play a "farsa trivial en XI tiempos" ("*Historia*," 16).

20. Ibid.

21. Severino João Albuquerque, *Violent Acts*, 25.

22. Boorman observes that although the theme of *Historia de un número* appears

in the literatures of countless other countries, Plá may have seen Paraguay as a particularly significant site for its presentation: "Paraguay, it seems, is not excepted from the problems and concerns besetting contemporary man and may, indeed, even offer a more concentrated view of those universal and interchangeable ills" ("Contemporary Latin American Women Dramatists," 75).

CHAPTER 7: GAMES AND HISTORICAL-POLITICAL REALITIES

1. My translation. Nieves Martínez de Olcoz, "Decisiones de la máscara neutra: Dramaturgia femenina y fin de siglo en América Latina," *Latin American Theatre Review* 31, no. 2 (1998): 8–9.

2. Jacqueline Eyring Bixler, "El teatro de la crisis: Nueva dramaturgia mexicana," in *Tradición, modernidad y posmodernidad*, ed. Osvaldo Pellettieri (Buenos Aires: Galerna, 1999), 111. Nonetheless, Bixler also points out the singular characteristics of Mexico's theater of crisis: its origin is political, arising from the events of 2 October 1968 with the Tlatelolco massacre, and it has its own set of political and economic circumstances. Dramatists whose texts emerge from these events include both Jesusa Rodríguez and Sabina Berman, in addition to Estela Leñero, Leonor Azcárate, Víctor Hugo Rascón Banda, Ricardo Pérez-Quitt, and Hugo Salcedo ("El teatro de la crisis," 111–12).

3. Marguerite Feitlowitz's description of the play's creation could well be another scene in the drama. Gambaro wrote *Información para extranjeros* in 1971–1973, hid the play in her house, and smuggled it out when she fled Argentina into exile. "For years," Feitlowitz states, "the play circulated in samizdat among theater people in Europe, but when companies offered productions, Gambaro refused permission, fearing repercussions against family members still in Argentina. An early version appeared in a small Italian theater journal. . . . The play was published in Buenos Aires in 1987 . . . but it has not been produced there, nor are the prospects very good" ("The Theater of Griselda Gambaro," in *Information for Foreigners: Three Plays by Griselda Gambaro*, ed. and trans. Marguerite Feitlowitz [Evanston, Ill.: Northwestern University Press, 1992], 5–6). In *Exorcising History*, Jean Graham-Jones adds in a note that *Información para extranjeros* has never been staged in its entirety, in keeping with Gambaro's wishes (*Exorcising History: Argentine Theater Under Dictatorship.* Lewisburg, Pa.: Bucknell University Press, 2000], 202 n. 6).

4. Griselda Gambaro, *Información para extranjeros*, in *Teatro 2* (Buenos Aires: Ediciones de la Flor, 1987), 69. Subsequent quotations from this work are cited parenthetically in the text. The groups do converge in Scene 20. Dick Gerdes, discussing the numerous possibilities from which the spectator can view the play, asserts that "It becomes apparent that although the scenes are experienced in a different sequence for each group, the total effect of the scenes is the same" ("Recent Argentine Vanguard Theatre: Gambaro's *Información para extranjeros*," *Latin American Theatre Review* 11, no. 2 (1978): 12).

5. Diana Taylor observes that Gambaro "calls attention to the way that the public's perception is directed and controlled by those in power" (*Theatre of Crisis*, 136–37). Taylor specifically emphasizes the ways in which the guide ties into "a rampant national misogyny" and participates in the violence: "While this may be Hell, this Guide is no Virgil" (137).

6. Feitlowitz, "The Theater of Griselda Gambaro," 6.

7. Taylor, *Theatre of Crisis*, 146.

8. The couplet does not translate literally, but Argentines will recognize the evocation of Rosas's command to kill one's political enemies. See also Feitlowitz, "The Theater of Griselda Gambaro," 7.

9. For a related discussion of the metatheatrical techniques of this play, see Rosalea Postma's "Space and Spectator in the Theatre of Griselda Gambaro: *Información para extranjeros*," *Latin American Theatre Review* 14, no. 1 (1980): 41.

10. Moretta, "Spanish-American Theatre," 5–6.

11. In the United States, 66 percent of the subjects shocked their pupils to "death"; in Germany, the percentage rate was 85 percent (Feitlowitz, "The Theater of Griselda Gambaro," 11 n. 10).

12. Postma, "Space and Spectator," 43.

13. Marguerite Feitlowitz, trans., *Information for Foreigners*, 122.

14. Feitlowitz tells us that the author of these verses is a young Greek writer who was disappeared ("The Theater of Griselda Gambaro," 8).

15. Taylor, *Theatre of Crisis*, 144. Gerdes offers further confirmation, stating that the "effect of the play is based on the juxtaposition of acts of human violence and references to children's games. The impact of this strange parallelism can be explained through Antonin Artaud's theory of cruelty, composed of surprise (with physical violence) and assaults on human sensitivity, making the sensation of fear more acute. . . . To juxtapose violence and the playful world of children touches the very primitive and archetypal roots of man; it is a situation which defies human reason" ("Recent Argentine Vanguard Theatre," 13). He later adds, "There is a thin line separating premeditated violence of mature man (torture) and the impulsiveness of a child, whose motives are not always political, but stem rather from man's primitive nature in general" (15).

16. Taylor, *Theatre of Crisis*, 143. *Información para extranjeros*, adds Taylor, "signals not only a new kind of theatre but a new kind of world being created before our eyes. Not only is theatre an arena for intense political confrontation, as attested by the policing of theatres, censorship of scripts, and harassment of writers and practitioners, but political violence is itself played out theatrically, on the public streets, in private houses, on human bodies" (136). This is a "dangerous theatre, one that provokes audiences to resent and reject theatrical manipulation, one that shocks and disrupts, that breaks the frames of theatrical traditions in order to make the invisible visible once again" (145).

17. The text, like so many others by Rodríguez, is published in *Debate feminista* (*Sor Juana en Almoloya [Pastorela Virtual]. Debate Feminista* 12 [1995]; subsequent quotations from this work are cited parenthetically in the text). The journal gives Rodríguez credit for authorship but adds, "Con la colaboración de Tito Vasconcelos, Manuel Poncelis y Liliana Felipe" (395). Each year, Rodríguez produces a *pastorela* (pastourelle) that serves as a satirical review of the year (Mark and Blanca Kelty, "Interview with Jesusa Rodríguez," *Latin American Theatre Review* 31, no. 1 [1997]: 123). She explains her use of the form: "La pastorela a mí me permite dos vertientes que me interesan mucho. Mis principales enemigos son la iglesia católica y el Estado . . . [la pastorela] te permite atacar esas dos vertientes" [The pastourelle allows me to explore two dimensions that interest me a great deal. My principal enemies are the Catholic Church and the State . . . the pastourelle allows you to attack both dimen-

sions] ("Interview" 124–25). Not coincidentally, *Sor Juana en Almoloya* allows Rodríguez to attack both dimensions at once.

18. According to Mark and Blanca Kelty ("Interview with Jesusa Rodríguez," 123), Rodríguez wrote, directed, or acted in more than 180 satirical works between the time that her theater/bar/cabaret (an ex-chapel, part of a house once owned by Salvador Novo) opened in 1991 and the time of the interview (1997). Rodríguez sees her work as "'periodístico,' un género que 'recoge la opinión pública, humor popular'" ["journalistic," a genre that "captures public opinion, popular humor"]. She adds that times of greatest national crisis—economic, ideological, social, and political—produce the best material and highest attendance for her type of spectacle (123). Rodríguez and her company, the Divas, are daring; as Jean Franco puts it, "In a country in which shame and decorum cement public life, Jesusa is shameless and unafraid" ("A Touch of Evil: Jesusa Rodríguez's Subversive Church," in *Negotiating Performance*, ed. Diana Taylor and Juan Villegas [Durham, N.C.: Duke University Press, 1994], 164). Kirsten Nigro comments that Rodríguez identifies herself in Mexico with a theater that could be termed "alternative," opposing official cultural institutions, which takes place in "performance" spaces or in theater-bars like the Hijo del Cuervo, or in the type of space for which she herself is the impresario: the Teatro de la Capilla and El Hábito bar, in Coyoacán" (my translation, "Un revuelto de la historia, la memoria y el género: Expresiones de la posmodernidad sobre las tablas mexicanas," *Gestos* 9, no. 17 [1994]: 34). Discussing "Cielo de abajo," Nigro presents a fascinating exploration of the postmodern experience in the theater. Further examinations of Jesusa Rodríguez, Liliana Felipe, and their theater/cabaret projects may be found in studies by Gastón A. Alzate (see especially the introduction and chapter on Rodríguez and Felipe in *Teatro de cabaret: imaginarios disidentes* [Irvine, Calif.: Gestos, 2002]), Johannes Birringer ("Border Media: Performing Postcolonial History," *Gestos* 21 [1996]), Nieves Martínez de Olcoz ("Decisiones de la máscara neutra"), Diana Taylor ("*High Aztec* or Performing Anthro Pop," *The Drama Review* 37, no. 3 [1993]), and Jean Franco ("A Touch of Evil: Jesusa Rodríguez's Subversive Church").

19. Amalia Gladhart, "Monitoring Sor Juana: Satire, Technology, and Appropriation in Jesusa Rodríguez's *Sor Juana en Almoloya*," *Revista hispánica moderna* 52 (1999): 214.

20. My translation, Kelty, "Interview," 124.

21. As Gladhart observes, Salinas's widely disseminated letter, which "protests accusations that he was involved in the assassination of Luis Donaldo Colosio, denies responsibility for Mexico's economic crisis, and generally decries his own transformation into 'el villano favorito,'" was published in *La Jornada* on December 4, 1995 ("Monitoring Sor Juana," 215).

22. Gladhart captures the essence of the game: "The costume accords Salinas the false humility of the Bishop of Puebla's pseudonym and prepares the ground for Sor Juana's far from docile letter" ("Monitoring Sor Juana," 217). She adds, "Costuming Salinas as Sor Filotea underscores his alleged helplessness . . . and suggests that Salinas's vulnerability is as much a pose as was that of the Bishop of Puebla. The 'mask' in the case of Rodríguez's performance already exposes and inverts power relations, as Salinas-as-nun becomes an object of ridicule even before Sor Juana begins her reply" (218).

23. Ibid., 221.

24. Ibid., 223.

25. Sor Juana tries to defend her previous efforts to make the play acceptable to the censors ("Disculpe, procuradora, pero ya le quité el *table dance* de María Magdalena" [Forgive me, Procuratrix, but I already took out Mary Magdalene's table dance], 406), but the Procuradora, citing article after article of the law of public spectacles, even accuses Sor Juana's play of lewdness because the baby Jesus in a nativity scene is naked: "Bebé o lo que sea de todos modos le cuelgan sus porquerías" [Whether he's a baby or not, the family jewels are hanging out] (407).

26. The edict further condemns Sor Juana to physical torture and to the emotional torture of having to write hagiographies of "saints" Enrique Krause, Raúl Velasco, and Jorge Serrano Limón.

27. As owner of the Televisa network, Azcárraga incurs Rodríguez's wrath; she states in an interview, "En México aparece un tercer enemigo visible que sería Televisa y los monopolios de información" [In Mexico, a third visible enemy appears: Televisa and the monopolies of information] (Kelty, "Interview," 125).

28. Jacqueline Eyring Bixler, "Pretexts and Anti-PRI texts": Mexican Theatre of the 90s," in *Todo ese fuego (Homenaje a Merlin H. Forster) / All that fire (Studies in honor of Merlin H. Forster)*, ed. Mara L. García and Douglas Weatherford. (Mexico City: Universidad Autónoma de Tlaxcala, 1999), 45.

29. *Krisis* premiered in 1996; it was published in *Tramoya* in 1997. Bixler explains its origin: the text was based on a 1994 farce, *El gordo, la pájara y el narco*. A series of particularly shocking events in 1994—narcoterrorism, rebellions, assassinations, and electoral fraud—led Berman to convert her farce into the play we know as *Krisis* ("El teatro de la crisis," 114). Bixler adds that in *Krisis*, Berman breaks the reverential silence that had surrounded the presidency of Carlos Salinas de Gortari and the official silence that had followed the assassination of the candidate Luis Donaldo Colosio (117). Many of those same arguments can also be seen in Bixler's "Power Plays and the Mexican Crisis: The Recent Theatre of Sabina Berman," in *Performance, pathos, política de los sexos: Teatro postcolonial de autoras latinoamericanas*, ed. Heidrun Adler and Kati Röttger (Vervuert: Iberoamericana, 1999).

30. In a telling scene, when a group of poor citizens comes to protest the upcoming vote to raise their taxes, one of the politicians treats them like children, trying to convince them that the crisis really represents nothing more than a number of great opportunities, a reading clearly rendered ironic for the vast majority of Mexicans.

31. For a clear explanation of the historical and political crises presented in the drama, see Mario A. Rojas, "*Krísis* (sic) de Sabina Berman y el escenario político mexicano" (in *Tradición, modernidad y posmodernidad*, ed. Osvaldo Pellettieri [Buenos Aires: Galerna, 1999]) and Andres Oppenheimer's *Bordering on Chaos: Guerrillas, Stockbrokers, Politicians, and Mexico's Road to Prosperity* (Boston: Little, Brown, 1996). Noting the connection between Berman's drama and a specific project aimed at exposing Mexican socioeconomic and political problems, Timothy G. Compton links the play to the "Teatro Clandestino" project begun in 1995 and headed by Luis de Tavira, an initiative that teamed prominent playwrights with equally prominent directors and actors to produce plays dealing with current events in Mexico deemed *urgentes*, including politics, economic crises, AIDS, drug traffic and abuse, and poverty ("Mexico City Theatre: Summers 1995 and 1996," *Latin American Theatre Review* 30, no. 1 [1996]: 135).

32. Jacqueline Eyring Bixler, "The Postmodernization of History in the Theatre of Sabina Berman," *Latin American Theatre Review* 30, no. 2 (1997): 57–58.

33. In "El teatro de la crisis," Bixler suggests that the personal and political actions of the play are so inextricably linked that they suggest that the Mexican crisis may be not only political in nature, but also moral (115).

34. Sabina Berman, *Krisis*, in *Tramoya* 52 (July–September 1997): 55. Subsequent quotations from this work are cited parenthetically in the text.

35. Compton's performance review of *Krisis* describes the opening movie as "featuring five young boys precociously playing cards as if at a high stakes Vegas casino" ("Mexico City Theatre," 14). This obvious contrast with the printed version's Monopoly game may have resulted from an attempt to create an image that would be more "stageable" for the members of the audience who were far from the stage. The Mexican version of Monopoly is overtly symbolic, but the idea of gambling at cards is equally suggestive, with the five boys' ability to control the country and themselves presented as fragile—a house of cards destroyed just as surely as the Seijas household at the end of the play. Both versions—both games—set the stage for the political and financial game playing that will take place later in the drama.

36. The math does not quite add up: the printed version states that thirty-six years have passed since the scene takes place, but scene 2 is labeled "1994," or thirty-four years from the first scene's setting.

37. As Bixler says, "Life in Mexico is a power play, whether it be at the level of sex or that of politics. It is the same old game of Monopoly, with the same tactics and the same struggle between traditional values and the forces of democracy and modernity" ("Power Plays," 92).

38. My translation, Bixler, "El teatro de la crisis," 115.

39. In a recurring motif that Pedrero initiates, the indigenous woman is worthy only of the boys' scorn: "A ver si aprendes a hablar en español. Es totonaca" [Let's see if you're learning to speak Spanish. She's a Totonac indian] (53).

40. Because Pedrero uses the literal and metaphoric "in your face" executions as an emblem of his power game; he employs the technique on all those who cross him. Planning the details of Polo's assassination, his final part of the execution order is "Y hazme un favor: que le disparen a la cara" [And do me a favor: have them shoot him in the face] (80).

41. As Rojas notes, the scene could be a parodic allusion to the type of empty political rhetoric that recycles quotations from famous men and recontextualizes them to suit a purpose that has nothing to do with the original incident motivating the quote in the first place ("*Krisis*" 128).

42. Two reports of *Krisis* in performance add to the appreciation of the drama's rich texture. Compton describes the 1996 staging in the Telón de Asfalto theater, with Berman directing and with a "dazzling set and lighting design" by Philippe Armand, which allowed for "seamless jumps in theatrical spaces and times, and made possible the unraveling of an extremely complex web of politics, intrigue, double-dealing, womanizing, and assassinations. A farcical tone prevailed despite the play's weighty thematics and its undisputable similarities to actual Mexican politics" ("Mexico City Theatre," 145). He adds enthusiastically, "The acting in *Krisis* was superb, the sound effects aggressive (deafening but appropriate), the plot complex and gripping, the thematics gutsy, the combination of seriousness and comedy delightful, and the audience enthusiastic and abundant. In short, *Krisis* was nothing short of brilliant theatre" (145). Although he focuses less on the actual staging of the play, Ronald Burgess sees *Krisis* as a political farce that "recalls the political satires that disappeared from bars

years earlier, now raised to a new level of sophistication by Berman, but reminiscent of earlier times, nonetheless" ("Five Summers of Mexican Theater," *Latin American Theatre Review* 30, no. 2 [1997]: 70), which suggests an interesting parallel to Jesusa Rodríguez's satirical work in her bar, El Hábito.

43. Obviously, these plays come from only two countries, and it is equally clear that each nation has its own individual history and political issues, making it impossible to generalize too much about the applicability of any single political discussion across the board. Still, knowing it would be beyond the scope of this book to describe a representative drama from every country in the Hispanic world, I have tried to find three that speak to the concerns that often defy national boundaries: state-sponsored terrorism and repression, violence and torture, assassinations, and political corruption.

CHAPTER 8: CONCLUSIONS

1. Huizinga, *Homo Ludens*, 13.
2. Ann Witte, *Guiding the Plot*, 65.
3. Hans-Georg Gadamer, *Truth and Method* (New York: Crossroad, 1988), 86; Gene Koppel, "Maggie Moran, Anne Tyler's Madcap Heroine: A Game Approach to *Breathing Lessons*," *Essays in Literature* 18, no. 2 (1991): 283, 285.
4. See Bretherton, "Representing the Social World," x.
5. Ruth E. Burke, *The Games of Poetics: Ludic Criticism and Postmodern Fiction* (New York: Peter Lang, 1994), 177.
6. Witte, *Guiding the Plot*, 4.
7. Diana Taylor, *Disappearing Acts: Spectacles of Gender and Nationalism in Argentina's "Dirty War"* (Durham, N.C.: Duke University Press, 1997), ix.

Bibliography

Abel, Lionel. *Metatheatre: A New View of Dramatic Form.* New York: Hill and Wang, 1963.

Adler, Heidrun, and Kati Röttger, eds. *Performance, pathos, política de los sexos: Teatro postcolonial de autoras latinoamericanas.* Vervuert: Iberoamericana, 1999.

Ahern, Maureen, ed. and intro. *A Rosario Castellanos Reader.* Austin: University of Texas Press, 1988.

Albuquerque, Severino João. *Violent Acts: A Study of Contemporary Latin American Theatre.* Detroit: Wayne State University Press, 1991.

Aldis, Owen. *Play Fighting.* New York: Academic, 1975.

Alzate, Gastón A. *Teatro de cabaret: imaginarios disidentes.* Irvine, Calif.: Gestos, 2002.

Andrade, Elba, and Hilde F. Cramsie, eds. *Dramaturgas latinoamericanas contemporáneas: Antología crítica.* Madrid: Verbum, 1991.

André, María Claudia. "Conversaciones sobre vida y teatro con Susana Torres Molina." *Latin American Theatre Review* 35, no. 2 (2002): 89–95.

Argentine National Commission. *Nunca más: The Report of the Argentine National Commission on the Disappeared.* New York: Farrar, Straus and Giroux, 1986.

Auslander, Philip. *From Acting to Performance: Essays in Modernism and Postmodernism.* London: Routledge, 1997.

Austin, Gayle. *Feminist Theories for Dramatic Criticism.* Ann Arbor: University of Michigan Press, 1990.

Austin, John L. *How to Do Things with Words.* Edited by J. O. Urmson and Marina Sbisà. 2nd ed. Cambridge: Harvard University Press, 1975.

Bakhtin, Mikhail M. Chap. 3 in *Rabelais and His World.* Translated by Helene Iswolsksy. Cambridge: MIT Press, 1968. Reprint, "The Role of Games in Rabelais." *Yale French Studies* 41 (1968): 124–32.

Barthes, Roland. *The Pleasure of the Text.* Translated by Richard Miller. New York: Hill and Wang, 1975.

Bassnett, Susan, ed. *Knives and Angels: Women Writers in Latin America.* London: Zed, 1990.

Bateson, Gregory. "A Theory of Play and Fantasy." In *Ritual, Play and Performance: Readings in the Social Sciences/Theatre,* edited by Richard Schechner and Mady Schuman, 67–73. New York: Seabury, 1976.

Bauman, Kevin. "Metatexts, Women, and Sexuality: The Facts and (Ph)allacies in Torres Molina's *Extraño juguete.*" *Romance Languages Annual* 2 (1990): 330–35.

Bellver, Catherine. "Game-Playing and Reading *Ultraísta* Poetry." *Hispanófila* 118 (1996): 17–27.

Benson, Nancy A. "Play Theory and an Elizabethan Sonnet Sequence." In *The Many*

Faces of Play, edited by Kendall Blanchard, 150–60. Champaign, Ill.: Human Kinetics, 1986.

Berman, Sabina. *Krisis*. In *Tramoya* 52 (July-September 1997): 51–100.

Betsko, Kathleen, and Rachel Koenig, eds. *Interviews with Contemporary Women Playwrights*. New York: Beech Tree, 1987.

Birringer, Johannes. "Border Media: Performing Postcolonial History." *Gestos* 21 (1996): 49–66.

———. *Theater, Theory, and Postmodernism*. Bloomington: Indiana University Press, 1991.

Bixler, Jacqueline Eyring. "For Women Only? The Theater of Susana Torres Molina." In *Latin American Women Dramatists: Theater, Texts, and Theories*, edited by Catherine Larson and Margarita Vargas, 215–33. Bloomington: Indiana University Press, 1998.

———. "The Game of Reading and the Creation of Meaning in *El amasijo*." *Revista Canadiense de Estudios Hispánicos* 12, no. 1 (1987): 1–16.

———. "Games and Reality on the Latin American Stage." *Latin American Literary Review* 12 (1984): 22–35.

———. "Los juegos crueles de Egon Wolff: ¿Quién juega?" *Alba de América* 7, no. 12–13 (1989): 245–61.

———. "The Postmodernization of History in the Theatre of Sabina Berman." *Latin American Theatre Review* 30, no. 2 (1997): 45–60.

———. "Power Plays and the Mexican Crisis: The Recent Theatre of Sabina Berman." In *Performance, pathos, política de los sexos: Teatro postcolonial de autoras latinoamericanas*, edited by Heidrun Adler and Kati Röttger, 83–99. Vervuert: Iberoamericana, 1999.

———. "Pretexts and Anti-PRI texts: Mexican Theatre of the 90s." In *Todo ese fuego (Homenaje a Merlin H. Forster) / All that fire (Studies in honor of Merlin H. Forster)*, edited by Mara L. García and Douglas Weatherford, 35–47. Mexico City: Universidad Autónoma de Tlaxcala, 1999.

———. "El teatro de la crisis: Nueva dramaturgia mexicana." In *Tradición, modernidad y posmodernidad*, edited by Osvaldo Pellettieri, 111–18. Buenos Aires: Galerna, 1999.

Blanchard, Kendall, ed. *The Many Faces of Play*. Champaign, Ill: Human Kinetics, 1986.

Blau, Herbert. *The Audience*. Baltimore: Johns Hopkins University Press, 1990.

———. "Universals of Performance; or, Amortizing Play." In *The Eye of Prey: Subversions of the Postmodern*. Bloomington: Indiana University Press, 1987.

Bloom, Harold. "The Dialectics of Poetic Tradition." In *Twentieth Century Literary Theory*, edited by Vassilis Lambropoulos and David Neal Miller, 163–73. Albany, N.Y.: SUNY Press, 1987.

Bockus Aponte, Barbara. "Estrategias dramáticas en *El eterno femenino* de Rosario Castellanos." *Latin American Theatre Review* 20, no. 2 (1987): 49–58.

Boling, Becky. "From Pin-Ups to StripTease in Gambaro's *El despojamiento*." *Latin American Theatre Review* 20, no. 2 (1987): 59–65.

———. "Reenacting Politics: The Theater of Griselda Gambaro." In *Latin American*

Women Dramatists: Theater, Texts, and Theories, edited by Catherine Larson and Margarita Vargas, 3–22. Bloomington: Indiana University Press, 1998.

Boorman, Joan Rea. "Contemporary Latin American Women Dramatists." *Rice University Studies* 64, no. 1 (1978): 69–80.

Boyle, Catherine M. "Griselda Gambaro and the Female Dramatist: The Audacious Trespasser." In *Knives and Angels: Women Writers in Latin America*, edited by Susan Bassnett, 145–57. London: Zed, 1990.

Bretherton, Inge. "Representing the Social World in Symbolic Play: Reality and Fantasy." In *Symbolic Play: The Development of Social Understanding*, edited by Inge Bretherton, 1–41. London: Academic Press, 1984.

Bruckner, D. J. R. "Woman's Many Lives in 'El Eterno Femenino.'" *New York Times* 25 March 1990, 63.

Burgess, Ronald D. "Five Summers of Mexican Theater." *Latin American Theatre Review* 30, no. 2 (1997): 61–72.

———. *The New Dramatists of Mexico, 1967–1985*. Lexington: University Press of Kentucky, 1991.

Burke, Ruth E. *The Games of Poetics: Ludic Criticism and Postmodern Fiction*. New York: Peter Lang, 1994.

Butler, Judith. *Bodies That Matter*. London: Routledge, 1993.

———. *Gender Trouble: Feminism and the Subversion of Identity*. New York: Routledge, 1999.

Caillois, Roger. *Man, Play, and Games*. Translated by Meyer Barash. New York: Free Press of Glencoe, 1961. Originally published as *Les jeux et les hommes* (Paris: Librairie Gallimard, 1958).

Cajiao Salas, Teresa, and Margarita Vargas, eds. *Women Writing Women: An Anthology of Spanish-American Theater of the 1980s*. Albany, N.Y.: SUNY Press, 1997.

Calderwood, James L. *Metadrama in Shakespeare's Henriad*. Berkeley: California University Press, 1979.

———. *Shakespearean Metadrama*. Minneapolis: Minnesota University Press, 1971.

Carlson, Marvin. *Performance: A Critical Introduction*. London: Routledge, 1996.

Casas, Myrna. *El gran circo eukraniano*. TS. 1988.

———. *The Great USkrainian Circus*. In *Women Writing Women: An Anthology of Spanish-American Theater of the 1980s*, edited and translated by Teresa Cajiao Salas and Margarita Vargas, 125–86. Albany, N.Y.: SUNY University Press, 1997.

Case, Sue-Ellen. *Feminism and Theatre*. New York: Methuen, 1988.

Castellanos, Rosario. *El eterno femenino*. Mexico City: Fondo de Cultura Económica, 1986.

———. *The Eternal Feminine*. In *A Rosario Castellanos Reader*, edited by Maureen Ahern and translated by Diane E. Marting and Betty Tyree Osiek, 271–367. Austin: University of Texas Press, 1988.

Castillo, Debra A. *Talking Back: Strategies for a Latin American Feminist Literary Criticism*. Ithaca: Cornell University Press, 1992.

Castillo, Susan D. "*El juego*: texto dramático y montaje." *Latin American Theatre Review* 14, no. 1 (1980): 25–33.

Chick, Garry E. "Play in Games and Sports." In *The Many Faces of Play*, edited by Kendall Blanchard, 188–90. Champaign, Ill.: Human Kinetics, 1986.

———. "Play in Literature." In *The Many Faces of Play*, edited by Kendall Blanchard, 122–23. Champaign, Ill.: Human Kinetics, 1986.

Chocrón, Isaac. Introduction to *El juego* by Mariela Romero, 7–10. Caracas: Monte Ávila, 1977.

———. Prologue to *Vida con mamá* by Elisa Lerner, 9–12. Caracas: Fundarte, 1981.

Chrzanowski, Joseph. "El teatro de Mariela Romero." *Revista Canadiense de Estudios Hispánicos* 7, no. 1 (1982): 205–11.

Chumbley, Robert, ed. *A Polylogue on Play*. In *Sub-Stance* 25 (1980).

Cohen, David. *The Development of Play*. New York: New York University Press, 1987.

Cohen, Steven A., ed. *The Games We Played: A Celebration of Childhood and Imagination*. New York: Simon and Schuster, 2001.

Compton, Timothy G. "Mexico City Theatre: Summers 1995 and 1996." *Latin American Theatre Review* 30, no. 1 (1996): 135–50.

Cortés, Eladio. "*Felipe Angeles*: Theater of Heroes." In *A Different Reality: Studies on the Work of Elena Garro*, edited by Anita K. Stoll, 80–89. Lewisburg, Pa.: Bucknell University Press, 1990.

Cypess, Sandra Messinger. "Dramaturgia femenina y transposición histórica." *Alba de América* 7, no. 12–13 (1989): 283–304.

———. "From Colonial Contructs to Feminist Figures: Re/visions by Mexican Women Dramatists." *Theatre Journal* 41 (1989): 492–504.

———. "The Plays of Griselda Gambaro (Argentina)." In *Dramatists in Revolt*, edited by Leon F. Lyday and George W. Woodyard, 95–109. Austin: University of Texas Press, 1976.

———. "Visual and Verbal Distances in the Mexican Theater: The Plays of Elena Garro." In *Woman as Myth and Metaphor in Latin American Literature*, edited by Carmelo Virgillo and Naomi Lindstrom, 44–62. Columbia: University of Missouri Press, 1986.

Dauster, Frank. "El teatro de Elena Garro: Evasión e ilusión." *Revista Iberoamericana* 30 (1964): 81–89.

———, ed. *Perspectives on Contemporary Spanish American Theatre*. Lewisburg, Pa.: Bucknell University Press, 1996.

Derrida, Jacques. *Of Grammatology*. Translated by Gayatri C. Spivak. Baltimore: Johns Hopkins University Press, 1976.

———. "The Theater of Cruelty and the Closure of Representation." In *Writing and Difference*. Chicago: University of Chicago Press, 1978.

Diamond, Elin, ed. Introduction to *Performance and Cultural Politics*. London: Routledge, 1996.

DiPuccio, Denise M. "The Merging of *La(s) dama(s) boba(s)*." *Gestos* 9 (1990): 53–63.

———. "Radical and Materialist Relationships in Torres Molina's *Extraño juguete*." *Letras femeninas* 11, no. 1–2 (1995): 153–64.

Dolan, Jill. *The Feminist Spectator as Critic*. Ann Arbor, Mich.: UMI Research Press, 1988.

————. "Geographies of Learning: Theatre Studies, Performance, and the 'Performative.'" *Theatre Journal* 45, no. 4 (1993): 417–41.

Dorfman, Ariel. "My House is On Fire." In *My House is On Fire*, translated by Ariel Dorfman and George Shivers, 45–56. New York: Viking, 1990.

Driskell, Charles B. "Theatre in Buenos Aires:1976–77." *Latin American Theatre Review* 11, no. 2 (1978): 103–10.

Duvignaud, Jean. *Le jeu du jeu*. Paris: Balland, 1980.

Egan, Robert. *Drama within Drama: Shakespeare's Sense of His Art*. New York: Columbia University Press, 1975.

Ehrmann, Jacques, ed. *Game, Play, Literature*. Yale French Studies 41 (1968). Reprint, Boston: Beacon, 1968.

————. "Homo Ludens Revisited." In *Game, Play, Literature*, edited by Jacques Ehrmann, 31–57. Boston: Beacon, 1968.

Eidelberg, Nora. "La ritualización de la violencia en cuatro obras teatrales hispanoamericanas." *Latin American Theatre Review* 13, no. 1 (1979): 29–37.

————. *Teatro experimental hispanoamericano 1960–1980. La realidad social como manipulación*. Minneapolis, Minn.: Institute for the Study of Ideologies and Literature, 1985.

Eidelberg, Nora, and María Mercedes Jaramillo, eds. *Voces en escena: Antología de dramaturgas latinoamericanas*. Medellín, Colombia: Universidad de Antioquia, 1991.

Elam, Keir. *The Semiotics of Theatre and Drama*. London: Methuen, 1980.

————. *Shakespeare's Universe of Discourse: Language-Games in the Comedies*. Cambridge: Cambridge University Press, 1984.

Esslin, Martin. "Violence in Modern Drama." In *Brief Chronicles: Essays on Modern Theatre*. London: Temple Smith, 1970.

Feitlowitz, Marguerite. "The Theater of Griselda Gambaro." In *Information for Foreigners: Three Plays by Griselda Gambaro*, edited and translated by Marguerite Feitlowitz, 1–11. Evanston, Ill.: Northwestern University Press, 1992.

————, trans. *Information for Foreigners*, by Grislda Gambaro. In *Information for Foreigners: Three Plays by Griselda Gambaro*. Evanston, Ill.: Northwestern University Press, 1992.

Fink, Eugen. *Le jeu comme symbole du monde*. Paris: Editions de Minuit, 1966.

————. "The Oasis of Happiness: Toward an Ontology of Play." *Yale French Studies* 41 (1968): 19–30.

Flores, Yolanda. *The Drama of Gender: Feminist Theater by Women of the Americas*. New York: Peter Lang, 2000.

Foster, David William. "Identidades polimórficas y planteo metateatral en *Extraño juguete* de Susana Torres Molina." *Alba de América* 7, no. 12–13 (1989): 75–86.

————. *Violence in Argentine Literature: Cultural Responses to Tyranny*. Columbia, Mo.: University of Missouri Press, 1995.

Franco, Jean. "Self-Destructing Heroines." *The Minnesota Review* 22–23 (1984): 105–15.

————. "A Touch of Evil: Jesusa Rodríguez's Subversive Church." In *Negotiating*

Performance, edited by Diana Taylor and Juan Villegas, 159–75. Durham, N.C.: Duke University Press, 1994.

Fraser, John. *Violence in the Arts*. Cambridge: Cambridge University Press, 1974.

Gadamer, Hans-Georg. *Truth and Method*. New York: Crossroad, 1988.

Galván, Delia. "*Felipe Angeles* de Elena Garro: Sacrificio heroico." *Latin American Theatre Review* 20, no. 2 (1987): 29–35.

———. "Feminism in Elena Garro's Recent Works." In *A Different Reality: Studies on the Work of Elena Garro*, edited by Anita K. Stoll, 136–46. Lewisburg, Pa.: Bucknell University Press, 1990.

Gambaro, Griselda. *El campo*. Buenos Aires: Insurrexit, 1967.

———. *El despojamiento*. In *Teatro 3*, 170–81. Buenos Aires: Ediciones de la Flor, 1989.

———. *Información para extranjeros*. In *Teatro 2*, 67–128. Buenos Aires: Ediciones de la Flor, 1987.

———. *Information for Foreigners: Three Plays by Griselda Gambaro*, edited and translated by Marguerite Feitlowitz. Evanston, Ill: Northwestern University Press, 1992.

———. *Los siameses*. In *9 dramaturgos hispanoamericanos: Antología del teatro hispanoamericano del siglo xx*, edited by Frank Dauster, Leon Lyday, and George Woodyard, 93–143. Vol. 2. Ottawa: Girol, 1979.

Garro, Elena. *El árbol*. México: Colección Teatro de Bolsillo, 1967.

———. *La dama boba*. In *Un hogar sólido*, 171–246. Xalapa: Universidad Veracruzana, 1983. First published in *Revista de la Escuela de Arte Teatral*, no. 6. (Mexico City: Instituto Nacional de Bellas Artes, 1963).

———. *Felipe Ángeles*. México: UNAM, 1979. Also published in *Coatl: Revista Literaria* (Guadalajara), 1967.

Geertz, Clifford. "Deep Play: Notes on the Balinese Cockfight." In *The Interpretation of Cultures*, 412–53. New York: Basic Books, 1973.

George, David. "On Ambiguity: Towards a Post-Modern Performance Theory." *Theatre Research International* 14, no. 1 (1989): 71–85.

Gerdes, Dick. "Recent Argentine Vanguard Theatre: Gambaro's *Información para extranjeros*. *Latin American Theatre Review* 11, no. 2 (1978): 11–16.

Giella, Miguel Angel. "El victimario como víctima en *Los siameses* de Griselda Gambaro: Notas para el análisis." *Gestos* 2 (1987): 77–86.

Gilbert, Sandra M. "What Do Feminist Critics Want? A Postcard from the Volcano." In *The New Feminist Criticism: Essays on Women, Literature, and Theory*, edited by Elaine Showalter, 29–45. New York: Pantheon, 1985.

Gladhart, Amalia. *The Leper in Blue: Coercive Performance in Contemporary Latin American Theater*. Chapel Hill: University of North Carolina Press, 2000.

———. "Monitoring Sor Juana: Satire, Technology, and Appropriation in Jesusa Rodríguez's *Sor Juana en Almoloya*." *Revista Hispánica Moderna* 52 (1999): 213–26.

———. "Nothing's Happening: Performance as Coercion in Contemporary Latin American Theatre." *Gestos* 18 (1994): 93–112.

———. "Playing Gender." *Latin American Literary Review* 24, no. 47 (1996): 59–89.

Glickman, Nora. "Parodia y desmitificación del rol femenino en el teatro de Diana Raznovich." *Latin American Theatre Review* 28, no. 1 (1994): 89–100.

———. "El teatro del absurdo de Diana Roznovich." In *Antología crítica del teatro breve hispanoamericano: 1948–1993*, edited by María Mercedes Jaramillo and Mario Yepes, 188–94. Medellín, Colombia: Editorial Universidad de Antioquia, 1997.

Goffman, Erving. "Performances." In *The Presentation of Self in Everyday Life*. New York: Doubleday, 1959.

Gorfain, Phyllis. "Hamlet and the Tragedy of Ludic Revenge." In *The World of Play*, edited by Frank E. Manning, 111–24. West Point, N.Y.: Leisure, 1983.

Gorostiza, Carlos. *¿A qué jugamos?* Buenos Aires: Sudamericana, 1969.

Graham-Jones, Jean. "Decir 'no': El aporte de Bortnik, Gambaro y Raznovich al Teatro Abierto '81." In *Teatro argentino durante el Proceso (1976–1983): Ensayos críticos-Entrevistas*, edited by Juana A. Arancibia and Zulema Mirkin, 181–97. Vol. 2. Buenos Aires: Vinciguerra, 1992.

———. *Exorcising History: Argentine Theater Under Dictatorship*. Lewisburg, Pa.: Bucknell University Press, 2000.

———. "Myths, Masks, and Machismo: *Un trabajo fabuloso* by Ricardo Halac and . . . *y a otra cosa mariposa* by Susana Torres Molina." *Gestos* 20 (1995): 91–106.

Greene, Gayle, and Coppélia Kahn. "Feminist Scholarship and the Social Construction of Woman." In *Making a Difference: Feminist Literary Criticism*, edited by Gayle Green and Coppélia Kahn, 1–36. London: Methuen, 1985.

Grice, H. Paul. "Logic and Conversation." In *Syntax and Semantics. Vol. III: Speech Acts*, edited by Peter Cole and Jerry L. Morgan, 41–58. New York: Academic Press, 1975.

Grossberg, Lawrence. "Identity and Cultural Studies: Is That All There Is?" In *Questions of Cultural Identity*, edited by Stuart Hall and Paul Du Gay, 86–107. London: Sage, 1996.

Hall, Stuart. Introduction to *Questions of Cultural Identity*, edited by Stuart Hall and Paul Du Gay. London: Sage, 1996.

Hallie, Philip P. *The Paradox of Cruelty*. Middletown, Conn.: Wesleyan University Press, 1969.

Harris, J. C. "Beyond Huizinga: Relationships between Play and Culture." In *Play as Context*, edited by A. T. Cheska, 26–36. West Point, N.Y.: Leisure, 1981.

Hart, Lynn, ed. *Making a Spectacle: Feminist Essays on Contemporary Women's Theatre*. Ann Arbor: University of Michigan Press, 1989.

Hind, Emily. "Entrevista con Sabina Berman." *Latin American Theatre Review* 33, no. 2 (2000): 133–39.

Holzapfel, Tamara. "Griselda Gambaro's Theatre of the Absurd." *Latin American Theatre Review* 3, no. 1 (1970): 5–11.

Homan, Sidney. *When the Theater Turns to Itself: The Aesthetic Metaphor in Shakespeare*. Lewisburg, Pa.: Bucknell University Press, 1981.

Hornby, Richard. *Drama, Metadrama, and Perception*. Lewisburg, Pa.: Bucknell University Press, 1986.

Huizinga, Johan. *Homo Ludens: A Study of the Play Element in Culture.* Boston: Beacon, 1962.

Hutchinson, Peter. *Games Authors Play.* New York: Methuen, 1983.

Jaramillo, María Mercedes, and Mario Yepes, eds. *Antología crítica del teatro breve hispanoamericano: 1948–1993.* Medellín, Colombia: Universidad de Antioquia, 1997.

Jones, Ann Rosalind. "Writing the Body: Toward an Understanding of *l'écriture féminine.*" In *The New Feminist Criticism: Essays on Women, Literature, and Theory,* edited by Elaine Showalter, 361–77. New York: Pantheon, 1985.

Jones, Anny Brooksbank, and Catherine Davies, eds. *Latin American Women's Writing: Feminist Readings in Theory and Crisis.* Oxford: Clarendon, 1996.

Kelty, Mark, and Blanca Kelty. "Interview with Jesusa Rodríguez." *Latin American Theatre Review* 31, no. 1 (1997): 123–27.

Keyssar, Helene. *Feminist Theatre: An Introduction to Plays of Contemporary British and American Women.* New York: Grove, 1986.

Koppel, Gene. "Maggie Moran, Anne Tyler's Madcap Heroine: A Game Approach to *Breathing Lessons.*" *Essays in Literature* 18, no. 2 (1991): 276–87.

Kristeva, Julia. *The Kristeva Reader.* Edited by Toril Moi. New York: Columbia University Press, 1986.

Kronik, John. "Usigli's *El gesticulador* and the Fiction of Truth." *Latin American Theatre Review* 11, no. 1 (1977): 5–16.

Lancy, David F., and B. Allan Tindall, eds. *The Study of Play: Problems and Prospects.* West Point, N.Y.: Leisure Press, 1975.

Larson, Catherine. "El juego de la historia en *Felipe Ángeles.*" In *Baúl de recuerdos: Homenaje a Elena Garro,* edited by Robert K. Anderson and Mara L. García, 73–84. Tlaxcala, México: Universidad Autónoma de Tlaxcala Press, 1999.

———. "Lope de Vega and Elena Garro: The Doubling of *La dama boba.*" *Hispania* 74 (1991): 15–25.

———. "'No conoces el precio de las palabras': Language and Meaning in Usigli's *El gesticulador.*" *Latin American Theatre Review* 20, no. 1 (1986): 21–28.

———. "The Play's the Thing: Theater and the Ludic in Dramas by Griselda Gambaro, Carlos Gorostiza, and Maritze Wilde." *Hecho Teatral* 3 (in press).

———. "Playwrights of Passage: Women and Game-Playing on the Stage." *Latin American Literary Review* 19 (1991): 77–89.

Larson, Catherine, and Margarita Vargas, eds. *Latin American Women Dramatists: Theater, Texts, and Theories.* Bloomington: Indiana University Press, 1998.

Lerner, Elisa. *Vida con mamá.* Caracas: Fundarte, 1981.

Lindenberger, Herbert S. *Historical Drama: The Relation of Literature and Reality.* Chicago: University of Chicago Press, 1975.

Lockert, Lucía Fox. "El eterno femenino en la obra de Rosario Castellanos." In *Actas del 7° Congreso de la AIH,* edited by Giuseppe Bellini, 461–66. Vol. 1. Rome: Bulzoni, 1982.

López, Liliana B. "Diana Raznovich: Una cazadora de mitos." In *Dramas de mujeres,* edited by Halima Tahan, 291–306. Buenos Aires: Ediciones Ciudad Argentina, 1998.

Luiselli, Alessandra. "La voz en off de Sor Juana: *Tren nocturno a Georgia* y el teatro mexicano al comienzo del milenio." *Latin American Theatre Review* 33, no. 2 (2000): 5–20.

Lyday, Leon F., and George W. Woodyard, eds. *Dramatists in Revolt: The New Latin American Theater*. Austin: University of Texas Press, 1976.

Magnarelli, Sharon. "Acting/Seeing Woman: Griselda Gambaro's *El despojamiento*." In *Latin American Women's Writing: Feminist Readings in Theory and Crisis*, edited by Anny Brooksbank Jones and Catherine Davies, 10–29. Oxford: Clarendon, 1996.

———. "Humor and Games in *El gato eficaz* by Luisa Valenzuela: The Looking-Glass World Revisted." *Modern Language Studies* 13, no. 3 (1983): 81–89.

Maguire, Jack. *Hopscotch, Hangman, Hot Potato, & Ha Ha Ha: A Rulebook of Children's Games*. With a foreword by Bob "Captain Kangaroo" Keeshan. New York: Simon and Schuster, 1990.

Mahieu, Roma. "The Games They Play (At Siesta Time)." In *Two Plays*, translated by Silvia Ehrlich Lipp. Canada: Concordia University Press, 1977.

———. Interview. *Clarín* (Buenos Aires), 12 June 1979. Cited in Martha Martínez's "Seis estrenos del teatro argentino en 1976." *Latin American Theatre Review* 11, no. 2 (1978): 95–101.

———. *Juegos a la hora de la siesta*. TS. 1976.

Martínez, Martha. "Seis estrenos del teatro argentino en 1976." *Latin American Theatre Review* 11, no. 2 (1978): 95–101.

———. "Tres nuevas dramaturgas argentinas: Roma Mahieu, Hebe Uhart y Diana Raznovich." *Latin American Theatre Review* 13, no. 2 (1980): 39–45.

Martínez de Olcoz, Nieves. "Decisiones de la máscara neutra: Dramaturgia femenina y fin de siglo en América Latina." *Latin American Theatre Review* 31, no. 2 (1998): 5–16.

———. "Escrito en el cuerpo: mujer, nación y memoria." In *Performance, pathos, política de los sexos: Teatro postcolonial de autoras latinoamericanas*, edited by Heidrun Adler and Kati Röttger. Vervuert: Iberoamericana, 1999.

Mazziotti, Nora, et al. *Poder, deseo y marginación: Aproximaciones a la obra de Griselda Gambaro*. Buenos Aires: Puntosur, 1989.

McNab, Pamela J. "Humor in Castellanos's *El eterno femenino*: The Fractured Female Image." *Latin American Theatre Review* 33, no. 2 (2000): 79–92.

Meeker, Joseph W. *The Comedy of Survival: Literary Ecology and a Play Ethic*. 3rd ed. Tucson: University of Arizona Press, 1997.

Meier, Klaus V. "Play and Paradigmatic Integration." In *The Many Faces of Play*, edited by Kendall Blanchard, 268–88. Champaign, Ill: Human Kinetics, 1986.

Méndez-Faith, Teresa. "*Historia de un número* de Josefina Plá: ¿Farsa trivial en XI tiempos o alegoría teatral para todos los tiempos . . . ?" In *Antología crítica del teatro breve hispanoamericano*, edited by María Mercedes Jaramillo and Mario Yepes, 15–22. Medellín: Universidad of Antioquia, 1997.

———. "Sobre el uso y abuso del poder en la producción dramática de Griselda Gambaro." *Revista Iberoamericana* 51, no. 132–33 (1985): 831–41.

Mergen, Bernard, ed. *Cultural Dimensions of Play, Games, and Sport.* Champaign, Ill.: Human Kinetics, 1986.

Milleret, Margo. "Daughters *vs.* Mothers on Latin American Stages." In *Todo ese fuego (Homenaje a Merlin H. Forster) / All that fire (Studies in honor of Merlin H. Forster),* edited by Mara L. García and Douglas Weatherford, 135–47. Mexico City: Universidad Autónoma de Tlaxcala, 1999.

Molinaro, Nina L. "Discipline and Drama: Panoptic Theatre and Griselda Gambaro's *El campo.*" *Latin American Theatre Review* 29, no. 2 (1996): 29–41.

Monasterios, Rubén. *Un enfoque crítico del teatro venezolano.* Caracas: Monte Avila, 1975.

Mora, Gabriela. "*La dama boba* de Elena Garro: Verdad y ficción, teatro y metateatro." *Latin American Theatre Review* 16, no. 2 (1983): 15–21.

Moretta, Eugene L. "Spanish-American Theatre of the 50's and 60's: Critical Perspectives on Role Playing." *Latin American Theatre Review* 13, no. 2 (1980): 5–30.

Morrissette, Bruce. "Games and Game Structures in Robbe-Grillet." *Yale French Studies* 41 (1968): 159–67.

Muncy, Michèle. "Encuentro con Elena Garro." Interview. *Hispanic Journal* 7, no. 2 (1986): 69–76. Translated by Anita K. Stoll under the title "The Author Speaks. . . . ," in *A Different Reality: Studies on the Work of Elena Garro,* edited by Anita K. Stoll, 23–27. Lewisburg, Pa.: Bucknell University Press, 1990.

Muñoz, Willy O. "El juego de las máscaras." In *Antología crítica del teatro breve hispanoamericano: 1948–1993,* edited by María Mercedes Jaramillo and Mario Yepes, 530–33. Medellín, Colombia: Editorial Universidad de Antioquia, 1997.

Nelson, Robert J. *Play Within a Play: The Dramatist's Conception of His Art: Shakespeare to Anuoilh.* New Haven: Yale University Press, 1958.

Nigro, Kirsten. "Breaking [It] Up Is [Not] Hard to Do: Writing Histories and Women Theatre Artists in Latin America." *Gestos* 14 (1992): 127–39.

———. "Discurso femenino y el teatro de Griselda Gambaro." In *Ensayos críticos sobre Griselda Gambaro y José Triana,* edited by Diana Taylor, 65–73. Ottawa: Girol, 1989.

———. "Un revuelto de la historia, la memoria y el género: Expresiones de la posmodernidad sobre las tablas mexicanas." *Gestos* 9, no. 17 (1994): 29–41.

———. "Rosario Castellanos' Debunking of the *Eternal Feminine.*" *Journal of Spanish Studies: Twentieth Century* 8, no. 1–2 (1980): 89–102.

Norbeck, Edward. "Anthropological Views of Play." *American Zoologist* 14 (1974): 267–73.

———. "The Study of Play: Johan Huizinga and Modern Anthropology." In *The Study of Play: Problems and Prospects,* edited by D. F. Lancy and B. A. Tindall, 1–10. West Point, N.Y.: Leisure, 1976.

———, ed. *The Anthropological Study of Human Play. Rice University Studies* 60, no. 3 (summer 1974).

O'Connor, Patricia W. *Dramaturgas españolas de hoy: Una introducción.* Madrid: Espiral/Fundamentos, 1988.

Opie, Iona Archibald, and Peter Opie. *Children's Games in Street and Playground.* Oxford: Clarendon, 1970.

————. *Children's Games with Things.* Oxford: Oxford University Press, 1977.

Oppenheimer, Andres. *Bordering on Chaos: Guerrillas, Stockbrokers, Politicians, and Mexico's Road to Prosperity.* Boston: Little, Brown, 1996.

Pavlovsky, Eduardo, intro. *Extraño juguete* by Susana Torres Molina, 9–10. Buenos Aires: Apex, 1978.

Pellettieri, Osvaldo, ed. *Tradición, modernidad y posmodernidad.* Buenos Aires: Galerna, 1997.

Pérez-Firmat, Gustavo. "Apuntes para un modelo de la intertextualidad en literatura." *Romanic Review* 69 (1978): 1–14.

Piaget, Jean. *Play, Dreams and Imitation in Childhood.* Translated by C. Gattegno and F. M. Hodgson. New York: Norton, 1962.

Picón Garfield, Evelyn. "Una dulce bondad que atempera las crueldades: *El campo* de Griselda Gambaro." *Latin American Theatre Review* 13, no. 2 (summer 1980): 95–102.

Pinsky, Robert. "The Game." In *The Games We Played: A Celebration of Childhood and Imagination,* edited by Steven A. Cohen, 19–21. New York: Simon and Schuster, 2001.

Plá, Josefina. *Historia de un número.* In *Teatro breve hispanoamericano contemporáneo,* edited by Carlos Solórzano, 45–63. Madrid: Aguilar, 1967.

Postma, Rosalea. "Space and Spectator in the Theatre of Griselda Gambaro: *Información para extranjeros.*" *Latin American Theatre Review* 14, no. 1 (1980): 35–45.

Pross, Edith E. "Open Theatre Revisited: An Argentine Experiment." *Latin American Theatre Review* 18, no. 1 (1984): 83–94.

Raznovich, Diana. *Casa matriz.* In *Salirse de madre,* edited by Hilda Rais, 161–86. Buenos Aires: Croquiñol, 1989.

———— *Casa matriz.* In *Jardín de otoño, Casa matriz y De atrás para adelante,* with a prologue by Diana Taylor. Madrid: Consorcio Casa de América, 2001.

————. *Casa matriz* (Segunda versión). In *Antología crítica del teatro breve hispanoamericano: 1948–1993,* edited by María Mercedes Jaramillo and Mario Yepes, 159–87. Medellín, Colombia: Universidad de Antioquia, 1997.

————. *Defiant Acts: Four Plays by Diana Raznovich/Actos desafiantes: cuatro obras de Diana Raznovich.* Edited by Diana Taylor and Victoria Martínez. Lewisburg, Pa.: Bucknell University Press, 2002.

————. *Dial-a-Mom.* In *Women Writing Women: An Anthology of Spanish-American Theater of the 1980s,* edited by Teresa Cajiao Salas and Margarita Vargas, 215–41. Albany: SUNY Press, 1997.

Rizk, Beatriz J. "El arte del performance y la subversión de las reglas del juego en el discurso de la mujer." *Latin American Theatre Review* 33, no. 2 (2000): 93–111.

Rodríguez, Jesusa. *Sor Juana en Almoloya (Pastorela Virtual). Debate Feminista* 12 (1995): 395–411.

Rojas, Mario A. "*Krísis* (sic) de Sabina Berman y el escenario político mexicano." In *Tradición, modernidad y posmodernidad,* edited by Osvaldo Pellettieri, 119–34. Buenos Aires: Galerna, 1999.

Romero, Mariela. *El juego.* Caracas: Monte Ávila, 1977.

———. *Esperando al italiano*. In *Las risas de nuestras medusas*, edited by Susana Castillo. Caracas: Fundarte, 1992.

Roster, Peter, and Mario Rojas, eds. *De la colonia a la postmodernidad: teoría teatral y crítica sobre teatro latinoamericano*. Buenos Aires: Editorial Galerna/ IITCTL, 1992.

Rotella, Pilar V. "Games People Play: Oppressors and Oppressed in Three Plays by Latin American Women Writers (Castellanos, Hernández, Gambaro)." Paper presented at the Midwest Modern Language Association Conference, Chicago, Ill., November 1991.

Roven, Glen. "On With the Show." In *The Games We Played: A Celebration of Childhood and Imagination*, edited by Steven A. Cohen, 49–54. New York: Simon and Schuster, 2001.

Salter, Michael A., ed. *Play: Anthropological Perspectives*. West Point, N.Y.: Leisure, 1978.

———. "Winds of Change." In *The Study of Play: Problems and Prospects*, edited by David F. Lancy and B. Allan Tindall, 7–9. West Point, N.Y.: Leisure Press, 1975.

Schechner, Richard. *Essays on Performance Theory: 1970–1976*. New York: Drama Book Specialists, 1977.

———. "Victor Turner's Last Adventure." In *The Anthropology of Performance*, by Victor Turner, 7–20. New York: PAJ Publications, 1986.

Schechner, Richard, and Mady Schuman, eds. *Ritual, Play, and Performance: Readings in the Social Sciences/Theatre*. New York: Seabury Press, 1976.

Schleuter, June. *Metafictional Characters in Modern Drama*. New York: Columbia University Press, 1979.

Schmeling, Manfred. *Métathéâtre et intertexte: Aspects du théâtre dans le théâtre*. Paris: Lettres Modernes, 1982.

Schwartzman, Helen B. *Transformations: The Anthropology of Children's Play*. New York: Plenum, 1978.

Schwartzman, John. "Paradox, Play and Post-modern Fiction." In *Play and Culture*, edited by Helen B. Schwartzman, 38–48. West Point, N.Y.: Leisure Press, 1980.

———. "Playing Around with Words: Human and Postmodern Fiction." In *The Paradoxes of Play*, edited by John W. Loy, 50–57. West Point, N.Y.: Leisure, 1982.

Searle, John R. *Expression and Meaning: Studies in the Theory of Speech Acts*. Cambridge: Cambridge University Press, 1979.

Seda, Laurietz. "El hábito no hace al monje: Travestismo, homosexualidad y lesbianismo en . . . y a otra cosa mariposa de Susana Torres Molina." *Latin American Theatre Review* 30, no. 2 (1997): 103–14.

———. Review of *Antología crítica del teatro breve hispanoamericano (1948–1993)*, edited by María Mercedes Jaramillo and Mario Yepes. *Latin American Theatre Review* 35, no. 1 (2001): 181–83.

Senelick, Laurence, ed. *Gender in Performance: The Presentation of Difference in the Performing Arts*. Hanover, N.H.: Tufts University Press, 1992.

Sieber, Sharon. "The Deconstruction of Gender as Archetype in Rosario Castellanos' *El eterno femenino*." *Feministas Unidas* 17, no. 2 (1997): 6–10.

States, Bert O. "Performance as Metaphor." *Theatre Journal* 48, no. 1 (1996): 1–26.

Stevens, Camilla. "Traveling Troupes: The Performance of Puerto Rican Identity in Plays by Luis Rafael Sánchez and Myrna Casas." *Hispania* 85, no. 2 (2002): 240–49.

Stoll, Anita K. "Elena Garro's/Lope de Vega's *La dama boba*: Seventeenth-Century Inspiration for a Twentieth-Century Dramatist." *Latin American Theatre Review* 23, no. 2 (1990): 21–31.

———. "Playing a Waiting Game: The Theater of Mariela Romero." In *Latin American Women Dramatists: Theater, Texts, and Theories*, edited by Catherine Larson and Margarita Vargas, 41–52. Bloomington: Indiana University Press, 1998.

———, ed. *A Different Reality: Studies on the Works of Elena Garro.* Lewisburg, Pa.: Bucknell University Press, 1990.

Tahan, Halima, ed. *Dramas de mujeres.* Buenos Aires: Ediciones Ciudad Argentina, 1998.

Tantanián, Alejandro. *Juegos de damas crueles.* Caraja-ji. Buenos Aires: Universidad de Buenos Aires, 2000.

Taylor, Diana. *Disappearing Acts: Spectacles of Gender and Nationalism in Argentina's "Dirty War."* Durham, N.C.: Duke University Press, 1997.

———. "Fighting Fire with Frivolity: Diana Raznovich's Defiant Acts." In *Performance, pathos, política de los sexos: Teatro postcolonial de autoras latinoamericanas*, edited by Heidrun Adler and Kati Röttger. Vervuert: Iberoamericana, 1999.

———. "*High Aztec* or Performing Anthro Pop." *The Drama Review* 37, no. 3 (1993): 142–52.

———. "Negotiating Performance." *Latin American Theatre Review* 26, no. 2 (1993): 49–57.

———. *Negotiating Performance: Gender, Sexuality, and Theatricality in Latin(o) America.* Durham, N.C.: Duke University Press, 1994.

———. "Theater and Terrorism: Griselda Gambaro's *Information for Foreigners.*" *Theatre Journal* 42, no. 2 (1990): 165–82.

———. "The Theater of Diana Raznovich and Perceptitide in *El desconcierto.*" In *Latin American Women Dramatists*, edited by Catherine Larson and Margarita Vargas, 113–25. Bloomington: Indiana University Press, 1998.

———. *Theatre of Crisis: Drama and Politics in Latin America.* Lexington: University Press of Kentucky, 1991.

———. "Violent Displays: Griselda Gambaro and Argentina's Drama of Disappearance." In *Information for Foreigners: Three Plays by Griselda Gambaro*, edited by Marguerite Feitlowitz, 161–75. Evanston, Ill.: Northwestern University Press, 1992.

———, ed. *En busca de una imagen: Ensayos críticos sobre Griselda Gambaro y José Triana.* Ottawa: Girol, 1989.

Torres Molina, Susana. *Extraño juguete.* Buenos Aires: Apex, 1978.

———. *. . . y a otra cosa mariposa.* Buenos Aires: Búsqueda, 1988.

Triana, José. *La noche de los asesinos.* In *9 dramaturgos hispanoamericanos*, edited by Frank Dauster, Leon Lyday, and George Woodyard, 136–201. Vol. 1. Ottawa, Canada: Girol, 1979.

Turner, Victor. *The Anthropology of Performance*. New York: Performing Arts Journal Publications, 1986.

———. "Carnival, Ritual, and Play in Rio de Janeiro." In *Time out of Time: Essays on the Festival*, edited by Alessandro Falassi, 74–90. Albuquerque: University of New Mexico Press, 1987.

———. *Dramas, Fields, and Metaphors: Symbolic Action in Human Society*. Ithaca: Cornell University Press, 1974.

———. *From Ritual to Theatre: The Human Seriousness of Play*. With a preface by Richard Schechner. New York: Performing Arts Journal Publications, 1982.

———. *Schism and Continuity in an African Village: A Study of Ndembu Village Life*. Manchester, Eng.: Manchester University Press, 1957.

Unruh, Vicky. "A Moveable Space: The Problem of Puerto Rico in Myrna Casas's Theater." In *Latin American Women Dramatists: Theater, Texts, and Theories*, edited by Catherine Larson and Margarita Vargas, 126–42. Bloomington: Indiana University Press, 1998.

Usigli, Rodolfo. *El gesticulador: Pieza para demagogos en tres actos*. Edited by Rex Edward Ballinger. Englewood Cliffs, N.J.: Prentice-Hall, 1963.

Vandenberg, Brian. "Mere Child's Play." In *The Many Faces of Play*, edited by Kendall Blanchard, 115–20. Champaign, Ill.: Human Kinetics, 1986.

Versényi, Adam. *Theatre in Latin America: Religion, Politics, and Culture from Cortés to the 1980s*. Cambridge: Cambridge University Press, 1993.

Villegas, Juan. "La irrupción del circo en el teatro." In *Propuestas escénicas de fin de siglo: FIT 1998*, edited by Juan Villegas, 151–72. Irvine, Calif.: Gestos, 1999.

Vodanović, Sergio. *El delantal blanco*. In *En un acto*, edited by Frank Dauster and Leon F. Lyday, 1–14. 3rd ed. Boston: Heinle and Heinle, 1990.

Wade, Gerald. "The 'Comedia' as Play." In *Studies in Honor of Everett W. Hesse*, edited by William C. McCrary and José A. Madrigal, 165–77. Lincoln, Neb.: Society of Spanish and Spanish American Studies, 1981.

Weisinger, Herbert. "*Theatrum Mundi*: Illusion as Reality." In *The Agony and the Triumph: Papers on the Use and Abuse of Myth*. East Lansing: Michigan State University Press, 1964.

Weisz, Gabriel. *El juego viviente: Indagación sobre las partes ocultas del objeto lúdico*. Mexico City: Siglo Veintiuno, 1986.

Wilde, Maritza. *Adjetivos*. In *Antología crítica del teatro breve hispanoamericano: 1948–1993*, edited by María Mercedes Jaramillo and Mario Yepes, 511–29. Medellín, Colombia: Editorial Universidad de Antioquia, 1997.

Witte, Ann. *Guiding the Plot: Politics and Feminism in the Work of Women Playwrights from Spain and Argentina, 1960–1990*. New York: Peter Lang, 1996.

Wittgenstein, Ludwig. *The Blue and Brown Books*. New York: Harper and Row, 1958.

———. *Philosophical Investigations*. Translated by G. E. M. Anscombe. Oxford: Basil Blackwell, 1953.

Yovanovich, Gordana. "Play as a Mode of Empowerment for Women and as a Model for Poetics in the Early Poetry of Nicolás Guillén." *Hispanic Review* 68 (2001): 15–31.

Zalacaín, Daniel. "Circularidad y metateatro en la escena hispanoamericana: algunas piezas representativas." *Hispanófila* 86 (1986): 37–54.

———. "El personaje fuera del juego en el teatro de Griselda Gambaro." *Revista de estudios hispánicos* 14 (1980): 59–71.

Zayas de Lima, Perla. "Susana Torres Molina, la mujer y el mito." In *Dramas de mujeres*, edited by Halima Tahan, 327–45. Buenos Aires: Ediciones Ciudad Argentina, 1998.

Index